COLLECTIVE ACTION

COLLECTIVE ACTION

RUSSELL HARDIN

Published for Resources for the Future
By The Johns Hopkins University Press
Baltimore and London

Published for Resources for the Future
By The Johns Hopkins University Press, Baltimore, Maryland 21218

Library of Congress Cataloging in Publication Data
Hardin, Russell, 1940-
  Collective action.

  Bibliography: p.
  Includes index.
  1. Social choice. I. Title.
HB846.8.H37 1982 302′.13   81-48247
ISBN 0-8018-2818-X   AACR2
ISBN 0-8018-2819-8 (pbk.)

This book is a product of RFF's Quality of the Environment Division, Clifford S. Russell, director. It was edited by Dorothy Sawicki and designed by Elsa Williams. The index was prepared by Lorraine and Mark Anderson.

CONTENTS

FOREWORD

In his preface to this book, Russell Hardin asks why it is that the analysis of collective choice behavior has become such a large academic industry over the past fifteen years. He provides several possible answers, two of which are especially important in explaining the continuing interest of Resources for the Future in the field. The major spur to our undertaking and supporting of collective choice research came from observing how frequently sound economic and engineering reasoning about environmental problems led to prescriptions for policies and public institutions that came to nothing in the real world of public decisions.

To cite only one prominent example, the idea that river basin commissions should be created and made responsible for water quantity and quality management has considerable appeal on the basis of an efficiency analysis of these problems. But, few river basin commissions have in fact been created, and those that were had structures more or less guaranteeing that the efficient basin management solutions could never be adopted. In particular, the commissions usually had state members, and each state had one vote, if not an effective veto. Efficiency, which required upstream treatment to benefit downstream cities and recreational users, did not appeal to upstream states unless downstream treatment was extracted as a quid pro quo. Thus, uniform treatment became the politically feasible choice.

This rather commonplace sort of frustration and attendant education was intensified for us by the general mistrust of executive power and revival of interest in legislatures, representation, and legislative decision processes that grew out of the Vietnam angst and the Nixon years. Even environmental economists were not immune to those powerful social currents.

We were also influenced by our reading of the developing public choice literature. As Hardin says, it seemed that researchers were beginning to understand collective choice phenomena in generalizable ways.

Bringing the threads of our substantive, applied interests together with those of the theoretical public choice literature has not been easy. Indeed, it continues to be a goal rather than an accomplishment. One reason for this is simply the difficulty of the job. Public choice theory is notoriously abstract, even by the standards of much of the rest of economics; data and natural experiments relevant to testing the theory are hard to come by; and the policy experiments of the effort often constitute major constitutional changes rather than modest tinkering with a particular law—discouraging easy interaction with politicians and administrators. Finally, RFF began its effort in this direction just as the golden days of academic funding of the 1960s and 1970s became clouded by inflation, the severe stock market decline of 1973–74, and the shift of government priorities toward quick answers to energy questions.

Nevertheless, RFF has continued to encourage the application of public choice ideas to areas in which we have substantive interest. The resulting publications include Oran Young's *Compliance and Public Authority* (1979) and two edited volumes of papers: *Collective Decision Making* (1979) and *Public Choice and Rural Development* (1981).

RFF is especially pleased to bring out Hardin's book because it does bring theory and substantive areas together in a graceful and accessible way. It conveys the excitement inherent in this attempt to improve our society's understanding of the deep but commonplace difficulties that dog us in every policy area.

Clifford S. Russell
February 1982

PREFACE

This is a study of the problem of collective action in social contexts, which is the Prisoner's Dilemma writ large. The study passes from thin to thick, from static to dynamic, or from the analysis of discrete exchange to that of relational exchange. The early chapters (2 through 7) are an analysis of collective action as though it were a one-shot Prisoner's Dilemma. The later chapters (9 through 14) analyze collective action when it is directed at an ongoing problem or is otherwise part of ongoing relationships so that "conventions" may govern behavior. The two are dramatically different. The first has the flavor of a logical game, while the latter takes on the character of a nearly anthropological investigation of minute interrelationships. The conclusion of the first analysis is that collective action must generally fail unless it need not be collective at all (as when we can all let George do it, with confidence that George *will* do it). The conclusion of the second analysis is not so simple: collective action can succeed, even in very large groups, but the considerations that may play a role in success are complex and numerous; on the other hand, collective action can also fail, even in small groups.

Throughout the text I use many actual examples of collective action and collective action problems, from those concerning very small groups to those of the magnitude of mass movements, from trivial problems to profoundly important issues. Hence, the analysis cuts across what some consider to be unrelated substantive realms. But the point is to explain participation—contributions to collective actions—and there is no reason to parcel the theory according to the boundaries of substantive problems. The generalization of the explanation of participation leads to its greater

xiii

power in dealing with any particular realm of participation in actions for collective benefit.

Throughout the discussion I frequently consider the American civil rights, antiwar, women's, and environmental movements of the past two or three decades. Each of these has been diverse and conflict ridden, and each has had numerous organized groups within it. Unfortunately, none of these groups has been studied well enough to test all the claims I make, and many of my claims remain unproved. Possibly the best studied of all public interest groups for present purposes has been the Sierra Club, which was founded in 1892 as a nature appreciation club. From the beginning it has been involved in the politics of conservation, and now, with its 180,000 members, it is at the center of the wider politics of environmentalism.

The analysis of collective action has become a large industry over the past decade or two. One might wonder why. Perhaps, in part, the answer is simply that we have finally begun to understand it in generalizable ways. But in part the answer must also be that the problem of collective action has become more important: one might note with irony that from about the time—at the height of the civil rights movement—that Mancur Olson's *The Logic of Collection Action* was published, with its thesis that large groups must generally remain latent, successful collective actions seem to have become commonplace. Why should that have happened? Among the easy answers are that certain kinds of organizations and collective action have become less costly and that many collective actions are obviously the product of increasing affluence. Another answer is that government has come to play a larger role in providing groups their goods—but this larger role itself may be primarily a response to increased demands. Finally, one might suppose that new problems have arisen, although this involves a very difficult comparative judgment. In any case, if the rise of new problems has been an important stimulus to collective action in recent times, those new problems must especially be of concern to the affluent.

Finally, a brief word on the type of analysis that follows. One afternoon some time ago, I was involved in a conversation around a table at the Hoover Institution. We were debating the meaning of a word. Uncharacteristically for an economist, one of my colleagues noted that this was essentially a factual question, which should therefore be settled by reference to the relevant factual authority: Webster's dictionary. He fetched the dictionary and read us the following definition: "one who believes that human conduct is motivated wholly by self-interest." Simultaneously several of us said "economist." The word whose definition we had sought and just heard was, of course, "cynic." Most of the analysis that follows is an economic theory of individual contribution to group action, and one may indeed find it cynical. I am generally concerned with pushing cynical explanations to their limit, to see what they cannot explain as well as what they can; I am not sure what to feel about the fact that they can explain as much as they can. Of those who instantly said "economist" that day, I was the only noneconomist. I said it with a slightly accusing tone. The others, I am convinced, said it with pride. I have since occasionally wondered who was more in the right.

It is a pleasure to acknowledge the assistance of many people in bringing this book into being. Edward Banfield and Edwin Haefele were instrumental in getting me started, and I thank them warmly for their initial aid and comfort. Along the way, some forcible nudges from Aaron Director and Jack Nagel helped put my arguments on a coherent path. And Brian Barry and Clifford Russell gave me the final impetus to finish a work that was too long in progress.

Six research assistants contributed substantially toward this book: James R. Knickman and David Luery from the University of Pennsylvania; James R. Horney from the University of Maryland; and David Shiveley, Robert Latham, and Brian Downing from the University of Chicago. For information on the early history of the Prisoner's Dilemma and on the Sierra Club, I am grateful to Merrill M. Flood and Don Coombs, respectively; they both responded with generosity and alacrity to requests by mail from someone they had never met. Various officials of the Sierra Club were similarly helpful over the telephone.

In addition to most of those named above, several colleagues and readers gave me the benefit of (sometimes severely) critical commentary on various parts of the manuscript: Hayward Alker, Steven Brams, Stephen Elkin, Jerry Kelly, Robert Cameron Mitchell, Joe Oppenheimer, Charles E. Osgood, Ben Page, Sam Postbrief, Duncan Snidal, Karol Soltan, Michael Taylor, Eric Uslaner, Jean-Roger Vergnaud, Steven Walt, Oran Young, and the editorial staff of Resources for the Future. I only hope that by way of reciprocating I have given most of them equally critical commentaries.

Three institutions have provided financial support at various stages to give me time free to work on this project: Resources for the Future, The Hoover Institution of Stanford University, and the General Research Board of the University of Maryland. To all of these people and institutions, I am grateful.

In acknowledging the force of those who helped to bring this book about, I should also include my colleagues in the Department of Political Science at the University of Chicago. They offered me a swift kick and a warm welcome in the relevant order, and in between they provided the atmosphere in which to write two-thirds of what follows. But they are sufficiently convinced of their stimulating qualities that I am hesitant to praise them here. I am also hesitant to praise my wife Joan and my son Joshua for their stimulating qualities, but I must note that they, too, provided their own timely kicks and welcomes. Indeed, this work began only shortly before Joshua did, and its growth has been far outpaced by his.

INTRODUCTION

Since people cause pollution, we are told, people can stop pollution. The slogan seems to be logically impeccable—and yet it also seems specious. Why? It is logically impeccable because it is factually true in a trivial sense: if enough people would do certain things, which it is physically possible for them to do, pollution would stop. And it is specious because the intention behind the slogan goes beyond this trivial sense. That intention is more nearly captured in another claim, of a form with which we are all too familiar: if we wanted to stop pollution, we would. This claim is an easy analogue of such commonly valid claims as, "If I wanted another helping, I would take it."

However, the preceding analogy is misleading. Indeed, it is an instance of the fallacy of composition:

> We are committing the fallacy of composition when we argue from the premise that every man can decide how he will act to the conclusion that the human race can decide how it will act (for example, with regard to the rate of increase of population or the choice between war and peace). . . . This, or a similar fallacy, is committed whenever we assume, without adequate reason, that we can speak about groups in the same ways in which we can speak about their members, that we can speak of a nation having a will or interests. . . . Of course, it may be possible to do this; there may be predicates applicable (in the same sense) to a group and to its members, but this cannot be assumed without evidence. It may also be possible to introduce a different but useful sense in which a predicate normally applied to individuals may be applied to a group; but if so, the new sense must be explained.[1]

[1] J. L. Mackie, "Fallacies," p. 173.

1

When taking an editorial tone, virtually everyone seems ready to argue from the fallacy of composition. And in certain contexts of central importance in social philosophy and political science, scholars have commonly fallen prey to the fallacy: they have assumed that if an action is in the collective interest of a group and if the members of the group are rational, then the group must be (in the same sense) collectively rational, which is to say that the group must act in its interest just as each of its rational members would do.

This book is an effort to decompose group action into individual actions in order to explain collective outcomes in terms of individual motivations. Although it can make good sense to say that an individual is rational, there is no obviously useful new sense in which we can typically say that a group is rational. Yet, one of the more widely accepted doctrines of modern political science—the group theory of politics—was based on a presumption from the fallacy of composition: that a group of people with a common interest will take action to further that interest. That doctrine has collapsed in the face of two major developments, discussed extensively in the text that follows: Mancur Olson's logic of collective action[2] and game theory's Prisoner's Dilemma. In the latter, there is a dilemma precisely because what it makes sense for an individual to do is not what it would make sense for the group to do—if one could meaningfully speak of what the group should do.

The Prisoner's Dilemma gets its name from the story of two prisoners who are separately interrogated. Naturally, there is insufficient evidence to convict them of the crime that the police suspect them of having committed. Unless they confess, the worst conviction they risk is for illegal possession of firearms, for which they would each be sentenced to a year in jail. But the police and the prosecuting attorney are devious, and they offer each prisoner the following deal: you can turn state's witness to help us put your partner away for ten years, and we'll let you off free. The only hitch is that, if both of you confess, we'll convict both of you of armed robbery and ask the judge for a lenient sentence of only six years for each of you. To confess or not to confess—that is your dilemma. If you are narrowly self-interested, you are better off confessing no matter what your partner does. Since you both must see the issue this way, you may both spend six years in jail. But if you could act together as a group with a single mind, you would act in the group's interest and hold out so that you both would spend only a year in jail. If, however, you reason from the fallacy of composition

2 Mancur Olson, Jr., *The Logic of Collective Action.*

while your partner acts from self-interest, you will rest ten years in jail. It would be a painful lesson in logic.

Reasoning from the fallacy of composition is a characteristic tendency in the social sciences and in social philosophy, but it is rivaled in pervasiveness and destructiveness by another form of fallacious reasoning that has not been graced with a standard name. We might call this form of reasoning the fallacy of static generalization. In trying to understand dynamic social relationships, we generalize from our understanding of static relationships. Again, an analysis of Prisoner's Dilemma shows why the generalization can be wrong. The prisoners in the story above face their dilemma once only, and they face it in isolation from other aspects of their relationship with one another. You and I, however, may repeatedly face a smaller version of their dilemma. We may therefore quickly realize that our self-interest now dictates that we cooperate rather than defect (which, in the case of the prisoners, would be not to confess rather than to confess). Since your cooperation tomorrow may depend on my cooperation today, I have incentive to cooperate today.

Obviously, our iterated Prisoner's Dilemma has more in common with many social problems than does the one-shot version. In social contexts we typically face ongoing collective action problems rather than once-only actions that are isolated from other interactions. To understand these requires an analysis of incentives that depend on dynamic relationships, incentives that would not arise except in dynamic contexts. Note that the distinction between dynamic and static understanding is not merely that between the diachronic and synchronic accounts of historically minded social theorists. More important than the past in many dynamic explanations is the future, because such explanations are based on the strategic implications of present choices—these implications, often in the future, give incentive to make particular choices in the present. When such incentives motivate action, generalization from static analyses of only the incentives in the present interaction (or single play of our Prisoner's Dilemma) will often be fallacious.

At the group level we tend to think in individual terms, and in dynamic contexts we tend still to think in static terms. Of course, it is generally easier to reason in individual and static terms—such reasoning typically involves fewer relationships and demands less knowledge. Strategic reasoning can be complex and difficult. Indeed, it may strain one's capacity to keep relevant facts and relationships in mind simultaneously. A determined effort to classify these into clearly defined and, as nearly as possible, logical categories is perhaps the only way to achieve a successful overview and explanation of interesting social behaviors.

SYNOPSIS

In the chapters that follow, the analysis builds from the simplest to the most complex problems, beginning with static, one-shot problems that involve symmetric relationships among the participants, going on to more complex static problems, and ending with dynamic problems.

Chapter 1 establishes the general problem with a review of its intellectual history and the assumptions on which its analysis is based.

Chapter 2 discusses the analytical traditions—game theory and the theory of public goods—that have contributed to the contemporary understanding of the problem. It also demonstrates the equivalence of the logic of collective action and the Prisoner's Dilemma. And it discusses the major explanations of successful collective actions in common contexts in which the logic of collective action seems to imply failure.

Chapter 3 discusses, for the static case, the range of effects that group size can have on the prospects for success and failure of groups.

Chapter 4 considers important dimensions of the types of goods and types of provision involved in diverse collective action problems. For example, one of the most important classes of such problems involves the good of electoral victory, which is a step good, that is, a good that can be provided only in discrete steps rather than over a continuous range of levels. Another important class includes many of the most important collective actions in contemporary politics: those directed at the elimination of bads rather than at the provision of goods.

Chapter 5 complicates the static analysis further by bringing in various asymmetries that significantly affect the likelihood, forms, and prospects for success of collective action.

Chapters 6 and 7 then augment the static analysis by considering extrarational motivations for individual contributions to collective ends. Chapter 6 shows that there is no simple rule of fairness for cooperation that would readily cover any group of individuals who actually were inclined to be fair in cooperating with one another, rather than to be narrowly self-seeking. Chapter 7 discusses an array of other reasons for the successes of actual groups: moral motivations, the desire to live one's own history by participating in the movements of one's time, and ignorance and misunderstanding.

Chapter 8, which is transitional, finishes the static analysis with discussion of some analyses that, although strictly static, are based on artificially dynamic assumptions.

Chapter 9 opens the dynamic analysis of collective action. It establishes the fundamental importance of strategic interaction over time in motivating cooperation for collective and therefore for individual benefit.

The argument from this point forward is exclusively based on the Prisoner's Dilemma version of the collective action problem, because it better represents the strategic interaction. In iterated as opposed to single-play Prisoner's Dilemma, cooperation is often rational even for narrowly self-interested people. The argument here is based on the 2-person version of Prisoner's Dilemma.

Chapter 10 generalizes the argument for cooperation in iterated Prisoner's Dilemma from 2-person to *n*-person interactions, which may be resolved by conventional "agreement," or contract by convention. Since collective action problems often resemble iterated, rather than single-play, Prisoner's Dilemma, it may often be possible to resolve them cooperatively despite the apparent logic of their static representation.

Chapter 11 discusses conditions that allow for the conventional resolution of collective action problems when these are not iterated in strictly identical form.

Chapter 12 surveys considerations that constrain the likelihood of cooperative resolution of collective action problems by contract by convention.

The final two chapters bring various discussions together. Chapter 13 discusses the relationship of contract by convention to traditional perspectives in social theory, especially to exchange theory. And chapter 14 surveys the role of contract by convention in politics and in democratic theory.

Throughout the book, the concern is with groups whose members share a common interest: the provision of a collective good. As I argue in chapter 2, contrary to a common misconception, the good need not be a public good in the narrow, technical sense in which that term has been defined in economics (see chapter 2, section on "Public Goods"). Collective action can be directed at the provision of virtually any good, no matter how "private" or "public" the good. What is of concern is how it is provided: collectively.

Furthermore, the interest is always with collective action, whatever form it may take, rather than with substantively defined classes of groups. A theory of collective action is a theory of when there will be individual action toward collective ends and not simply a theory of organized groups. Such a theory should explain both successes and failures of collective action and therefore, of course, it should explain the presence or absence of relevant organizations. It should also contribute, as in chapters 5 and 14, to the explanation of certain biases in levels of group activity and in political outcomes. Indeed, it may even help to explain, as in chapter 13, differences in the force with which various moral norms are held.

1

THE BACK OF
THE INVISIBLE HAND

Every individual contributing to the general productiveness of society, says Adam Smith, "intends only his own gain, and he is in this, as in many other cases, led by an invisible hand to promote an end which was no part of his intention. Nor is it always the worse for the society that it was no part of [the individual's intended end]. By pursuing his own interest he frequently promotes that of society more effectually than when he really intends to promote it."[1] Collective interest, according to Smith, is best served by unfettered private interest-seeking: we live as well as we do because others seek to profit from providing the goods and services we want.

One may sense, however, that all too often we are less helped by the benevolent invisible hand than we are injured by the malevolent back of that hand; that is, in seeking private interests, we fail to secure greater collective interests. The narrow rationality of self-interest that can benefit us all in market exchange can also prevent us from succeeding in collective endeavors.

Smith recognizes the working of the back of the invisible hand, but he seems to think it crucial in only three realms: national defense, the administration of justice, and the erection and maintenance of "certain public works and certain public institutions, which it can never be for the interest of any individual, or small number of individuals, to erect and maintain: because the profit could never repay the expense to any individual or small number of individuals, though it may frequently do

[1] Adam Smith, *The Wealth of Nations*, bk. 4, chap. 2, p. 423.

6

much more than repay it to a greater society."[2] It is in these realms that he therefore sees the need for a state apparatus. But excluding this brief passage and the final quarter of the work, which discusses how the state should finance its operations in these areas, *The Wealth of Nations*—a voluminous 400,000 words—is almost entirely concerned with the benevolence of the invisible hand, and hence, with the disruptions that state intervention must generally cause.

The problem of the back of the invisible hand has become known as the problem of collective action, or the Prisoner's Dilemma, or the free rider problem, or the condition of common fate, depending on the context or discipline in which it is used. This multiplicity of terms reveals a failure to generalize the nature of the problem. It has been generalized only recently, most notably—as discussed in the following chapter—in the game-theoretic Prisoner's Dilemma (which was developed in about 1950, although research on Prisoner's Dilemma got under way seriously in the mid-sixties) and in Mancur Olson's *The Logic of Collective Action,* published in 1965. Because earlier writers had failed to abstract from particular examples, they often failed to grasp the significance of the problem and also to recognize other instances of it. (William Baumol notes that "writers, sometimes even those who had considered these ideas elsewhere in their writings, continued to make mistakes and omissions which greater familiarity with the analysis in question might have prevented."[3])

Although not generalized until recently, the problem of collective action has been recognized in a remarkable variety of contexts over many centuries. One may read the logic of collective action out of (or into) Glaucon's devil's advocacy against Socrates over the relationship between justice and interest. Glaucon notes that, given the ring of Gyges with its power to make him invisible, not even the supposedly just man "would stay on the path of justice or . . . keep away from other people's property and not touch it, when he could with impunity take whatever he wanted from the market, go into houses and have sexual relations with anyone he wanted . . . ," and so forth.[4] With greater or

[2] Ibid., chap. 9, p. 651. Depending on the restrictions he intends in the double use of "certain"—"certain public works and certain public institutions"—Smith might seem to license massive state action in this third realm. For a survey of classical political economy theories of the state, see William J. Baumol, *Welfare Economics and the Theory of the State,* esp. chap. 12.

[3] Ibid., p. 143. As Stigler says of Ricardo, they all too often lacked "that instinct for symmetry and generality which we now associate with the formal theorist" (George J. Stigler, *Essays in the History of Economics,* p. 185).

[4] Plato, *The Republic,* bk. 2, 360b–c. The devil in the drama is Thrasymachus. Glaucon retracts his devil's advocacy in bk. 10, 612b.

less charity in interpretation, one can also find it stated by numerous political philosophers and political economists from the time of Hobbes to that of Sidgwick and Pareto, with especially elegant examples of the problem invented by Hume and J. S. Mill. And philosophers are not alone in recognizing the problem. Novelist Joseph Heller, in *Catch-22,* portrays a character's acute awareness of his self-interest in this incident: facing Major Major Major Major's rebuke for not wishing to fly any more bombing missions over Italy, Yossarian contends that the bombs he could drop would make little or no difference to his eventual well-being, while the risks involved in dropping them might make an enormous difference to him. Likewise, nineteenth-century novelist Anthony Trollope, in *Phineas Finn,* has Finn aware that one man's contribution to a demonstration in favor of the ballot would put the man more at risk than it would benefit him.[5] Indeed, it might be expected that any insight as important and clear as the logic of collective action should be contained in an adage of long standing, and it is: everybody's business is nobody's business. It even appears as a notice conspicuously posted in restaurants: A 15% service charge will be included in bills for parties of six or more.[6]

What is the logic of collective action? Suppose with Pareto "that if *all* individuals refrained from doing A, every individual as a member of the community would derive a certain advantage. But now if all individuals *less one* continue refraining from doing A, the community loss is very slight, whereas the one individual doing A makes a personal gain far greater than the loss that he incurs as a member of the community."[7] This is the logic of collective action: if I am narrowly self-interested, I would presumably not refrain from doing A. I may refrain, but only if my not refraining would adversely affect the behavior of enough others to reduce my advantage from communal refraining by more than it would cost me not to refrain. For example, suppose smog in our metropolis could be prevented if all of us would voluntarily pay to have certain antipollution devices installed in our cars, and suppose further that a referendum to require such devices would pass by a nearly

[5] Joseph Heller, *Catch-22,* p. 107. Finn, like Yossarian, could only be rebuked by the voice of duty: "Look here, Mr. Finn; I don't believe the sea will become any fuller because the Piddle runs into it out of the Dorsetshire fields; but I do believe that the waters from all the countries is what makes the ocean. I shall help; and it's my duty to help" (Cited in Stanley I. Benn, "The Problematic Rationality of Political Participation," p. 291).

[6] Group tipping has naturally been studied—by a group. See Stephen Freeman, Marcus R. Walker, Richard Borden, and Bibb Latané, "Diffusion of Responsibility and Restaurant Tipping: Cheaper by the Bunch."

[7] Vilfredo Pareto, *The Mind and Society,* vol. 3, pp. 946–947 (sec. 1496).

unanimous vote. Voluntary action would not solve our smog problem if too many of us were narrowly rational.

There is extensive evidence of this logic at work: we do not voluntarily clean up our car exhausts or stop burning wood in our fireplaces; we seldom join our neighbors to clean up our blocks or to shovel snow from our alleys and sidewalks; we contribute, at most, trifling sums to collective causes we support, and most of us contribute nothing; most of us in the United States generally do not vote in most elections; fishing nations collectively destroy open-sea fisheries; if we possessed the ring of Gyges and could make ourselves invisible long enough, perhaps most of us would pluck flowers from public grounds until the public ceased to plant flowers.

Nevertheless, the most pervasive and important instance of this logic is probably overwhelmingly beneficial. The logic of collective action is, in another guise, merely the logic of the efficiency of market exchange: the existence of large numbers of sellers makes collusive agreements to raise prices virtually impossible (unless they are backed by state sanctions). It is in this guise that Smith most clearly sees the logic. If the amount of capital of the grocery trade sufficient to meet demand in a town "is divided between two different grocers, their competition will tend to make both of them sell cheaper, than if it were in the hands of one only; and if it were divided among twenty, their competition would be just so much the greater, and the chance of their combining together, in order to raise the price, just so much the less." [8] It is the incapacity for collusion that makes sellers finally efficient, causes better products to drive out poorer ones, and leads to most of what Smith holds dear in capitalism: economic growth and progress. Of course, that incapacity also prevents sellers from earning the greater profits they covet.

NARROW RATIONALITY

The argument of the logic of collective action is based on the strong assumption that individual actions are motivated by self-interest—or on the assumption of what I will commonly call narrow rationality or, more briefly, rationality. Obviously, individual actions are motivated by concerns in addition to self-interest. But collective action for mutual benefit is, in an analogous sense, narrowly rational for a group or organization. Hence, it should not surprise us to find that many of those who want their collective interests to be served may weigh their own

[8] Smith, *Wealth of Nations*, bk. 2, chap. 5, p. 342; see also bk. 1, chap. 10, pt. 2, p. 126. See also Stigler, *Essays*, pp. 234–240, on perfect competition.

self-interests heavily, even too heavily to cooperate in serving their collective interests.

The notion of narrow rationality is parodied by William Gaddis in his novel *JR*. (Since Gaddis's fiction does not make him a living, he also writes speeches for the heads of corporations—he can perhaps be trusted to have a rich understanding of the motivations that move narrowly rational souls.) One of the elderly Bast sisters in *JR* begins to tell "the whole story" of how the Basts achieved their propertied state:

> Well, Father was just sixteen years old. As I say, Ira Cobb owed him some money. It was for work that Father had done, probably repairing some farm machinery. Father was always good with his hands. And then this problem came up over money, instead of paying Father Ira gave him an old violin and he took it down to the barn to try to learn to play it. Well his father heard it and went right down, and broke the violin over Father's head. We were a Quaker family, after all, where you just didn't do things that didn't pay.[9]

Grandfather Bast's view notwithstanding, one has an interest in increasing one's resources only because the resources make it possible to satisfy certain of one's wants. To be narrowly rational means to act in a self-interested way—when one's interests are at stake. It does not mean never to play the violin.

There is another commonplace meaning of "rationality" that is used in wider contexts, but which I do not use here. Crudely stated, it is that one is rational if, after considering all of one's concerns—moral, altruistic, familial, narrowly self-interested, and so forth—one then chooses coherently in trading each off against the others, or even in refusing to make certain trade-offs. Another way of conceiving this notion is to suppose that one's mind is departmentalized, that one is a synthesis of several selves, each concerned with particular material and all governed by an overall regulator who, in making present choices of how to act, assigns systematic weights to all the selves, according as they have already been more or less differentially satisfied. One could meaningfully say of such a regulator that it was rational or irrational. My use of "rational" in this work is less profound and less interesting than such an alternative. I merely use rational to mean "efficient in securing one's self-interest." I do not thereby imply that rationality governs all human behavior or even all political behavior. Indeed, at issue throughout the analysis (especially in chapters 6 and 7 and also in chapters 10 through

[9] William Gaddis, *JR*, p. 4.

14) is the extent to which behavior that is extrarational in this narrow sense would affect or evidently does affect outcomes in collective action situations.

Part of the appeal of the assumption of narrow rationality is almost methodological: it is easy to accommodate in analysis, and it is relatively easy to assess in generalizable behaviors. An additional appeal might be, as is sometimes claimed, that it explains a very large fraction of behavior in certain realms. One can too easily overrate the size of that fraction even in the most explicitly economic contexts. But often the assumption of narrowly rational motivation yields predictions that are the most useful benchmark by which to assess the extent and the impact of other motivations. Occasionally it yields predictions which so nearly fit behavior that investigation need go no further in order to satisfy us that we have understood why certain outcomes, and not others, occur.

The logic of collective action does just this in many contexts, although not in others. It yields a notoriously poor explanation of voting behavior, since it suggests that almost no one would voluntarily vote in, say, American national elections. It helps us understand why half of eligible Americans do not vote, but it does little to help us understand the other half. The logic of collective action is, however, unquestionably successful in predicting negligible voluntary activity in many fields, such as the contemporary environmental movement. Then what about the apparent contradiction to this logic represented by the Sierra Club and other environmental organizations? The answer, as I argue at greater length below, especially in chapter 7, is that environmentalists contribute woefully little to their cause given the enormous value to them of success and given the repeated survey results that show the strong commitment of a large percentage of Americans to that cause. Environmentalists annually spend less on their apparently great cause than 25,000 two-pack-a-day smokers spend on cigarettes. The amount spent is a trivium, and one might find it inconceivable except that it makes clear sense on a narrowly rational analysis. One could go on to note even more embarrassing statistics showing how little Americans have spent on such honored causes as civil rights, the contemporary women's movement, gun control (as opposed to anticontrol), and so forth.

Admittedly, there are groups such as the Sierra Club, the National Association for the Advancement of Colored People, and women's organizations that do not seem to fit the narrow logic of collective action. Not only do they not seem to fit, but I think it is clear that some of them do not fit that logic. Nevertheless, some aspects of such organizations (and their associated movements) may make sense on narrowly rational grounds. For example, the waxing and possible waning of the women's movement may be explained in part by changing self-interest motivations of women over the past decade (see "The By-Product Theory" in chapter 2). The women's and the civil rights movements may both have suffered from the difficulty of achieving complex goals by contract by convention, that is, by tacit coordination, as argued in chapter 13 (see "Explicit Contract Versus Contract by Convention").

Another issue has often been implicitly confused with the implications of the logic of collective action. If qualitative groups such as environmentalists and civil rights supporters are very poorly mobilized, it may be asked why there has been so much legislation on their behalf. Part of the answer is obvious: a large number of voters with strong views have clout even if they do not organize (see "Political Entrepreneurship" in chapter 2). Another part of the answer is that political outcomes are not a simple balancing of resources available to antithetical interests. The limited contributions of environmentalists are far more effective than the burnt-up expenditures of 25,000 smokers—on occasion, they even count for more than the vastly greater political expenditures of various industries. Politics is more interesting than the problem of collective action.

STATIC AND DYNAMIC ANALYSES

Most of the discussion of collective action is relatively static. Each individual faces a choice problem, each choice being associated with its own costs and benefits, as expressed in the passage from Pareto quoted above. The technical discussions in chapters 2 through 6 are static in this sense. The general conclusion of the static analysis is Olson's: larger groups are less likely than smaller ones to succeed in providing themselves collective benefits. In chapter 3 I redefine the notion of group size not in terms of the group's absolute number of members, but in terms of the number of its members who, taken as a group themselves, could all benefit if they alone provided the whole group's good. When I use the terms "small groups" and "large groups" after that, I mean small and large as defined in chapter 3. In this sense, the oil industry with its hundreds of firms may often be an extremely small group, because, for instance, Exxon alone would benefit enough from influencing a government decision to outweigh its costs of exercising influence. Similarly, those concerned with the environment in the United States may number 100 million, but a much smaller subgroup, perhaps less than 1 percent of the whole group, may be efficacious in benefiting the subgroup beyond what the subgroup expends on the effort.

Social life is sometimes, but not always, captured in static analyses. In particular, many of the most interesting collective action problems are clearly dynamic in that they recur or are ongoing, so that there is not a single choice, but rather a sequence of choices, to be made. Hence, each person's future choices may be contingent, indeed, may be *made* contingent, on others' current choices.

The dynamic analysis of collective action has almost entirely been done either qualitatively, or in the context of repeated plays of the Prisoner's Dilemma, or iterated Prisoner's Dilemma. Brian Barry argues forcefully that much of political life is analogous to an iterated—not to single-play—Prisoner's Dilemma.[10] Iterated Prisoner's Dilemma, which is often called the Prisoner's Dilemma supergame, has been studied extensively both experimentally and analytically, especially by Anatol Rapoport and Albert Chammah and by Michael Taylor.[11] The most striking result of iteration is that two players who should rationally "defect" (that is, not cooperate) in a 2-person single-play game, commonly should cooperate in iterated play. In general, in an *n*-person single-play Prisoner's Dilemma, defection is narrowly rational. In iterated play it may not be. Whether it is depends on how many others' choices are likely to be affected by one's own choice. As *n* becomes very large, it is increasingly unlikely that cooperation will be narrowly rational even in iterated play. Hence, in the dynamic analysis, narrow rationality can lead to cooperation in Prisoner's Dilemma (or collective action), whereas in the static analysis, narrow rationality logically rules out cooperation. Still, cooperation becomes less likely as *n* increases in iterated play. Hence, in either analysis, the logic of collective action militates against cooperation in large enough groups.

Chapters 9 through 14 present a dynamic analysis of group action. That analysis, being largely strategic, is based on the Prisoner's Dilemma version of the problem of collective action, since games capture strategic interactions better than other extant analytical representations. The analogy between coordination for mutual advantage in an iterated coordination game—to achieve a "convention"—and cooperation in an iterated Prisoner's Dilemma—to achieve a "contract by convention"—is the basis of the dynamic analysis in chapters 10 through 14. In general, when relevant conditions obtain, a contract by convention can produce a high level of cooperation even in relatively large groups.

[10] Brian Barry, *Political Argument*, pp. 254–255.
[11] Anatol Rapoport and Albert M. Chammah, *Prisoner's Dilemma;* and Michael Taylor, *Anarchy and Cooperation.*

CAVEATS

There is a growing literature on what is called a modified theory of collective action. The modified theory takes account of more variables in an individual's so-called expanded calculus of whether to contribute. Avoiding a feeling of guilt, cultivating a feeling of goodness, and numerous other variables are summed in as additional costs and benefits of contributing or not contributing to a collective action. There are two strong objections to such an expanded calculus. First, the results are too flimsy to be worth the effort, since most of the relevant behavior may be explained already by the narrowest assessment of costs and benefits, and the host of motivations underlying the additional elements of behavior to be explained is sure to be far more crudely measured than the narrowest cost–benefit motivation. Second, the focus of the theory usually is shifted from explaining the behavior of a particular group to explaining the behavior of those in the group who *do* join in cooperative enterprise, especially in an interest group organization, so that it is not the logic, but the problem, of collective action that has been modified.

The issue of additional variables to be included in the logic of collective action is related to a larger issue in general decision theory. To attempt a complete decision theory of human behavior would be absurd—certainly at this time, but probably also in principle. Only in an assumed context can one sensibly be asked whether one's action was rational. To make a more complete assessment would require packing the context and much of the social history that has brought that context about into one's decision calculus. No decision theorist in his right mind would attempt to do so. Since it is unarguable that we will draw the line somewhere, the issue is not whether, but where. One widely touted philosophy of science criterion has been parsimony. Although it has obvious appeal in mathematics and in mathematical physics, the criterion is often either silly or without meaning in social explanation. In part, however, it may be a surrogate for some notion of economy, some complex combination of the marginal "cost" of additional bits of understanding and the quality of those bits. For example, in the modified logic of collective action, the additional bits are minuscule, extremely costly, and of painfully inferior quality. Qualitative accounts carry us farther than such trivializing quantification.

A central issue in group theories of politics is the difference between an interest group and an organization that represents an interest, although in the vocabulary of political science the two commonly run together. The logic of collective action is not a theory about interest group organizations. Rather, it is a theory about whether there will be interest group organizations or any other kind of collective action. A group theory of politics might take interest group organizations for granted and go on from there to explain certain political outcomes. The general explanation of collective action starts with individual motivations in determining what kinds of collective actions are likely to be undertaken and what kinds are not. Hence, with the logic of collective action, there is no reason to separate analysis substantively by groups and group organizations. Rather, certain aspects of that split are to be explained. There is not a unique motivational theory for explaining why people join political organizations. Indeed, our understanding of group politics is likely to be enhanced by the general understanding of motivations to action that is not political in the obvious sense of trying to influence government decisions.

In the analyses that follow, I am not concerned with systematically considering *how* groups' goods may be supplied to them, but rather with treating of the internal incentives that motivate groups to action. In analyzing these incentives, something must be known of the cost functions to the groups for the provisions of their goods. These functions will obviously turn on, say, whether the groups have to buy their own goods or whether they can use government to force others to buy the goods. Environmentalists could achieve little or nothing without the help of government. However, the issue of internal incentives turns not on how much the final provision costs (environmental protection now costs tens of billions of dollars per year in the United States), but on how much a collective action which can cause such provision costs. Some kinds of collective action are relatively cheap today because they need only be directed at influencing government, not at, say, contracting with the steel industry. Similar actions might have been outrageously expensive in the past because they could not easily have influenced government.

Finally, if it is not immediately obvious, I should note that I am generally concerned in all of what follows with groups whose members share a common interest. All Americans do not comprise a group on such issues as protective tariffs, environmental regulations, and civil rights policies. Presumably they do form a group on the issue of whether American nuclear weapons should be used to devastate American cities. It is often, but not always, the case that collective action is of interest to a group primarily because some other group has an ongoing interest that is being served to the detriment of the first group. Sometimes, however, as in Hume's example of a thousand neighbors who would benefit from draining a meadow (see chapter 3), there is no antagonistic interest, but there is still an obstacle to collective action: individual rationality.

2

COLLECTIVE ACTION AND PRISONER'S DILEMMA

Two major analytical traditions have contributed to the understanding of the problem of collective action: the theory of public goods and game theory. The theory of public goods is the older tradition. Almost exclusively European in its beginning, it culminated in a few pages of notation and comments by Paul Samuelson that have been the centerpiece of discussion since their appearance in the mid-fifties.[1] Olson's statement in *The Logic of Collective Action* is ostensibly based on Samuelson's analysis. Game theory took form between 1940 and 1942, appearing virtually whole from the minds of John von Neumann and Oskar Morgenstern.[2] In some respects, the theory per se has been less important than the framework on which it was constructed—a framework that has come to dominate even verbal accounts of social interaction. That framework (specifically, the form in which individual games are represented, especially the payoff matrix, described in this chapter) has influenced much of subsequent social psychological research, one of whose most important strains has been work in the Prisoner's Dilemma, which was invented in about 1950 by Merrill Flood and Melvin Dresher.[3]

The relevance of the theory of public goods and Prisoner's Dilemma to the analysis of collective action is discussed in this chapter. As

[1] Paul A. Samuelson, "The Pure Theory of Public Expenditure."

[2] For Morgenstern's half of the inside story of the writing of *The Theory of Games and Economic Behavior*, see Oskar Morgenstern, "The Collaboration Between Oskar Morgenstern and John von Neumann on the Theory of Games."

[3] Merrill M. Flood, University of Michigan, Ann Arbor, Mich., personal communication, 1975.

16

already exemplified, there are numerous instances of the recognition of collective action problems appearing in various literary forms over many centuries; but the generalization of the problem stems from the two recent theoretical advances referred to above. Similarly, how to make collective action work successfully has often been grasped at least tacitly, but general understanding of devices that might work in particular contexts has followed on the generalization of the problem of collective action itself. The chief of the devices, the use of certain selective incentives to induce individuals to join in group cooperation, is central to Olson's "by-product theory," discussed below. In certain circumstances, political entrepreneurs, also discussed below, can help a group gain its collective good even while the group fails to cooperate.

PUBLIC GOODS

Public goods are defined by two properties: *jointness of supply* and *impossibility of exclusion*. If a good is in joint supply, one person's consumption of it does not reduce the amount available to anyone else. Such nonphysical goods as ideas may often be seen as joint, but it is not easy to think of physical goods that are fully joint. For example, air might historically have seemed like a good in joint supply, but today it is hard to deny that if enough people consume it in various ways, what is left for others to use is greatly altered.[4]

If a good is characterized by impossibility of exclusion, it is impossible to prevent relevant people from consuming it. Again, it is not easy to think of pure cases of goods characterized by impossibility of exclusion

---

[4] The characteristic of air that might mislead one to think it is in joint supply is rather that it is commonly in superabundant supply. It is this characteristic of land that underlies Locke's theory of property. He argues that "every Man has a *Property* in his own *Person*. . . ." Hence, "The *Labour* of his Body, and the *Work* of his Hands, we may say, are properly his. Whatsoever then he removes out of the State that Nature hath provided, and left it in, he hath mixed his *Labour* with, and joyned to it something that is his own, and thereby makes it his *Property*. . . . For this *Labour* being the unquestionable Property of the Labourer, no Man but he can have a right to what that is once joyned to, at least where there is enough, and as good left in common for others" (*The Second Treatise of Government*, par. 27). The final proviso may seem today to wreck the theory, but when "all the World was *America*" (Ibid., par. 49) the "*appropriation* of any parcel of *Land*, by improving it," was no "prejudice to any other Man, since there was still enough, and as good left; and more than the yet unprovided could use. So that in effect, there was never the less left for others because of his inclosure for himself" (Ibid., par. 33). Land is clearly not in joint supply and never was, but it was once in plentiful supply.

(although one can easily name goods from which de facto no relevant person is excluded—for example, most interstate highways in the United States are open to all legally qualified drivers and vehicles). Large bodies of law have as their purpose to erect exclusionary barriers where the naive might have thought exclusion impossible: the law can simply mandate punishment for anyone caught consuming a particular good.[5]

It is instructive to contrast public goods as defined by Samuelson with private consumption goods. For a private good, total consumption is the sum of individual consumptions, whereas for a public good, consumption is the same for every individual. If X is total consumption of a good, and x_i is individual i's consumption, then for a private good we have $X = \sum x_i$, and for a public good, $x_1 = x_2 = \ldots = x_i = \ldots$.[6]

Conceptually it would generally not make sense to speak of the sum of individual consumptions of a public good, unless the good was a strictly physical good in de facto infinite supply, as one might have described, say, air in pre-Columbian America. One might say that Proust and his publishers offered up a public good when they published *Remembrance of Things Past*, but one would be reluctant to claim either that members of the relevant public consume it in equal measure, or that there is any "sum of individual consumptions" of it. It could make sense, however, to say that my consumption of it does not impair yours. Nevertheless, we may often impute a "collective value" to the collective consumption of a public good, in the crude sense that a group enjoying a public good might be thought willing to pay some amount for the privilege. In this case, if the good is a *pure public good* in the sense that additional consumers do not detract at all from the consumption of previous consumers, then the value of the good is a function of the number of consumers, whereas the cost of providing the good is constant. If too few people would enjoy such a public good, it might be too costly for its "collective value."

Because it is hard to imagine pure cases of Samuelson's public goods, Ezra Mishan ruefully comments that "we are left with the problem of reconciling ourselves to a neat definition of collective goods that is apparently inapplicable to nearly all the familiar instances of collective

[5] See further, Duncan Snidal, "Public Goods, Property Rights, and Political Organizations," for a succinct, articulate discussion of these issues. See also the readings by Samuelson and Head and the introductions to them in Brian Barry and Russell Hardin, eds., *Rational Man and Irrational Society?*

[6] Paul A. Samuelson, "Diagrammatic Exposition of a Theory of Public Expenditure," p. 350.

goods." [7] Although it is not easy to think of examples of physically consumed, pure public goods, one can easily list goods that seem similar to public goods over some range of the number of consumers. For example, a large swimming pool is often called a *shared good*. For present purposes, however, the finer distinctions are unnecessary. But since very few of the goals or goods that groups seek can accurately be described as pure public goods, it is probably best not to confuse the analysis of collective action by treating it as a problem in the provision of public goods. Therefore, I will generally refer to *collective* or *group* goods.

There is a further reason for avoiding the technical issues of public goods. Contributing as he was to the theory of public finance, Samuelson provides an account of public goods that is concerned entirely with *consumption*. However, the issue of whether groups succeed or fail in providing themselves some collective good is instead concerned with *provision*. Their goods need to be collective only in the sense that they are collectively provided. Hence, the notion of public goods might seem irrelevant, and strictly speaking it is. But the problem of collective provision has probably been clarified, although also often confused, by conceiving of the goods that groups seek as public goods. Often it is technically wrong to do so except in some abstract sense. For example, unions seek better pay for their members. Clearly, more money every week for every worker is not a public good in joint supply, because one worker's wages are available to no other. It is the higher wage rate sought by the union that might be seen as a public good, if, once the rate is established, it benefits all the relevant workers so that one worker's receipt of the higher rate does not reduce the rate available to others.

Olson's analysis of collective action depends not on jointness, but only on the impossibility of exclusion, or more accurately, on the de facto infeasibility of exclusion. For example, if the law says that wage rates in a factory must be uniform for each job category, nonunion

---

[7] E. T. Mishan, "The Relationship Between Joint Products, Collective Goods, and External Effects," p. 334. Mishan goes on to note that it "is readily admitted that [costs] will tend to rise with the increase in the number of beneficiaries." The notion of public goods is parodied by Eugene Ionesco in a discussion of the human fear of death: "That strikes me as one of the fundamental acts of cruelty on the part of the divinity. . . . It would have been so much easier to distribute all the anxiety, despair, and panic equally among the billions of creatures on the face of the earth. In that case, our portion of anxiety would only be one three billionth of the total amount of human suffering. But no, in dying each of us bears with him the entire crumbling universe" (*The Hermit*, p. 91).

workers cannot easily be excluded from enjoying the benefits of union-negotiated wage increases. The central relationship between the analysis of public goods and the problem of collective action, then, is that the costliness or de facto infeasibility of exclusion from consumption of a collectively provided good usually eliminates any direct incentive for individual consumers to pay for the good.

THE LOGIC OF COLLECTIVE ACTION

In his simplest statement of the logic of collective action, Olson presents the straightforward equation of costs (C), gross benefits (V_i) to the individual i, and net benefits (A_i) to the individual from i's own contribution to a group's collective good: $A_i = V_i - C$. If $A_i > 0$ for some i, the group is _privileged_ and presumably will succeed. If $A_i < 0$ for _all i_, the group is _latent_, and it will fail unless other non-collective-good (selective) incentives are available to induce contributions.[8]

Olson then applies this arithmetic analysis to various classical interest groups: unions, professional associations, industry lobbies, and farm lobbies. He concludes that these groups are generally latent, and must therefore depend for their success on selective incentives to induce contributions from their members. For example, unions often benefit from union shop rules that compel workers to join or at least to pay dues. Professional associations depend on their private goods, such as journals, low-cost group insurance, investment counseling, and, most important for many associations, restrictive licensing. Industry groups depend on asymmetries among their member firms to obtain cooperation in lobbying on general-interest issues that have some special, even firm-specific, implications (discussed further in chapter 5). Of course, industry groups are often also privileged. For example, Exxon's interest in industrywide tax benefits is great enough to justify Exxon's activities independently of the industrywide group.

In his analysis, Olson sets out to do two things: (1) He wishes to show that the rational incentive to an individual in a latent group is _not_ to contribute to the group's provision of its collective good to itself. (Because this is a strictly logical point, it is obvious once the definition of the case is clearly seen.) (2) He wishes to show that large groups are less likely to succeed than small ones. (Here the point is not so obvious, partly because the definitions are not so clear. As it stands, his argument turns on facts rather than logic. It can, however, be reconstructed to yield a tautology with bite, which is the subject of chapter 3.)

[8] Mancur Olson, Jr., *The Logic of Collective Action,* chap. 1, esp. pp. 23, 49–50.

Return for a moment to Olson's first point. It is an important point, which for many seems to have been as surprising as Olson's presentation of it is compelling. Yet it was well understood before Olson's account, indeed before Samuelson's discussion of public goods. Among others, William Baumol had already (in 1952) spelled out the general argument with great clarity.[9] However, the effectiveness of his account is diminished because it is a discussion of several examples—farmers seeding clouds to cause rain, Hume's meadow-drainage problem (cited in chapter 3 at note 5), military preparedness, general education, public parks, public health facilities—without generalizing the problem. The example he considers at greatest length is more general and might readily have been generalized. He discusses the problem of investment in the future, noting that risk-aversion might deter individuals from making investments that would be socially beneficial. An individual's investment might prove to be unwise, and, even if wise, its benefits might go to someone else if the individual died or lost title to the fruits of his effort. Counter to this explanation of the tendency to underinvest in the future, Baumol then offers the far more general argument that

> the individual as a citizen, having his share of local pride, may desire an improvement in the general future state of welfare in the community. If, however, he alone directs his activities in a manner conducive to it, the effects of his action may be quite negligible. It is true that in the process he may also be improving the value of his own assets, but his private return must be discounted by a risk factor which does not apply in the calculation of the expected gain to the community. Thus neither private interest nor altruism (except if he has grounds for assurance that others, too, will act in a manner designed to promote the future welfare of the community) [see Hardin comment at note 10 below] can rationally lead him to invest for the future, and particularly the far distant future, to an extent appropriate from the point of view of the community as a whole. Taken as a commodity, improvement in the future state of the community as a whole is one that must serve a group demand and not just the demand of isolated individuals.[10]

The impact of Olson's account may be due in part to his having addressed political interest groups, thereby attracting the attention of social scientists other than economists. But that is not the whole

[9] William J. Baumol, *Welfare Economics and the Theory of the State*, pp. 90–93.

[10] Hardin comment: The parenthetical qualification evidently is intended to apply only to altruism, not to private interest. Unless enough others are sure to contribute as well, it is foolish of an altruist to give toward the provision of a collective benefit that cannot be obtained at the price of his contribution alone. Baumol, *Welfare Economics*, p. 92.

explanation. Anthony Downs had already fully grasped the logic of collective action in the context of one of the most commonplace of political goods: electoral victory (a problem discussed more fully in chapter 4 under "Step Goods").[11] Hence, the impact of Olson's account must be due in the largest part to the greater generality or abstractness of his presentation.[12] He stops speaking of draining meadows, seeding clouds, winning elections, restricting wheat production to raise prices and profits, investing in the future, and so forth, and presents an abstract equation relating costs and gross benefits to net benefits. That having been accomplished, discussion no longer has had to depend on anyone's particular examples, but on the best imaginable examples.

Olson's main conclusion—that latent groups will fail—is modified by three important considerations: entrepreneurship, the selective incentives (including solidary incentives) of the by-product theory, and extrarational behavior. As explanations of occasional group success, entrepreneurship and the by-product theory are (in part) consistent with the assumption of narrow self-interest, and are discussed in this chapter. Extrarational behavior, of course, violates that assumption, and is discussed later (especially in chapter 7).

GAME THEORY AND THE PRISONER'S DILEMMA

In the grandeur of the introductory remarks in his presidential address before the American Economic Association, Samuelson imagines himself a modern Galileo on trial, forced to renounce the use of mathematics in economics, while muttering, "But mathematics does indeed help." Indeed. He concludes that address by quoting William Blake: "Truth can never be told so as to be understood and not be believed."[13] Blake was writing too early and too poetically for us to say simply that he was wrong. But to make it right for us, who have read Wittgenstein and the logical positivists, we must read his assertion to be about logical "truth," not about contingent facts. Alas, the claim then loses much of its bite and its beauty. Although Blake would perhaps be offended at such depreciation of his intent, there is still some point to the modernized version. Often, an understanding of the underlying logical constraints of

[11] Anthony Downs, *An Economic Theory of Democracy.*

[12] In part it may have been due to the new receptivity of the audience. As discussed later in this chapter, research on Prisoner's Dilemma took off about 1965; see Anatol Rapoport, "Prisoner's Dilemma—Recollections and Observations."

[13] Paul A. Samuelson, "Economics and the History of Ideas," pp. 2, 18. (Blake's proverb is from "The Marriage of Heaven and Hell," ca. 1790–93.)

a situation and of their mathematical abstraction or generalization leads us to a broader understanding of contingent events.

If Samuelson were stood in the dock for his use of mathematics, beside him would be one of history's greatest mathematizers, von Neumann, and his colleague, Morgenstern, the creators of mathematical game theory, which has become one of the dominant frameworks for analyzing social interactions.[14] The greatest strength of game theory is that it makes the strategic aspects of social interactions explicit, even emphatic. Since it also renders them algebraically, it makes them seem incontrovertibly clear, so that it becomes second nature even for casual students of game theory to take strategic interactions into account. In this respect, the principal contribution of game theory to social scientists is not the abstruse theory, but merely the form in which individual games are represented, especially the payoff matrix, or strategic, game form. In strategic form, the strategic structures of some games are sufficiently obvious to remake the thinking of those who have once comprehended them.

Figure 2-1. Prisoner's Dilemma.

<table>
<tr><td colspan="3">Matrix 1
Row's and Column's payoffs</td><td colspan="2">Matrix 1a
Semigame: Row's payoffs</td></tr>
<tr><td>*Row*</td><td colspan="2">*Column*</td><td>*Row*</td><td></td></tr>
<tr><td></td><td>Cooperate</td><td>Defect</td><td></td><td></td></tr>
<tr><td>Cooperate</td><td>1,1</td><td>−2,2</td><td>Cooperate</td><td>1 | −2</td></tr>
<tr><td>Defect</td><td>2,−2</td><td>−1,−1</td><td>Defect</td><td>2 | −1</td></tr>
</table>

On the evidence of sheer volume of publications, the most interesting of all strategic structures is that of Prisoner's Dilemma (see figure 2-1). In its simplest form, Prisoner's Dilemma involves two players in interaction, each facing two possible strategies: that is, each can choose the strategy of cooperating, or that of defecting (not cooperating). Since the players can make their choices of strategy independently of each other, their two pairs of strategies produce four possible outcomes. Matrix 1 in figure 2-1 shows the four outcomes, represented by the four pairs of numbers, which are called payoff pairs.

Before explaining the payoff system, we should note the words "Row" and "Column" in figure 2-1; these represent the two players. *Row* and *Column* (according to the mnemonic *R*oman *C*atholic convention)

---

[14] John von Neumann and Oskar Morgenstern, *The Theory of Games and Economic Behavior*. The first edition was published in 1944.

receive the first and second payoffs, respectively, in each payoff pair: for instance, the 2,−2 pair indicates that Row receives a positive payoff, 2, and Column receives a negative payoff, −2, if Row defects while Column cooperates. The game involves strategic interaction because the players do not have complete control over their own payoffs.

The payoffs in Prisoner's Dilemma work like this: if both players cooperate, they each receive a positive payoff of 1 (represented by payoff pair 1,1 in matrix 1). If both defect, they each receive negative payoffs of −1 (−1,−1). If one cooperates and the other defects, the cooperator receives an even worse payoff, −2, while the defector does very well with a positive payoff of 2. There is, therefore, strong incentive to defect. Indeed, defection is a "dominant strategy" for each player. (In the usual definition, one strategy is said to dominate another if the first strategy always yields a payoff at least as good as and sometimes better than the second, no matter what any other player does.) Hence, if Row's choice does not influence Column's, then Row is better off defecting no matter what Column does. This is shown clearly by isolating Row's payoffs (see matrix 1a in figure 2-1): Row gets more in each column from defecting than from cooperating.

Flood and Dresher, who discovered Prisoner's Dilemma, were concerned with testing John Nash's solution for noncooperative games (games in which players are not allowed to collude).[15] The game they created was strategically equivalent to the game of matrix 1 in figure 2-1. It was later named Prisoner's Dilemma by A. W. Tucker, a game theorist at Princeton University. As it happened, Flood's and Dresher's experimental play of Prisoner's Dilemma did not provide a test of Nash's theory, but was far more interesting than such a test would have been. Rather than do a statistical count of large numbers of one-shot plays of Prisoner's Dilemma, they had two players face each other in a sequence of 100 plays, which provided opportunity for tacit collusion and therefore violated Nash's conditions. Their result was consistent with the analysis of iterated Prisoner's Dilemma presented in chapters 9 and 10—their players cooperated in a majority of the plays of the game (they were especially cooperative in the final half of the play).[16] The game, in both its one-shot and iterated versions, was next treated at length by R. Duncan Luce and Howard Raiffa. In the

[15] Nash's solution is discussed in R. Duncan Luce and Howard Raiffa, *Games and Decisions*, pp. 106–109.

[16] I am indebted to Merrill Flood for some of the early history. (Merrill M. Flood, University of Michigan, Ann Arbor, Mich., personal communication, 1975.) The Flood–Dresher results are published in Flood, "Some Experimental Games," pp. 11–17.

late fifties, experimental research on Prisoner's Dilemma began to take off, and it soared during the sixties, especially with the work of Anatol Rapoport and his colleagues.[17]

The appeal of Prisoner's Dilemma, as with the logic of collective action, has been its generality and its apparent power in representing manifold social interactions. Indeed, the problem of collective action and the Prisoner's Dilemma are essentially the same, as is shown in the next section. Again, although numerous specific Prisoner's Dilemma interactions had been commonly understood centuries before game theory, the understanding has now been generalized in such a clear manner that it can no longer easily be ignored when we turn from investigating one specific interaction to another.

COLLECTIVE ACTION AS A PRISONER'S DILEMMA

We have for the latent group, as with the Prisoner's Dilemma, a result that tells us that individual effort to achieve *individual* interests will preclude their achievement, because if the *collective* good is not provided, the individual member fails to receive a benefit that would have exceeded the individual's cost in helping purchase that good for the whole group. It will be useful to perform a game theory analysis of collective action to demonstrate that the logic underlying it is the same as that of Prisoner's Dilemma. First, however, since Olson's analysis was accomplished from the perspective of an individual in the group, let us consider a particular instance of collective action in the game of Individual vs. Collective.

Individual vs. Collective

Let us construct a game matrix (see figure 2-2) in which the row entries will be the payoffs for Individual, and the column entries will be the per capita payoffs for Collective, where Collective will be the group less Individual. The payoffs will be calculated by the prescription for rational behavior: that is, the payoffs will be benefits less costs. The group will comprise ten members whose common interest is the provision of a collective good of value twice its cost. There are two possible results if one member of the group declines to pay a share: either the total benefit will be proportionately reduced, or the cost to the members of the group will be proportionately increased. Let us

---

[17] Luce and Raiffa, *Games and Decisions,* pp. 94–102; Rapoport, "Prisoner's Dilemma."

assume the former, although either choice would yield the same analysis. For the sake of simplicity, let us also assume that there are no initial costs in providing the collective good and no differential costs as payments and resultant benefits rise, that is, exactly 2 units of the collective good will be provided for each unit paid by any member of the group.[18]

Figure 2-2. Individual vs. Collective.

Matrix 2
Individual's and Collective's
payoffs

Individual	Collective	
	Pay	Not pay
Pay	1,1	−0.8,0.2
Not pay	1.8,0.8	0,0

Matrix 2a
Semigame: Individual's
payoffs

Individual		
Pay	1	−0.8
Not pay	1.8	0

If all members of the group pay 1 unit (for a total cost of 10 units), the benefit to each member will be 2 units (for a collective good of 20). The individual payoffs will be benefit less cost, or 1 unit. In matrix 2 of figure 2-2, the first row shows the payoffs to Individual if Individual contributes (pays); the first column gives per capita payoffs to the remaining members of the group, that is, to Collective, if they pay. The second row shows the payoffs to Individual if Individual does not pay, and the second column indicates those for Collective if it does not pay. The various payoffs are readily calculated. For example, if Individual does not pay but Collective does, the total cost will be 9 units, the total benefit will be 18 units, and the per capita benefit will be 1.8 units (for Individual cannot be excluded from the provision of the collective good); consequently, Individual's payoff for this condition will be Individual's benefit less cost for a pleasant 1.8 units. From the payoffs for the game in matrix 2, one can see that it is evidently to Individual's advantage to choose the strategy of not paying toward the purchase of the collective good.

Since it is individuals who decide on actions, and since each member of the group sees the game matrix from the vantage of Individual, we can assume that Collective's strategy will finally be whatever Individual's strategy is, irrespective of what Collective's payoffs suggest. The dynamic under which Individual performs is clearly the same as that for the

[18] Within a broad range, this assumption entails only that the payoffs in the upper-right and lower-left cells in matrix 2 of figure 2-2 will contain payoffs only slightly higher or lower than might have been the case for a real-world problem. Consequently, the logical dynamics of the game are unaffected by the assumption.

Prisoner's Dilemma: the strategy of not paying dominates the strategy of paying. For no matter what Collective does, Individual is better off not paying, as is illustrated in matrix 2a of figure 2-2, which displays only the payoffs to Individual. It is clear that for Individual, not paying is invariably more lucrative than paying. Likewise, as was pointed out in the discussion of Prisoner's Dilemma, and as is shown in matrix 1a of figure 2-1, Row is better off defecting no matter what Column does. Matrices 1a and 2a are strategically equivalent; the preference orderings of the payoffs to Individual and to Row are identical, as the arrows in figure 2-3 show.

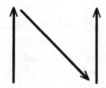

Figure 2-3. Preference ordering for Row and Individual.

n-Person Prisoner's Dilemma

For the theorist of *n*-person games, a more cogent analysis of the problem of collective action defined by the game of Individual vs. Collective would require a ten-dimensional matrix pitting the payoffs of each individual against all others. The payoffs can easily be calculated. The cell defined by all players paying would be $(1,1,1,1,1,1,1,1,1,1)$, and that defined by all players not paying would be $(0, \ldots, 0)$. Every other cell would have payoffs whose sum would be equal to the number m of players paying in that cell; each player i would receive a payoff of $(2m/10 - 1)$ if i paid, or $2m/10$ if i did not pay. Anyone able to visualize a ten-dimensional matrix can readily see that each player's dominant strategy is not to pay, because it yields the best payoff regardless of what the other players do. The rest of us can easily enough calculate that whereas the payoff to player i is $(2m/10 - 1)$ with m players including i paying, the payoff to i with $m - 1$ players not including i paying would be the preferred $2(m - 1)/10$ (in the latter case i's payoff is 0.8 units greater than in the former). Thus, once again, for each player i, the strategy of not paying dominates the strategy of paying. But playing dominant strategies yields all players the poor payoff $(0, \ldots, 0)$, and this solution is the only equilibrium for the game. (An outcome is an equilibrium if no player has an incentive unilaterally to switch strategies.)

The game now defined is simply 10-person Prisoner's Dilemma, to which any solution generalized from the game in its simplest form—2-person Prisoner's Dilemma—can be applied. To generalize the game further, n prisoners can be substituted for 10, and a ratio r of benefits to costs (with cost being 1 unit to each player) for the ratio of 2 assumed in Individual vs. Collective. The result is analogous, with the choice of not paying always yielding a payoff $(n - r)/n$ units higher than the choice of paying (the bonus increases as n increases); and if all pay, all receive payoffs of $(r - 1)$. Olson's privileged group would be the case in which r is greater than n in some player's perception (if costs are a matter of binary choice between paying a fixed sum for all players who pay, or paying nothing).

In this game there is only one equilibrium (at the payoff of 0 to every player, that is, all players not paying); but this equilibrium solution is not Pareto-optimal because some (indeed all) players could be made better off without making any worse off. Moving from the equilibrium to the payoff of $(r - 1)$ to every player (i.e., all players paying) would improve the payoff to every player. Among the seventy-eight strategically nonequivalent 2×2 games in the scheme of Rapoport and Guyer, Prisoner's Dilemma is unique in its class: it is the only game defined by the condition that it has a single stable equilibrium which, however, is Pareto-nonoptimal.[19] Hence, the generalized game of collective action defined above is analogous to Prisoner's Dilemma. (It should be clear that the reason for the equivalence of Prisoner's Dilemma and the game of collective action for a large, or latent, group is precisely the condition that in such a group one's contribution to the purchase of the collective good is of only marginal utility to oneself. Hence, one's payoff is increased by almost the amount one does not pay when one does not pay.)

Empirical Consequences

The significance of the result stated above is that any analysis prescribing a solution for Prisoner's Dilemma must prescribe a similar solution for the game of collective action. That means that the vast body of experimental and theoretical work on Prisoner's Dilemma is

---

[19] Anatol Rapoport and Melvin Guyer, "A Taxonomy of 2×2 Games." In terminology borrowed from physics, a *stable* equilibrium is one that will be restored after any perturbation. In 2-person Prisoner's Dilemma, if Row switches from a strategy of defection to one of partial or complete cooperation, Column will have no incentive to follow suit, but will continue to defect. Hence, Row will have strong incentive to revert to defection.

relevant to the study of collective action in general (and conversely that the growing body of work on collective action can be applied to the study of the Prisoner's Dilemma). In particular, any analysis of Prisoner's Dilemma yielding the conclusion that the mutual-loss payoff (which results when all defect) was not rational would, by implication, contravene Olson's claim that, for logical reasons, in a latent group "it is certain that a collective good will *not* be provided unless there is coercion or some outside inducements."[20] Since there are arguments to the effect that the rational solution to Prisoner's Dilemma is the payoff resulting from mutual cooperation, before turning to the rationale of group success, we should perhaps reconsider why it might be that, empirically, latent groups do generally seem to fail. Let us view the 10-person Prisoner's Dilemma defined above in the light of some 2-person Prisoner's Dilemma experimental results.

Whatever the rationales of players in experimental Prisoner's Dilemmas, we can probably safely generalize from the 2-person results to n-person behavior in some respects. In particular, we can probably conclude that cooperativeness will not increase, other things being equal, as n increases beyond 2 (but see chapter 3 for fuller discussion of the effects of increasing n).

Some experimental data suggest that about one-half of all players cooperate with, and one-half exploit, a 100 percent cooperative adversary-partner in 2-person Prisoner's Dilemma.[21] In the 10-person Prisoner's Dilemma described above, let us assume that this result would mean that five of the players would not pay even if the other five did pay. In this event, the benefit to each player would be 1 unit, and the cost to each of the five who pay would be 1 unit: hence, the payoff to those who pay would be 0. Consequently, even an analysis that prescribed cooperation, or paying, as the rational strategy—under the assumption that all players are rational—would allow nonpayment as a rational strategy to players in a real-world game in which habitual nonpayers drained off any positive payoff to those who pay.

Assuming the validity of the generalization of behavior from the Prisoner's Dilemma experimental data, in real-world games in which the law of large numbers applies and in which the perceived benefits of the collective good are not more than twice the costs, one can expect no provision of the collective good. In the intermediate group (where the statistics of large numbers do not apply), even with benefits considerably less than twice the costs, there is some statistical chance that a collective

[20] Olson, *The Logic,* p. 44.
[21] Anatol Rapoport, "Editorial Comments."

good will be provided. In either case, the prospects for success decline as the ratio (or perceived ratio) of benefits to costs decreases.

In game-theoretic solution theory, one generally assumes that the players are playing irrespective of the payoffs they might receive. Often in real contexts, however, part of the issue is *whether* to play, so that not playing must be included as an available strategy. For real instances of Prisoner's Dilemma and of collective action in particular, the issue is whether anyone will choose to play the game at all. In economic analyses, though not generally in game-theoretic analyses, the actual values of payoffs are not important; the only consideration is the rank ordering of payoffs. But clearly, the normal inducement to play a real-world game is the expectation of positive payoffs. Hence, if one is a rational player in a game of collective action, one does not refuse to pay merely because one's strategy of not paying is dominant and yields a higher payoff; rather, one refuses to pay because enough others in the group do not pay so that one would suffer a net cost if one did. Consequently, it would be irrational for one to play the game, and not playing means not paying.

The issue of group size and its theoretical effect on the degree of cooperation in collective action will be taken up in chapter 3. There the analysis will assume narrow self-interest. The evidence of Prisoner's Dilemma experimental games suggests that players are not wholly motivated by narrow self-interest even in that artificially narrow context, or that they define the gaming problems they face in terms other than those set down in their payoff schedules. Players may be trying to help or please the experimenter, as in Stanley Milgram's grisly experiments— subjects were encouraged to deliver supposedly fatal shocks to stooges who appeared to be screaming with pain[22]—or trying to second-guess the experimenter. Many subjects in game experiments may have altruistic attitudes toward their adversary-partners or may simply misunderstand what is at issue. On the evidence of many gaming experiments with students, I think the extent of misunderstanding is probably underrated. People's conscious statements of their perceptions of Prisoner's Dilemmas (and other problems) may be socialized into a "right" attitude, even while their behaviors are more narrowly self-interested. The overt, conscious nature of a game experiment may therefore provoke a more cooperative response than would everyday instances of Prisoner's Dilemmas. (For more extensive discussion of motivations at variance with narrow self-interest, see especially chapters 6 and 7.)

[22] Stanley Milgram, *Obedience to Authority*.

THE BY-PRODUCT THEORY

Groups that happen to have been organized previously for other reasons, for example, for sociability, can occasionally cooperate to promote their interests. However, over the long term, the essential difference between the actions of such groups and the actions of traditional, organized interest groups (whose political activity Olson characterizes as a by-product) is that the narrowly defined, spontaneous groups commonly require some coordinating event to stimulate group-oriented behavior. Once the event is past, the individuals' activities are no longer coordinated, and the group returns to its latent state even though its interest may not yet have been secured. The occasional instantaneous successes of such groups can then frequently be dissipated over time, as Murray Edelman argues.[23]

Many traditional interest groups succeed in providing their collective goods as by-products of organization based on other, selective (that is, private rather than collective good) incentives. Such groups remain organized over a long period of time and can put a fraction of their resources into providing collective goods such as higher wages, political lobbying, public relations, and so forth. The incentives that encourage and sometimes even compel membership and support range from nominal incentives such as low-cost group insurance and professional journals to potentially coercive incentives such as union shop rules and restrictive licensing.[24] Some of the most important traditional interest groups—industry groups—may require no selective incentives because they are privileged groups (for instance, the oil industry and the industries dominated by General Motors, Du Pont, AT&T, and IBM clearly are privileged with respect to certain of their industrywide interests). Other industry groups have selective incentives, such as a given firm's incentive to participate in lobbying on tariffs that could otherwise be deviously designed to benefit other firms in the industry preferentially (see further the discussion of asymmetries in chapter 5).

Many traditional forms of selective incentives used by groups to encourage membership, however, are no longer available. In part because of the success of traditional groups, government has taken over the provision of many of the goods used as selective incentives, such as group insurance, pensions, even club houses (public reservoirs and parks with easy-access highways undercut the attractions of group-outing lodges). An attractive incentive sometimes still available to many of the

[23] Murray Edelman, *The Symbolic Uses of Politics.*
[24] Olson, *The Logic,* chap. 6.

middle-class qualitative issue groups is group air travel at prices attractively lower than individuals outside groups can obtain. It is possible that the organized outings may be a greater incentive here than the reduced fares, and one should not be surprised that a major motivation for membership in the Sierra Club is to participate in outdoor activities. (It is important for later discussion, in chapter 7, to note that this seems earlier to have been the chief motivation, but that more members have recently joined primarily "to show general support of" the club's conservation activities.)[25] It seems unlikely that Sierra Club membership would fall off significantly if there were no bargain airfares.

There are other perhaps less obvious, but often more important, forms that selective incentives can take. For example, there are clear benefits from group participation in many contexts. There is a vast organizational literature on the extent to which individual members of an organization tend to become committed to the organization independently of commitment to its goals or values.[26] Among the sources of commitment to an organization are its social life with friendship ties and shared experiences, the sunk costs that one may have invested in mastering its structure, and so forth. Furthermore, one may simply enjoy activities which for the organization are merely means to its ends. On Helen Gouldner's account, the League of Women Voters benefits from strong commitments to its local chapters as a result of the pleasure members find in chapter activities. Many members evidently place high value on belonging to *some* organization and the league is the one.[27] The success of the national organization in even trying to affect the general level of political discussion seems to depend in large part on its federated structure, which provides valued local activities. If it merely solicited funds for its national purposes, it would not benefit from local selective incentives. Of course, it is in the nature of the league's national goals that local chapters serve those goals directly—to raise the level of political discussion and awareness means to raise it everywhere locally.

The more recent movement for women's liberation has also no doubt benefited substantially from selective incentives, especially perhaps from the uniquely interesting incentive of individual consciousness raising. This incentive is best provided by local, ongoing groups; the women's movement, like the league, has a naturally federated structure of local chapters, with the chief difference perhaps being that the movement is not so formally organized. If the women's movement has gone into

25 Don Coombs, "The Club Looks at Itself."
26 See esp. Philip Selznick, *Leadership in Administration;* and William H. Starbuck, "Organizational Growth and Development."
27 Helen P. Gouldner, "Dimensions of Organizational Commitment."

decline since its peak in the early- to mid-seventies, as many now assert, a principal reason may be that for very many committed women there is little more to be individually gained from continued consciousness raising. Hence, the federated structure of the movement is less able to motivate action, because action increasingly depends on public-spirited (collective good) motivation and decreasingly depends on the personal benefits to be gained from an improved self-image.[28]

Pleasure in the life of the group, or solidarity, may also be the most important selective incentive to participation in collective actions by those other than traditional interest groups. However, this incentive may have substantial implications with regard to group size that would often rule it out for very large scale groups unless, like the League of Women Voters and the contemporary women's movement, they could successfully organize federally to aggregate numerous smaller, local groups into a much larger, even national, group. There may be a double size effect for solidarity: there may be an optimum size much below or much above which participation would fail. For solidarity to grow in a group, a certain minimum number of members may be required, as some evidence for voluntary union participation suggests (see further the final paragraph of chapter 3).

There are two important shortcomings of the by-product theory. The first and lesser of these is that many of the selective incentives commonly associated with groups are not very powerful motivators. This is not true of solidarity, restrictive licensing, or union shop rules, but it is true of access to recreational facilities, receipt of journals, and group insurance, for example.[29] These latter are essentially private goods that often display increasing returns to scale as the number of "purchasers" increases, so that one might think a large group's organization could provide them at a "price" somewhat above marginal cost and thereby rake off a surplus for group-oriented activity. But if this is feasible, then markets should often develop to supply such goods more cheaply without any rake-off. As a perverse example, a union member would get a better price for group insurance sponsored by the company or the industry if the union were padding its price to include the equivalent of dues. If the origin of unions were principally explained by the by-product theory, one would probably have to conclude that their success was the

[28] Jo Freeman, *The Politics of Women's Liberation*, pp. 118, 128.

[29] Robert Cameron Mitchell suggests that such selective benefits are of little note in environmental organizations. (Mitchell, "National Environmental Lobbies and the Apparent Illogic of Collective Action," pp. 107–109.) But see Coombs, "The Club Looks at Itself," on the significance of outings to many Sierra Club members.

result of employers' failure: if American industrialists had been as quick-witted as the Fuggers of Augsburg, they might never have had to face unions on such nearly equal footing (but see the following paragraph). The Fugger family provided its workers with housing and other benefits whose unit costs must have been substantially lower than any "market" alternatives, because they were all provided on such a large scale. Certain postwar American electronics firms have openly attempted to undercut the appeal of unions through the use of similar devices.

The most obvious weakness of the by-product theory, however, is that although it can make sense of contributions to an ongoing political organization, it does not seem to explain how it is that many groups come to be organized in the first place. This would not be a problem if it seemed that organization for selective benefit reasons preceded organizational pursuit of collective benefits. But even limited knowledge of early efforts to organize labor or to organize professionals such as doctors[30] strongly suggests the contrary: many organizations were built in order to pursue collective benefits, and many of the selective incentives commonly discussed (such as union shop rules, restrictive licensing, group insurance, club houses, and professional journals) must generally have followed organization. They were the result—not the source—of group success. As Samuel Gompers said, the union shop naturally follows organization[31]—not vice versa.

Hence, Olson presents a compelling rational explanation of the survival of some organizations that provide their members with collective goods, but he leaves the origin of many such groups unexplained, and therefore the explanation of the success of their collective action is also in question. An obvious answer is perhaps that extrarational (i.e., not self-interested) motives stimulate original group organization (and perhaps even subsequent support), as is discussed in chapter 7. There are, however, two (partially) rational alternatives to that answer: (1) that original organization of latent groups is accomplished by political entrepreneurs acting in their own career interests, and (2) that groups often have complex collective interests, so they can cooperate beneficially on a very small scale for some parts of their interests, and then can use selective inducements to assist in organizing up to a larger scale for providing grander, but related, parts of their collective interests. The first of these possibilities is discussed in the next section, since it depends on an essentially static account of costs and benefits. The

---

[30] Jeffrey L. Berlant, *Profession and Monopoly,* esp. pp. 177–252.
[31] Samuel Gompers, "Discussion at Rochester, N.Y., on the Open Shop—'The Union Shop Is Right'—It Naturally Follows Organization."

second is discussed later, in the context of the dynamic analysis of collective action, because it requires interactions between various individuals' actions carried out over time (see chapters 8 through 14).

Finally, note a perverse aspect of the by-product theory: it implies only a tenuous connection between a group's interest and what the organization based on selective incentives does for that interest. This point is clearly understood in the literature on organizational commitment, which often concludes that in time an organization can subvert the values that initially led to its creation.[32] It has also been well understood in actual interest group contexts. For example, the abuse of pension funds by Teamsters Union officials might seem to many teamsters to be contrary to their collective interests. In general, if contributions to an organization are motivated by selective benefits, the contributions may continue even if the organization ceases to supply any collective benefits. This problem may be less severe for collective action organizations based on moral commitment rather than on selective benefits (see further, chapter 7).

POLITICAL ENTREPRENEURSHIP

The by-product theory generally, although not exclusively, explains how groups may maintain organization despite their apparently being latent. Another argument is that, through political entrepreneurship, groups may obtain collective benefits despite latency and even despite failure to organize at all. Political entrepreneurs are people who, for their own career reasons, find it in their private interest to work to provide collective benefits to relevant groups.

Political entrepreneurs work to the benefit of groups in two fundamentally distinct ways. First, they may be candidates for elective office who recognize that even though a group may not be organized, it may nevertheless exist as a latent group and that its members might be more inclined to vote for candidates who seek to provide the group some collective benefit.[33] Edmund Muskie and even Richard Nixon may have received some of their electoral support in the late sixties and early seventies from environmentalists who thought Muskie and Nixon would further their collective interest in various environmental policies. To this

[32] See Selznick, *Leadership;* and Starbuck, "Organizational Growth."

[33] Richard E. Wagner, "Pressure Groups and Political Entrepreneurs." See also Norman Frohlich, Joe A. Oppenheimer, and Oran R. Young, *Political Leadership and Collective Goods;* and Brian Barry, *Sociologists, Economists and Democracy,* pp. 37–40.

explanation of latent group success in obtaining collective benefits, one may object that the group members must often be stimulated to vote at all only by extrarational motivations having nothing to do with individual gain from the provision of collective benefits. Hence, narrowly rational behavior does not determine the result. This is a valid complaint against any claim that strictly rational behavior explains the whole outcome. But it does not undercut the argument that political entrepreneurship may lead to political action on behalf of a latent, unorganized group. More generally, it is not surprising that an admixture of individually extrarational moral behavior will produce collective benefits.

The second way political entrepreneurs may work to the benefit of groups is—just as entrepreneurial business leaders do—by founding and expanding organizations and by seeking collective benefits for organization members, in part, because their own careers will be enhanced by the size and prosperity of their organizations.[34] On the analogue of entrepreneurial business leaders, early union organizers and Nathan Smith Davis, an early and energetic organizer of the American medical profession,[35] may have been motivated partly by their own career interests. But, as with the by-product theory, the incentive of personal career may seem more suited to explaining ongoing than newly emerging organizations. Jimmy Hoffa owed his great power in the Teamsters Union in large part to his efforts to strengthen and expand the union, thereby enhancing the prosperity of its members. One may be less inclined to suppose that, say, Joe Hill, the "poet laureate" of the Wobblies who was executed in Utah in 1915 on a murder charge that was believed by many to be a frame-up for his strike activities, was motivated by his own career prospects as an eventual union leader. Hoffa's efforts on behalf of the Teamsters Union members might make rational sense independently of any extrarational concern he might have had for their well-being. In this respect, he is similar to Nixon and Muskie with their environmentalist policies, in that all three might sensibly have taken their stances even if they personally did not care about the issues. In the cases of both the politician and the leader of an ongoing union, action is heavily influenced by the fact that an electoral process is already organized and funded, so that neither the politician nor the union leader need pay the greater part of the costs for successful election. The later union leader's success and the leader's efforts at provision of collective benefits may be seen, however, as very much

[34] This is particularly argued in Frohlich, Oppenheimer, and Young, *Political Leadership.*
[35] Berlant, *Profession and Monopoly*, pp. 225–234.

the result of rational motivations by everyone concerned—the leader and the union membership—because there may be an extensive system of individual incentives to cause members to vote, and the career interest may be the principal motivation of the leader.

In sum, political entrepreneurship probably helps explain the fact that certain unorganized interests receive benefits, especially from government. Together with the distribution of propensity to vote, it may even help to explain certain biases in government programs toward the upper middle class, as is traditionally argued.[36] Nevertheless, groups can often control their own effects on policy more specifically when they actively lobby, campaign, or go to court than when they more nearly passively influence the choices of entrepreneurs. For organized groups, however, political entrepreneurship as an explanation of successful collective action generally suffers weaknesses similar to those of the by-product theory: it is most clearly a compelling explanation in the context of ongoing organizations, and is not well suited to explaining the origin of many organizations that serve collective interests. .

[36] See, for example, George J. Stigler, "Director's Law of Public Income Redistribution."

3

GROUP SIZE

The most controversial issue in the contemporary literature on collective action has probably been that of the effect of group size on the likelihood of group success. Indeed, Olson's central conclusion is stated in terms of group size: large groups will fail; small groups may succeed. In the original statement, this seems to be tautological but nevertheless to have bite.[1] It is seemingly tautological, being logically derived—hence the *logic* of collective action—but the extended controversy over the issue of size effects suggests that Olson's conclusion was not so clearly tautological. It will be useful here to go over the ground of the controversy in order to clarify the extent to which the size effects are tautologically derived (and hence unarguable) and the extent to which they are not.

OLSON'S TYPOLOGIES OF GROUPS

Let us begin with Olson's argument that the class of interest groups is descriptively dichotomized by a simple, clear rule. His achievement is then to show that this dichotomy correlates with the success or failure of groups. He grants that the correlation is weakened somewhat by considerations such as the intrusion of strategic interaction effects that

[1] Mancur Olson, Jr., *The Logic of Collective Action*, p. 44.

38

might cause "small" groups to fail, and by social relationships that might help "large" groups to succeed. But for many of the most important instances of groups that defy his correlation, he is able to give a consistent explanation in his by-product theory (discussed in the preceding chapter), thereby making his argument for the correlation all the more convincing.[2]

In his algebraic and graphic presentations, Olson's analysis is not about group size, but about latency.[3] Recall from chapter 2 that a group member *i* will contribute an amount *C* to the provision of a group collective good only if the return V_i to *i* from *i*'s contribution exceeds the contribution. In Olson's terms, A_i is the advantage to *i* of *i*'s contribution:

$$A_i = V_i - C$$

Now if A_i is positive for some *i*, the group is *privileged* and likely to succeed. If A_i is negative for all *i*, the group is *latent* and likely to fail. (Olson perhaps unintentionally indulges in persuasive definition when he calls the latter group latent. His central thesis is that a group that is latent in his sense is also latent in the usual sense of not being manifest. Anyone who wishes to disagree with Olson's theory must clumsily assert that some "latent" group is not latent.)

Having made this argument, Olson goes on to present a typology of groups by size so that he has two parallel typologies:

I	II
	Small
Privileged	Intermediate
Latent	Large

He then uses the terms "large" and "latent" almost interchangeably, as he does occasionally also the terms "small" and "privileged." The two typologies and the implication that failure of a group is a function of its large size are the source of unwarranted confusion—unwarranted at least in the sense that Olson's logic per se is much too clear and simple to cause confusion.

The confusion arises from the ill-conceived typology of groups by size,[4] which, oddly enough, seems superficially more compelling than

---

[2] Ibid., pp. 132–167.

[3] Ibid., pp. 22–23.

[4] In his technical analysis, Olson speaks of group size S_g as depending "not only upon the number of individuals in the group, but also on the value of a unit of the collective good to each individual in the group" (Ibid., p. 23). See further the discussion in this chapter at n. 7.

the dichotomy into privileged and latent groups—perhaps because size is more readily observable and intuitively apprehended than latency, and perhaps also because common sense suggests that there is a strong empirical correlation between groups' sizes and their prospects of failure. Hume argues as follows:

> Two neighbours may agree to drain a meadow, which they possess in common; because 'tis easy for them to know each others mind; and each must perceive, that the immediate consequence of his failing in his part, is, the abandoning the whole project. But 'tis very difficult, and indeed impossible, that a thousand persons shou'd agree in any such action; it being difficult for them to concert so complicated a design, and still more difficult for them to execute it; while each seeks a pretext to free himself of the trouble and expence, and wou'd lay the whole burden on others.[5]

Common sense does not generalize to a hard rule, however, and Hume's "impossible" is surely an exaggeration.

Olson's two typologies are based on arguments in distinctly different classes: typology I is based on an analytical (or economic) argument that divides *all groups* into privileged and latent categories; and typology II is based on empirical (or political–sociological) arguments that divide *latent groups* into smaller and larger categories. In order to draw the latter distinctions without confusing terminology here with Olson's terminology, for a moment let us use the synonyms big and little. A little latent group has political–sociological advantages to help it overcome latency. A big latent group does not. Little latent groups are equivalent to Olson's "intermediate" groups.

Because the social psychology and social structure of small groups may differ from those of large groups, one might expect that solidarity, moral suasion, or strategic interaction would work to the advantage of little, but not of big, latent groups. For example, in a little group the members can know each other's choices well enough to make others' choices contingent on their own. Although this is largely an empirical assertion, it seems probable that such contingent choosing would be much more difficult in very big than in little latent groups. (This subject is addressed in chapters 11 through 13.)

In this case, however, it is not merely the size of the group but also the ratio of benefits to costs that is important. If that ratio is very large, then a relatively small fraction of the whole group would already

---

[5] David Hume, *A Treatise of Human Nature*, bk. 3, pt. 2, sec. 7, p. 538.

stand to benefit, even if that fractional subgroup alone paid the full cost of the group good. Let us use k to designate the size of any subgroup that just barely stands to benefit from providing the good, even without cooperation from other members of the whole group.[6] In 2-person Prisoner's Dilemma, $k = 2$. If $k = 1$, the group is privileged in Olson's terms. In a nonsymmetric latent group, that is, one whose members place different values on the collective good, k may vary over a considerable range. It follows that a very large group may benefit from the sociological characteristics of little latent groups if k for the group is small. Hence, an intermediate group should be seen as one in which k, and not total group size, is small.[7]

Despite Hume's commonsense empirical correlation, it is easy to see that the division into privileged and latent groups does not imply any logical connection between group size and these two categories. One can easily define conditions under which the smallest of all possible groups (a two-member group) can be latent. And if it is logically possible that a privileged group can enjoy the provision of a good characterized by perfect jointness of supply,[8] then *eo ipso* that group could be expanded to any size whatsoever and it would still be a privileged group.

For the smallest of all possible latent groups, consider the symmetric group, each of whose two members would be willing to pay up to 3 units for a collective good that costs 4 units to supply. Hence, the total value of the good to the group is 6, for a group advantage of 2. With symmetric payoffs, a range of possible outcomes is given in figure 3-1, which is the familiar Prisoner's Dilemma. In the lower-right cell with no one paying, the good is not provided. In the other cells, the good is provided through payments of one player only or, in the upper-left cell, through equal payments from both. The payoffs represent benefits minus contributions.

[6] The designation follows Thomas C. Schelling, "Hockey Helmets, Concealed Weapons, and Daylight Savings"; and Schelling, *Micromotives and Macrobehavior*, pp. 213–243.

[7] This usage is in the spirit of Olson's own qualifications on the notion of group size. See n. 4 above.

[8] As has been stated, a good is in joint supply if its use or enjoyment by some does not impair its use by others (as my eating a hamburger would utterly ruin it for you), so that once the good is made available to one person it can be made available to others without further cost. If a good fits this definition completely, it is characterized by perfect jointness. If it does not fit perfectly, it may still be a good in joint supply which, however, suffers from crowding.

Figure 3-1. Prisoner's Dilemma with symmetric payoffs.

Row	*Column*	
	Pay	Not pay
Pay	1,1	−1,3
Not pay	3, −1	0,0

Now let the matrix be expanded to allow each player to contribute any amount from 0 to 4 units. If the sum of their contributions is less than 4 units, let a proportionate part of the project be completed, and let each value the result proportionately (for example, if half as much is contributed, each values the result half as much). By Olson's logic, this is a latent group, because A_i is less than 0 for both members. Therefore, if there are no sanctions against noncooperation, and if there are no benefits to be gained from cooperation other than the enjoyment of the greater or lesser completion of the project, the group will fail.

An example of an enormous privileged group? Suppose that a Greek shipping tycoon once dearly wanted to hear his favorite prima donna sing *Medea* at La Scala, but that the press of business kept him on the yacht. The magnate might have paid Radio Milano to broadcast the performance, and 50 million Italians would have been privileged to listen along with him. Should one think this example a frivolous abuse of logic, consider the actual case of billionaire Howard Hughes, whose tastes ran to watching westerns and aviation movies on television from midnight to 6:00 A.M. When he moved to Las Vegas where the local television station went off the air at 11:00 P.M., his aides badgered the station's owner to schedule movies through the night until the owner finally challenged a Hughes emissary: "Why doesn't he just buy the thing and run it the way he wants to?" Hughes obliged, paid $3.8 million for the station, and ran movies until 6:00 A.M.[9] The potential audience for these movies was a quarter of a million people.

EFFECTS OF SIZE ON LATENT GROUPS

The conclusion of Olson's analysis is that many potentially interesting groups are latent in his sense and therefore are likely to be latent in the sense of failing to cooperate for the group interest. Some groups will be able to secure collective goods as a by-product of their previous organization. Hence, a group that is latent in Olson's sense with respect to a particular collective good may nevertheless manifest cooperation to

[9] *Time Magazine*, Apr. 8, 1974, p. 42.

gain the good. With respect to groups that cannot achieve cooperation as a by-product of previous organization, however, Olson gives three arguments to explain why larger groups will fail to further their own interests:

1. The individual incentive not to contribute increases with group size;
2. Larger groups are less likely to be either privileged or intermediate (Olson, an economist, speaks of the likelihood of oligopolistic interaction);
3. The larger the number of people who must be coordinated, the higher the costs of organizing them to an effective level.[10]

The examples of the billionaires given above suggest that the claim in argument 2 is an empirical issue. An impertinent positivist might ask how it could be demonstrated. A pertinent answer is not obvious. In part, however, the issue turns on whether there are goods that are perfectly joint, but not very expensive (a question discussed further in chapter 8).

The claim in argument 3 is also an empirical issue, but it seems more readily subject to demonstration. Moreover, it seems likely that it would survive tests for many classes of collective goods. Nevertheless, for some very important classes of goods there is another effect, which may well counter and even far outweigh the costs of initial group organization. The production functions for many goods show enormously increasing returns to scale over a large initial range of the number of consumers. The average cost of such a good might be greater than its average value to a group member until the group finally reaches a large enough size. As the group size increases thereafter, average cost might continue to fall for some time, so that the excess of value over cost increases considerably. In this case, the larger the group, the larger may be the incentive to an entrepreneur or a subgroup of fixed size to organize the group for collective benefit. A similar argument would apply in the case of a perfectly joint good if there were increasing returns to scale in organizing the group. In addition, many formerly latent groups have been very resourceful at overcoming organization costs by "piggybacking" their causes onto extant organizations.[11] Many of the currently active environmental lobbying organizations were originally just conservation and nature appreciation organizations, whose infrastructures have since been borrowed by environmentalists at very low start-up costs to the environmental

[10] Olson, *The Logic,* p. 48. Note that here Olson seems to use "large" in its commonsense meaning rather than in the technical sense of n. 4 above.

[11] I owe the term "piggybacking" in this context to Bernard Grofman.

movement. Similarly, the Southern civil rights movement of the fifties
and sixties was largely piggybacked onto churches, especially black
Southern churches, and church organizations.

Finally, to return to argument 1, that claim is not true for the case
of perfectly joint goods, but it is true for goods with some degree of
crowding (a good suffers from "crowding" if the ratio of individual
benefit to total cost declines as the number of people who use or enjoy
the good increases). But, in any case, it is a somewhat peculiar assertion, since the issue is whether the incentive to cooperate is positive.
If the incentive is negative, one will not contribute no matter *how*
negative. It may be true that I would *more* rather not contribute to
group B than to group A, but I would rather *not* in either case. (There
is a sense in which it does matter how large the disincentive is. A small
negative incentive can be overcome with a small side-payment. For
goods that suffer crowding, a large enough group might have to receive
side-payments almost equaling their contributions.)

Despite its peculiarity, the claim in argument 1 has been the subject
of extensive commentary. James Buchanan, in an argument generalized
from his earlier analysis of clubs, categorically agrees with Olson that
larger groups are more likely to fail than smaller groups.[12] Norman
Frohlich and Joe Oppenheimer, analyzing a group seeking a pure public
(that is, perfectly joint) good, show that Olson is wrong.[13] In an earlier
version of my argument in chapter 2 that collective action is a Prisoner's
Dilemma, I show that the disincentive to contribute increases with group
size.[14] Although they do not address disincentives per se, John Chamberlin and Martin McGuire both agree and disagree with Olson, depending on various conditions; and Joel Guttman disagrees.[15]

The apparent disagreement in these findings lies in the implicit *ceteris
paribus* clauses of the authors. It is not logically possible to increase
group size, *n, ceteris paribus*. As *n* increases, something else must
change: for instance, average cost (especially for perfectly joint goods),
individual valuation, total cost, or level of supply. When we unpack
the meaning of the sentence "Large groups are more likely to fail than

[12] James M. Buchanan, *The Demand and Supply of Public Goods*, pp. 88–90;
and Buchanan, "An Economic Theory of Clubs."

[13] Norman Frohlich and Joe A. Oppenheimer, "I Get By with a Little Help
from My Friends."

[14] Russell Hardin, "Collective Action as an Agreeable n-Prisoners' Dilemma."

[15] John Chamberlin, "Provision of Collective Goods as a Function of Group
Size"; Martin C. McGuire, "Group Size, Group Homogeneity, and the Aggregate
Provision of a Pure Public Good Under Cournot Behavior"; and Joel M. Guttman,
"Understanding Collective Action: Matching Behavior."

small groups," it appears, contrary to its superficial sense, to be at least ambiguous. Among its possible interpretations are these:

1. If the size of group A is increased, so is the likelihood of its failure; and

2. If A and B are groups each with a similar common interest, and A is larger than B, then A is more likely to fail than is B.

The second meaning seems to be more useful than the first. Consider, for example, that 100 American gun owners could not contribute adequate funds for lobbying against gun control to justify, in their 100-member group interest, the lobbying effort. But 10 million gun owners apparently can. The highly joint good of preventing gun control costs too much for a very small group to yield net benefits, but it does not cost too much for a very large group. For this good, the large group therefore has some (perhaps minuscule) chance of success in voluntarily providing itself its lobbying effort; the small group has none. In the terminology from the text above at note 6, k for the interest is very large.[16] It is not easy to think of interesting cases of collective goods that would yield net benefits for both very small and very large groups. (Presumably, few would consider a tycoon's love of late-night movies or of an operatic voice politically interesting.) Hence, when we assert that large groups are more likely to fail than small groups, it is generally not useful to suppose that we mean, as in interpretation 1 above, that increasing the size of a given group increases the probability of its failure.

To appreciate the richness of this ambiguity and of the implications of increasing n, it is instructive to compare the cases implicit in the arguments of Buchanan, of Frohlich and Oppenheimer, and of Hardin. In table 3-1, row 1 presents values of relevant variables for a small group of five members. The next three rows present values of the same variables for groups of 100 members. The shift from row 1 to row 2, then, represents Buchanan's case[17] with total cost and sum of individual benefits (C and nV_i, respectively, where V_i is the value of the collective good to an individual i) held constant. (This condition might roughly be expected to obtain if the individual benefits consisted, for example, of the status inherent in belonging to an exclusive club—if the club

16 If the American gun manufacturers are counted as members of the group, k is quite small, perhaps 1. A cynical view of the National Rifle Association is that its members are being taken for a ride by the gun manufacturers. It is not a free ride.

17 Buchanan, *Demand and Supply*, pp. 88–90.

$\dfrac{nV_i}{C} \gtrless r$

TABLE 3-1. COSTS AND BENEFITS FOR 5- AND 100-MEMBER GROUPS

Row	n (number of members)	C (total cost of good)	r (ratio of group benefit to C)	V_i (value of good to i)	C/n (cost per individual)	$rC = nV_i$ (sum of individual benefits)	V_i/C (return to i per dollar)	$1 - V_i/C$ (disincentive to pay \$1)	k
1	5	5	4	4	1	20	0.8	0.2	2
2	100	5	4	0.2	0.05	20	0.04	0.96	26
3	100	5	80	4	0.05	400	0.8	0.2	2
4	100	100	4	4	1	400	0.04	0.96	26

expanded, the status of membership would be diluted, and individual benefits would fall.) The shift from row 1 to row 3 presents the case of Frohlich and Oppenheimer[18] with the value of the good to an individual (V_i) and total cost (C) held constant. The shift from row 1 to row 4 presents the case of Hardin[19] with the value of the good to an individual group member and the ratio (r) of group benefit to total cost both held constant. In the shift from row 1 to 3, as group membership increases, the total amount of the good actually provided also increases. In the shift from row 1 to 2, however, as membership increases, the total amount of the good actually provided remains fixed. In the shift from row 1 to 4, as membership increases, both the total amount of the good provided *and* its cost increase. The variables in the columns of table 3-1 should be self-explanatory (some are provided merely for the reader's information), except perhaps for k in the last column: k is simply the smallest integer larger than C/V_i. As discussed above, k is the size of the smallest subgroup that could benefit more than the total cost of the whole group's good. Note that the variables n, C, and r, which head the first three columns, can change independently of one another, but that the variables heading all the other columns are determined once n, C, and r are fixed.

If we compare rows 1 and 3 of table 3-1, we see with Frohlich and Oppenheimer that the marginal benefit (V_i/C) to an individual from contributing and, hence, the marginal incentive (a disincentive: $1 - V_i/C$) to contribute remain constant as n increases. Under the *ceteris paribus* assumptions of Frohlich and Oppenheimer, k does not increase as n does. The group remains a "little" latent group no matter how large it is. Under the assumptions of Buchanan and of Hardin, k

[18] Frohlich and Oppenheimer, "I Get By."
[19] Hardin, "Collective Action."

increases almost proportionately with *n*, so that the group evidently ceases to be "little." From the sociological considerations in Olson's discussion of intermediate groups, we would expect prospects of failure to increase with *n* in the Buchanan and Hardin cases, but not in the Frohlich and Oppenheimer case.

Examples may help clarify the numbers of table 3-1. For Buchanan's case, comparing rows 1 and 2, consider the traditional pie. Five people might successfully cooperate to buy a pie so that each could have a share. If we set the same pie before 100 people, most will not find it worth the effort to get a share. But if they would not find it worth the effort to get a share, then they would not reckon it worth their while to help buy the pie for the crowd in the first place. This good suffers from crowding—the more who enjoy it, the less each enjoys it.

For the uncrowded pure public good case, comparing rows 1 and 3, suppose our collective good is clean air. Let's say that our air is polluted by the gases from a small marsh upwind. If 5 of us agree collectively to fill in the marsh for clean air, then surely 100 of us can succeed as well, even if only 10 percent of us pitch in. Whereas 90 holdouts against buying more expensive fuel would severely damage prospects for success of the group discussed in the next paragraph, 90 holdouts against filling in the marsh need not deter success. Note the de facto similarity between this example and Hume's argument cited above. Hume seems to assume more than merely that instead of having 2 neighbors interested in draining a particular meadow, 1,000 people want that *same* meadow drained. He seems to assume that the latter project is bigger, and that each of the 1,000 people has a smaller fractional interest in the project than do the 2 neighbors in the first project. That is, he is making the argument in interpretation 2 above about increasing group size while Frohlich and Oppenheimer are rebutting the argument in interpretation 1.

For a case consonant with what appears to be Hume's argument, comparing rows 1 and 4, suppose our collective good is again clean air. But our air is polluted because we burn a very cheap, very dirty fuel. If each would spend more for fuel, all would have cleaner laundry, windows, and lungs. If there are only 5 of us, we have a fair chance of full agreement on switching fuel. If there are 100 of us, there are likely to be very many Scrooges who hold out, so that reaching a comparable level of cleanliness of our air will be more difficult in the larger group.

We might conceive each of these shifts to be literal expansions from 5 to 100 members of groups enjoying their respective goods (as in the first of the two interpretations above of the supposed rule, "Large groups are more likely to fail than small groups"). If so, Buchanan's case (row 2) involves a good that exhibits limited jointness, while Frohlich and Oppenheimer's case (row 3) involves a good that exhibits perfect jointness. Whereas the latter good suffers no crowding, Buchanan's good could be called a "totally crowded" collective good. Totally crowded collective goods meet the condition of Samuelson's private consumption goods: [20] the sum of the enjoyments of individuals partaking of the good is a fixed quantity independent of n. One can nevertheless conceive of a good that is a totally crowded collective good and not simply a private good in this sense: that those who enjoy it cannot appropriate their shares and exchange them for commonplace private consumption goods.

Hardin's case (row 4) might also involve a good that exhibits limited jointness, but which is supplied at higher levels as more people join the group (much as Buchanan's group might simply have bought more pies as it grew). Alternatively, as in the example of the severe pollution problem, it might involve a good which is the elimination of some bad generated internally by the group. In the latter case, the magnitude of the bad may increase as group size increases, so that the cost of a given level of supply of the good (for example, cleanliness of the air) also increases with group size. Hence, although the good exhibits perfect jointness, the cost of providing it rises as the group grows.

Before leaving the comparisons in table 3-1, note that Olson qualifies his definition of group size by defining individual "size" as "the extent to which [the individual] will be benefited by a given level of provision of the collective good." [21] This is not a rigorous definition, but one can infer that under it the move from row 1 to row 3 does not involve an increase in group "size." That is to say, what Olson means by group size is not n, but something at least roughly in the spirit of k.

In summary, the distinction between privileged and latent groups is not a function of group size except in the following sense: a group is privileged if it has an efficacious subgroup of size $k = 1$; a group is latent if its smallest efficacious subgroup has more than one member, so that $k > 1$; a group is intermediate if k is greater than 1, but is "small," where the meaning of small is somewhat indeterminate and probably variable according to context. For example, in a study of union participation and activity, it was found that the highest level of average

20 Paul A. Samuelson, "The Pure Theory of Public Expenditure."
21 Olson, *The Logic,* p. 28.

participation occurred when shop size was around 200.[22] For smaller and for larger shop sizes, participation fell off. It may be that in such a context, where members are selecting not associates but jobs, there must be enough people to provide relevant diversity before enough interlocking friendships develop to lead to solidary ties. For sizes much larger than 200, free rider effects might set in. On a neighborhood block, however, a dozen or fewer people might successfully cooperate at a very high level (largely, perhaps, for the reasons discussed in chapter 10), while free rider effects might deter cooperation if the number of families on the block rose much higher, so that there would be little or no cooperation well before size reached 200 families.

[22] S. M. Lipset, Martin Trow, and James S. Coleman, *Union Democracy,* pp. 170–200, and fig. on p. 218. See also Schelling's related discussion of the "dying seminar," which dies for increasing lack of participation when participation falls below a certain level (*Micromotives,* pp. 91–92).

4

TYPES OF COLLECTIVE
ACTION PROBLEMS

In the Prisoner's Dilemma–collective action game presented in chapter 2 and discussed further in chapter 3, two important assumptions were made, namely, that individuals could either contribute a set amount (1 unit) or contribute nothing, and that the collective good could be supplied at varying levels. In many collective action problems, one or both of these may not apply. There are two additional important considerations that do not necessarily influence the game matrix or its strategic structure, but which often do influence the strategic possibilities in particular collective actions. First, although the literature chiefly discusses groups that are interested in the provision of goods, many collective action problems, especially those that are political issues, have as their best outcomes the elimination of harm rather than the provision of good or goods. Second, it often matters for the success of a group whether its good or bad is to be provided or generated *internally* or *externally,* that is, by the members of the group themselves or by an outside party.

DIMENSIONS OF COLLECTIVE ACTION PROBLEMS

One might draw up a typology of collective action problems on these three dimensions: (1) collective good versus collective bad,

Short portions of this chapter have appeared in an article by the author, "Group Provision of Step Goods," in *Behavioral Science* vol. 21 (1976) pp. 101–106.

(2) step (especially binary) contribution versus continuous levels of individual contribution, and (3) step (especially binary) provision versus continuous levels of provision of the good or bad. It is not difficult to find examples of real-life collective action problems to fit every one of the eight cells in such a typology. For example, a good somewhat undevoutly to be desired on a lazy, suburban, springtime Sunday morning is quiet. But one neighbor with a power mower can provide a step contribution/step provision/collective bad to twenty others. Some examples might yield ambiguous fits. In particular, one may often invert goods and bads, just as, with a bit of creaking in his logic, a robber with a gun might claim to be offering continued life rather than threatening quick death. And few goods or bads may be so clearly either step contribution or step provision as is the Sunday morning lawn mower.

The three dimensions listed above often have implications for strategic possibilities in games that define various collective action problems. The most obvious implication is that, as discussed in the next section, a pure step good is often not strictly a Prisoner's Dilemma, although this analytical fact often will not matter for behavior. If a collective action requires binary rather than continuous contributions from individual members of a group, there may be heightened interest in inducing a particular member to contribute—if I have already made my contribution (for example, by voting in an election) and am logically precluded from doing more under the rules or conditions of our collective action problem, then I may apply my energies to trying to get you to contribute. This effect may be even greater if our good is a step good (for example, qualifying a petition) that will be provided only if a certain level of contribution has been achieved.

Those not already uncomfortable with a three-dimensional typology might wish to add a fourth dimension: (4) internal provision versus external provision of the good or bad. The late-sleeping suburbanites suffer a bad produced externally by the power mower of an early rising neighbor, and if they wish to eliminate the bad, they must deal with that external agent. For many goods and bads, groups have a choice of collective actions directed internally (at themselves) or externally (at outside agents). For example, if users of a beach prefer to have it free of litter, they can individually not litter (internal direction), or they can have some agent regularly remove all litter (external direction). If our air is polluted primarily by our cars, we can clean it up; if it is polluted primarily by a factory, only the factory can clean it up. For either type of pollution, we might as a group prefer to organize a collective action to lobby government to intervene instead of attempting to do it ourselves or to deal with the factory. This is also true for goods: we may prefer organizing in order to lobby government to provide, say, recreation facilities instead of organizing them ourselves. Such preferences may be cynically motivated by a desire to shift costs for our benefits onto others, but they may also be motivated by compelling strategic considerations. Two such considerations are especially important. First, a collective action by a small fraction of a group might be adequate to engage government, but woefully inadequate to provide the group's good or eliminate its bad. And second, for an ongoing or recurrent problem, one-time organization to engage government may be considerably easier than continuous organization to regulate internal group action or such external agents as neighbors or firms.

Let us digress briefly on these two points. First, the barriers to a collective action adequate to engage government may be lower than the barriers to organizing the group to achieve its own provision. Government intervention as a means of securing a collective benefit in such cases may be referred to as the "Baumol solution" of the collective action problem, because Baumol has discussed it at some length with clarity and force.[1] He is concerned with giving an economic argument for the existence of the state as well as for state intervention in particular instances. It is the latter which is of interest here and to which the Baumol solution applies. He cites one of the best classical statements of the problem, an argument by J. S. Mill.[2] Mill discusses the problem of laborers in concerting a mutually beneficial refusal to work more than nine hours a day even if it was clear that they would then be paid at the same daily rate at which they were previously paid for ten hours' work. Mill argues:

> There are matters in which interference of law is required, not to overrule the judgment of individuals respecting their own interest, but to give effect to that judgment; they being unable to give effect to it except by concert, which concert again cannot be effectual unless it receives validity and sanction from the law.[3]

Why? Because, under the logic of collective action, voluntary cooperation cannot be assured.

> But suppose a general agreement of the whole class: might not this be effectual without the sanction of law? Not unless enforced by opinion with a rigor practically equal to that of law.[4]

[1] William J. Baumol, *Welfare Economics and the Theory of the State,* chaps. 10–14, esp. chap. 12.

[2] Ibid., chap. 12, pp. 149–152.

[3] J. S. Mill, *Principles of Political Economy,* bk. v, chap. xi, sec. 12, p. 963.

[4] Ibid., pp. 963–964.

In sum,

> Assuming then that it really would be the interest of each to work
> only nine hours if he could be assured that all others would do
> the same, there might be no means of their attaining this object
> but by converting their supposed mutual agreement into an engage-
> ment under penalty, by consenting to have it enforced by law.[5]

If it is feasible to achieve government intervention, which is a form of
external provision, a group may find it easier to obtain government
action than to provide its good internally. Hence, other things being
comparable, those collective action problems with which government can
be expected to concern itself are advantaged over those that government
would consider outside its domain. Coordination of traffic at major
intersections is far more efficiently achieved by traffic police or signals
enforced by police than by entirely voluntary coordination, and government has long been willing to take over that problem. Many activities,
however, are not subject to inexpensive (from the viewpoints of the
relevant groups) government intervention, and many of these are
therefore more severely subject to the logic of collective action.

Let us now turn to the second strategic consideration in a group's
decision to organize to lobby government instead of organizing itself.
Again, this second point involves the effects over time on a collective
action to overcome a recurrent problem. R. H. Coase has argued that,
in the absence of transactions costs (and, one should add, in the absence
of certain forms of strategic behavior which, outside game theory, are
commonly called extortion), overall social efficiency is not affected by
the distribution of property rights.[6] For example, whether the rights
to air are owned by polluters or breathers will not affect whether the air
will be polluted. If the cost of not polluting is not high, a firm will not
pollute in either case: if the firm owns the rights, breathers will see it
in their interest simply to pay the firm enough that it will prefer not to
pollute. If the cost of not polluting is high enough, the firm will pollute
in either case: if breathers own the rights, they will sell them to the firm.[7]
This result is the so-called Coase theorem. (Strategic behavior can

[5] Ibid., p. 964.

[6] R. H. Coase, "The Problem of Social Cost."

[7] Particular cases require more complex statements, but the results are similar.
For example, if breathers own the air, the cost of buying their rights might
bankrupt the firm if its increased costs made it no longer competitive. But it
would be bankrupted even if it owned the air rights, because the breathers could
pay its competitors to undercut it as much as they would have in the former
outcome.

wreck the result, since, for example, a firm with the right to pollute could pollute even at higher production costs in order to extract a profit from breathers when they offer to pay "enough" to end the pollution.) [8]

Suppose now that a firm has the right to pollute, but that pollution is inefficient in the sense that breathers and the firm could all be made better off if breathers paid to end (or reduce) the pollution. Suppose further that the breathers successfully overcame their collective action problem and offered to contract with the firm, and that the firm agreed. The contract would still have to be enforced, and if the breathers subsequently disbanded their organization, the firm might violate the contract. The costs of organizing the group of breathers in the original collective action and the possible enforcement of the contract would be among the transactions costs of achieving an efficient outcome, and they would presumably be high, not least for Prisoner's Dilemma reasons.

But consider how much higher the transactions costs of achieving an efficient outcome could be if the group's bad were internally generated. Collective action itself might be harder, because it might require a higher level of cooperation, as discussed above, to achieve similar results. But enforcement costs might be prohibitively higher, since each individual violator would have to be sued, and the costs of suing one violator might be far more than the benefit to be gained from compelling that violator to comply with the original contract. Even if property rights in air belonged to breathers, if pollution was generated by the breathers themselves (for example, by burning dirty fuel in their furnaces or cars), contracting with themselves to stop the pollution would often be prohibitively difficult, merely for collective action reasons. As in Mill's argument above, recourse to government intervention might succeed more easily than contractual efforts, but only if it were relatively easy to get the problem into the domain of government. (This issue raises difficult corollary issues, such as the possibility that government intervention might be so inexpensive to obtain that it would be inveigled even to achieve inefficient outcomes. It would be a reasonable inference from much interest group activity to claim that certain groups, especially business and professional groups, have commonly inveigled inefficient government intervention. Some corollary issues will be discussed below, especially in chapters 5 and 14.)

Two dimensions of the fourfold typology of collective action problems will be discussed at length below: step provision (as opposed to continuous provision) of goods, and collective bads (as opposed to goods).

[8] G. A. Mumey, "The 'Coase Theorem': A Reexamination."

The other two dimensions, step versus continuous levels of contribution, and internal versus external provision are best discussed in the context of the first two dimensions and in various later discussions of their strategic implications. Issues of equity (discussed in chapters 6 and 7) and the prospects for contract by convention (chapters 10 through 13) will often be less conflicted if the only choice of contribution is binary— to contribute or not to contribute. However, as is true of step goods (see next section), it may also happen that step contribution can blur into more nearly continuous contributions: for example, one may either pollute or not pollute, but it also matters *how much* one might pollute. Although in principle it need not do so, internal versus external provision often defines whether a collective action is political in the ordinary sense of being directed at influencing government action. This issue is discussed further in chapters 7, 8, and 14.

STEP GOODS

If contributions are binary in a step good collective action, then the good will be provided only if enough members, k, of the group contribute. (If the Sunday power mower example discussed above were in a small suburban compound, k could equal the total number of members of the neighborhood.) The structure of the collective action game would therefore not be particularly clarified by game-theoretic representation in this instance. Analytically more complex step goods would involve a quasi-continuum of possible contributions, such as in the case of goods to be purchased by a group.

The Collective Action Game for Step Goods

It is not a simple matter to represent as a game the collective action problem for a continuous contribution step good. As a first stage in such a representation, it is useful to restrict ourselves to a single-step symmetric game in which, additionally, all those who cooperate contribute equal shares, which sum to just enough to provide the good. Assume that we have a step good that can be supplied to an n-person group at total cost C and at ratio r of group benefits to cost. If $r > n$, it is in an individual's interest unilaterally to provide the good if others refuse to help pay the cost, so that the group is a privileged group. Let us assume $r < n$, so that we have a latent group.

If the good is provided at all, then some subset of the group must pay the total cost C. Assume perfect symmetry of benefits, so that each member of the group benefits by an amount rC/n if the good is pro-

Figure 4-1. Step good collective action game ($r = 3, n = 5, C = 5$).

Number besides i who pay	4	3	2	1	0
Payoff to i if i { pays	2.0	1.8	1.33	0.5	−2.0
does not pay	3.0	3.0	3.0	3.0	0
Number besides i who do not pay	0	1	2	3	4

vided. If m ($\leq n$) is the number of those who contribute toward supplying the good, then C/m is the average contribution. Assuming symmetry among the contributors, the payoff to the m contributors is $rC/n - C/m$, and to the noncontributors the payoff is simply rC/n. If all contribute, $m = n$, and the payoff to each player is $[(r - 1) C]/n$.

As an example, consider the case for $r = 3$, $n = 5$, $C = 5$, and $m = 1, 2, 3, 4, 5$, as given in the matrix in figure 4-1. The two payoff rows of the matrix exhibit the binary choice that an individual player i faces. For instance, if i chooses to join two others in paying for the good, i's payoff is 1.33, whereas if i does not join them, i's payoff in the cell directly below 1.33, is 3.0.

If we compare the upper row of payoffs with those in the lower row, we see that the payoff from not paying is always greater than the payoff from paying. Hence, the strategy of not paying dominates the strategy of paying. (As has been mentioned, one strategy is said to dominate another if the first strategy always yields a payoff at least as good as and sometimes better than the second, no matter what any other player does.) Since all individual players in this game face the same matrix, if all choose the dominating strategy, the payoff to each will be 0. Had all chosen the dominated strategy, each would have been better off, at a payoff of 2.0. Hence, this is a Prisoner's Dilemma, albeit somewhat contrived.

The matrix in figure 4-1 is too simple to capture the full range of possibilities in many instances of step, or lumpy, collective action games. Choice in real situations is sometimes binary—as in the choice of whether to vote or not to vote, in most analyses of Prisoner's Dilemma, or in a remarkable range of examples discussed by Schelling.[9] But in many other situations, as noted above, the choice is not merely whether, but also how much, as with charitable contributions or campaign work. For such cases, the individual faces an enormous range of choices from 0 to very large contributions.

[9] Thomas C. Schelling, "Hockey Helmets, Concealed Weapons, and Daylight Savings"; and Schelling, *Micromotives and Macrobehavior*, pp. 213–243.

In order to accommodate the nonbinary range of possibilities, the matrix in figure 4-1 can be expanded to allow i to choose to contribute anything from 0 to an amount equal to the cost of providing the group step good. For the general case of an n-person group, this new matrix will be n-dimensional, and if each individual could contribute at t different levels, the number of cells would be t^n. (If costs were infinitely divisible, there would not be payoff cells, but a continuum of payoff points. But infinite divisibility is an unrealistic notion in actual choice contexts. Hence, the terms "continuous" and "continuum," as used here, should not be given a mathematically literal sense.) Of course, many of the cells or points in the matrix of the nonbinary case would represent possibilities that one would not expect to result from actual group choice. For instance, the group members would have to contribute, wastefully, far more than was necessary to provide the group good in order to reach numerous cells in the matrix.

If one can picture the nonbinary matrix, the most interesting view comes from scanning the matrix of payoffs upward from the bottom row of 0 contribution to higher rows of increasing levels of contribution. If the dominating strategy is to contribute nothing, as in the usual analysis of the Prisoner's Dilemma and of latent groups, then the payoff in the bottom row of a column always should be greater than, or at least equal to, each payoff above it in the same column. This is not the case in the non-binary-choice step good matrix.

If other members of the group have already contributed the bulk of the cost of a step good, then an individual might stand to benefit more from final supply of the good than the additional increment required for its provision. Hence, the nonbinary matrix may include numerous local regions in which noncontribution is not the preferred strategy for an individual. If so, the matrix violates the defining characteristic of Prisoner's Dilemma. The perversity of such local regions follows from the fact that the good is lumpy, so that contributions totaling 99 percent of the cost of the good leave it just as thoroughly unprovided as would no contribution at all.

Smearing the Logic

There are two considerations which nevertheless suggest that the Prisoner's Dilemma outcome of noncooperation will follow from individualistically rational choice in providing step goods. First, the pristine elegance of a sharp-cornered step with a vertical riser may not commonly characterize real goods when those goods are lumpy. Slightly sloping the riser upward to the right, as in figure 4-2, will be enough to return the logic of the game to Prisoner's Dilemma in many instances.

Figure 4-2.

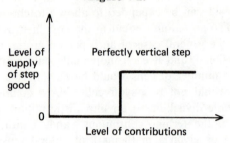

Level of supply of step good

Perfectly vertical step

0

Level of contributions

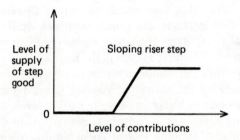

Level of supply of step good

Sloping riser step

0

Level of contributions

Second, one may not look for game-theoretic dominance, but rather for the expected value to oneself of one's contribution. This value may be less than the contribution, in which case contributing would be individually irrational even if not contributing is not a dominating strategy.

Norman Frohlich, Joe Oppenheimer, and Oran Young note that, under relevant patterns of expectations, "rational individuals may conclude that it is worthwhile to contribute toward the supply of the collective good."[10] If one expected that others' contributions would fall short of the cost of providing a step good, one might then calculate that one's benefit from one's own contribution would exceed that contribution. Similarly, for a relatively lumpy good with a sloping riser, if others' expected contributions would have pushed supply into the region of very steep slope in the graph of benefits against costs in figure 4-2, then an individual's returns from the individual's own contribution again might exceed the contribution.

However, the notion of expectations, or of expected value calculations,[11] suggests a contrary conclusion in the commonplace contexts of many groups. If members of a group must choose when they have deficient knowledge of how others are choosing, then their expectations

[10] Norman Frohlich, Joe A. Oppenheimer, and Oran R. Young, *Political Leadership and Collective Goods,* pp. 21–22.
[11] Ibid., p. 24.

that the group will push provision into the region of the step or of the steep slope may be considerably less than 1. The expected value of an individual's contribution then would be the value of a useful contribution discounted by the expectation that the individual's contribution will not be useful. This expected value will commonly be less than the contribution.

Of course, one can easily imagine circumstances under which group members' expectations about each other's behavior will be very nearly certain. But these circumstances are most likely to obtain in already organized groups in which the members are able tacitly or legally to contract with each other to contribute fair or assessed shares. Obviously, such collusion would often also suffice to resolve usual 2-person Prisoner's Dilemma games. Moderately anomic groups commonly face a twofold obstacle to cooperation: they cannot contract with themselves to cooperate, and they cannot be very confident of their expectations of each other's behavior. Again, for such a group, it may be individualistically rational not to cooperate even though noncooperation is not a dominating strategy in the group's payoff matrix.

A Step Good Collective Action: Election of a Candidate

There are few genuine single-step goods. One of the standard examples is a bridge—but bridges vary over a near continuum from terrifying Himalayan rope footbridges to the stupefying Verrazano-Narrows Bridge. Perhaps the most renowned of all genuine step good collective actions is the election of a candidate to office: two votes out of thousands or, in principle, even millions, can make the difference between success and failure. Electoral victory has other characteristics—especially that it is played as though it were a game with, at best, poor communication and that it can be seen as a one-shot rather than an ongoing game— which make it an excellent example of most of the analysis above.

Consider the costs and benefits of voting in a major statewide election in a state as large as Illinois. To simplify the calculations, however, assume an election for a single office rather than a simultaneous election for numerous offices. Suppose that there are likely to be about 4 million votes cast in the statewide gubernatorial contest, and that I keenly value the election of A over B—it is worth, say, a thousand dollars to me (a preposterous figure for the vast majority of the voters, including me). The more nearly I expect the election to be a toss-up, the more interested I am in voting. But maybe not interested enough.

As noted above, in general for large n, looking at the matrix to decide whether it is a Prisoner's Dilemma may be less compelling than determining the expected value to me of my contribution. In such a determination, the fact that some contribution might make the difference between provision and nonprovision of a step good is discounted by the low probability that a particular contribution will be the one that makes the difference. This is the central argument of Downs's analysis of whether to vote.[12] What is my expected probability that my vote will make a difference in the election of A over B? In part, of course, the answer is a function of my information about the likely behavior of others, although this is likely to take the form of aggregate rather than specific individual information. In the 1976 Illinois gubernatorial contest, Michael Howlett had little hope against James Thompson, who received 3 million votes, or 65 percent of the total cast. No voter could sensibly have been drawn to the polls solely on the chance of influencing the outcome in that race. In 1972, however, Daniel Walker defeated Richard Ogilvie by fewer than 80,000 out of 4.6 million votes cast, receiving 50.8 percent of the total vote.[13] A reliable poll should have called that election a toss-up.

Now suppose that a traditionally reliable poll shows a toss-up between A and B. With no better information than is provided by a preelection poll, there are various assumptions one might make in determining one's expected probability of making a difference in an election. If the poll says A has a 50 percent chance of winning, there is a substantial chance that A will win or lose, say, 53 percent of the vote with a not very sharply peaked normal distribution over the intervening range—in which case my vote could be expected to be worthless. To give my vote excessive benefit of any doubt, assume that I expect the 4 million other Illinois voters to enter the polls, flip 4 million fair coins, and vote for A when heads turns up and for B otherwise, while if I vote, I will vote for A. Given that I value A's election at a preposterous thousand dollars, my vote would be worth about forty cents to me.[14] If I would be willing to pay as little as fifty cents to avoid the hassle of going to the polls—let's say the phone company tallies votes at a charge of fifty cents to the voter's phone bill, and I would rather vote

---

[12] Anthony Downs, *An Economic Theory of Democracy*.

[13] Michael Barone, Grant Ujifusa, and Douglas Matthews, *The Almanac of American Politics 1978*, p. 224.

[14] Under the same assumptions, my vote would be worth about eighty dollars to me if the electorate numbered 100, eight dollars if it numbered 10,000 and only eight cents if it numbered 100 million, so that in a perverse twist, most voters could probably agree with George Wallace that there is not a dime's worth of difference between the major parties' candidates for president. I owe these calculations to Duncan Snidal.

by phone than trek to the polls—it would be irrational of me to vote strictly for my own benefit.

The example of voting as a collective action problem obviously undercuts the assumption of strictly self-interested behaviors, since over half of eligible Americans have voted in recent quadrennial elections.[15] But, considering how relatively few people turn out despite all the institutional and moral exhortations to do something so public and uncostly as to vote, one might expect that quieter instances of collective action problems would suffer substantially greater neglect.

COLLECTIVE BADS

The annual Avant-Garde Festival of New York has been called that only since the second festival. The festival director did not like the term "avant-garde," but "John Cage was sued by a lady who claimed that his music had permanently impaired her hearing. So we started calling it avant-garde the second year when our lawyers advised us that there should be something in the title to warn people they weren't going to hear Mozart."[16] For at least one person in New York, Cage's music constitutes a bad. What would make a bad the subject of collective action in the way that de facto impossibility of exclusion makes a good the subject of collective action?

The Collective Action Problem for Bads

For people in the auditorium where Cage's music was being performed, the music was in joint supply. If all those people had found it painful, as one woman did, presumably they would have left. But suppose they could not leave without incurring very high costs, so that they would prefer to stay even on pain of listening. Then they would be unable to reject the music, and it would be a collective bad—and heaven help the orchestra if the audience overcame its collective action problem.

A radiobroadcast is a collective good that, thankfully, one can easily reject, but from which one cannot easily be excluded. A broadcast by loudspeaker in a public place is a good that one cannot easily reject, and from which one cannot easily be excluded. Because the latter cannot easily be rejected, it is potentially a public bad. (However, as with the so-called impossibility of exclusion characteristic of collective

[15] For further discussion, see Brian Barry, *Sociologists, Economists and Democracy*, pp. 19–23.

[16] *Village Voice*, Sept. 15, 1975, p. 40.

goods, impossibility of rejection is not really the issue—rather, de facto infeasibility or costliness of rejecting a bad is sufficient to provoke collective action problems.) This essential asymmetry in the defining characteristics of collective goods and collective bads has consequences for the nature of the collective actions and the politics that they are likely to provoke.

Whether a particular provision is a good or a bad is, of course, an empirical, subjective issue. To those who enjoyed the constant sound of patriotic polemics and martial music in the public places of Berlin during the Third Reich, the broadcasts were a good. For those who, like the author of *The World of Silence*,[17] cherished occasional silence, presumably they were a bad.

While granting this distinction in individual valuations, one still might argue that there should be no asymmetry in the collective consequences of goods and bads. If the broadcasts are a bad, their absence is a good, and what people would do to prevent the bad is surely equivalent to what they would do to provide the obverse good. Many distinctions, such as gain versus loss, or threat versus exchange, which stand up to ordinary discourse, will wither under a persistent philosophical glare. Nevertheless, the ordinary discourse account may reveal distinctions that motivate behavior. A group's members may uniformly perceive either that they suffer from a bad or that they fail to benefit from a good, and although the logical account of costs and benefits might be strategically the same, the group's action may depend on whether its members see their problem as the elimination of a bad or the provision of a good.

Despite the formal equivalence of their payoff structures, cooperation to oppose a loss may be easier than cooperation to support a gain for several reasons. First, the goal of action is likely to be more clearly focused, for example, opposing a specific refinery or highway project rather than supporting "some constructive effort." This distinction may not generalize to some classes of bads, such as pollution, but even then it might often be compelling. The very real presence of pollution may focus and unify action for general antipollution policies to a degree that general desire for some general good may not; this is so because there may be various alternatives that many prefer in order to obtain some general good.

A second reason why cooperation to oppose a loss may be easier is that the way costs are exacted in controlling many collective bads differs from the way they are more commonly exacted in providing goods. In particular, many large-scale bads of political interest are controlled

17 Max Picard, *Die Welt des Schweigens.*

through regulation, which is a relatively inexpensive task for government and a relatively easy policy for public interest groups to request. Hence, the gain to a group from action to regulate a bad created by an external agent may be large relative to the costs of the action.[18]

A third reason is that if a bad comes from an external source, the prospects for collective action may be heightened by moral reaction to the inequity. (Hence, what might seem like goods are often defined as inequitable bads. This could serve the strategic purpose of enhancing the focus of action as well as of motivating more intense action.) Of course, this is a difficult empirical claim on which the evidence may be subtly distorted. It may be that in market societies, especially in the United States, the claim to government intervention is more compelling if we can credibly argue that our group's illfare is partly the doing of others. Government may be less inclined to respond to Mill's suggestion that we require legal sanctions (the Baumol solution) to effect action by us to achieve our ends. If this is true, it seems to be so only for large public interests and not for narrower business interests, as E. E. Schattschneider, C. E. Lindblom, and harsher critics claim.[19] Business has traditionally seen government's role as that of providing infrastructures and supports like general education, roads, canals, and tariff barriers, and even—when Prisoner's Dilemma effects have unprofitably heightened competition in an industry—regulation of the traditional kind, as with the Federal Communications Commission, Civil Aeronautics Board, Interstate Commerce Commission, early-day food regulation, and so forth. Furthermore, even if it has not been as commonly applied to public interests as to business interests at the American national level, the Baumol solution has been considerably more commonly applied in certain other market societies and at the American local government level. For example, American middle-class and upper-middle-class suburban governments have often seen their role as effectuating certain ends of the general populace in their communities. Nevertheless, it may be true that public—as opposed to business—interest groups in the United States have been more often organized to oppose bads than to support goods because government has generally been more responsive to the former efforts, as various market economists' theories of the state recommend.

A fourth reason why cooperating to oppose a loss may work better than doing so to support a gain is that people who would not cooperate

---

[18] See further, chap. 5, sec. on "Political Effects of Asymmetries"; and Russell Hardin, "Groups in the Regulation of Collective Bads."

[19] E. E. Schattschneider, *The Semi-Sovereign People;* and Charles E. Lindblom, *Politics and Markets.*

in a collective action to provide their group a good might nevertheless be averse to doing what would harm others. Hence, one might not give to a fund for cleaning a beach, but would still go to some trouble to avoid littering that beach. Many people voluntarily stopped using fluorocarbon aerosols as the ozone depletion theory was publicized, although the large-number logic of collective action should apply to such a case with a vengeance. J. N. Findlay's distinction between horatory ("Thou shalt aid") and minatory ("Thou shalt not harm") norms,[20] and his and others' claim for the greater force of the latter may be formidable considerations in social choice, even though they do not enter strict accountings of payoffs in game-theoretic representations of social interactions.

Fifth, many people are contractarians (as discussed in chapter 6)— that is, they play fair. Their impact may be especially important in relatively smaller groups, but it may occasionally be important even in a whole society. For contractarians in large groups, the first consideration above, that bads may be better-focused goals for collective actions, may be very important—there can be widespread agreement over what not to do even when there is little agreement over what to do.

Finally, there is a sixth consideration, which is better left for fuller discussion in chapter 5 ("Asymmetries in Collective Action"): it is the problem of hysteresis in individuals' perceptions of the relative sizes of their gains and losses. Losses are often apparently felt more acutely than gains of comparable magnitude. If this is true of losses in collective bad situations, then the effect may be to magnify the third consideration above (regarding moral reaction to an inequity), further compounding the sense of loss and therefore further motivating collective action.

In many respects, however, political dealings with collective bads may often be more difficult than dealing with collective goods. Once a public has voted or otherwise decided to supply itself a collective good, there is commonly little opposition thereafter to actually achieving that good (subject to the obvious caveat below). Opposition would be to the cost exactions, that is, generally to taxation. But taxation is highly institutionalized and is quite general, so that it is not always directly stipulated or perceived that a given act of tax collection is to enable a particular public expenditure. Dealing with collective bads, however, often requires direct exaction of costs at the various sources of the bads in a way that may well be hard to institutionalize, because it is often quite particular. Moreover, there is commonly a strong incentive

[20] J. N. Findlay, "The Structure of the Kingdom of Ends," pp. 424–426.

to cheat, often in a complex variety of ways—for example, many people in the United States disable pollution-control equipment in their cars, and many people in England burn natural wood in their fireplaces in smokeless districts. Many of these miscreants would probably be happy to vote a law that required everyone to obey the rules they just as happily break. With goods, the only cheating commonly is at taxation, so that detection mechanisms can be made increasingly sophisticated, and the *incentive for detection* may be far greater, because it has such general importance. Admittedly, however, in government projects the distinction between goods and bads often blurs in the meaningful sense that what some see as a good others see as a bad. For example, the completion of interstate highway I-95 through various Eastern cities was slowed or stymied by popular opposition partly before and partly independently of the concern with pollution and oil supplies that made the good of interstate highways seem less good, even bad, to many.

A Step Bad: Blackout

Bads, like goods, can be continuous or step, externally or internally produced. Auto pollution is an internally produced continuous bad for most of the population; refinery pollution is an externally produced continuous bad. A blackout is an internally produced step bad; the installation of a nuclear generator is an externally produced step bad for the neighboring communities. All of these bads except the blackout are externalities of activities otherwise seen as good—if these activities could be carried on without their bad effects at no additional cost, presumably they would be.

Collective actions over bads produced externally, that is, outside the group, may often be seen as strategically equivalent to collective actions over the provision of goods, but with some effect from the kinds of complications discussed above. Therefore, it is analytically more interesting to consider an internally generated bad to exemplify the collective action game for bads, and it is probably most interesting to consider a step bad. Excessive electrical demand threatening to bring down the supply system and black out a metropolitan area is an elegant, all-too-real instance of an almost perfectly voluntaristic problem in the creation of a collective bad, an internally produced step bad. On a hot summer afternoon, household air conditioning may overload the system by adding to usual consumption for other purposes and to commercial air conditioning.

Suppose it was advertised that our system could handle 80 percent of extant air conditioners at 5:00 P.M. on a hot weekday, so that if each household would voluntarily refrain from using air conditioning one day each workweek, there would be no failure. My household randomly selects (or is assigned) Monday. Now it is approaching 5:00 P.M. on Monday and we are sweating. If our only concern is our selfish benefit, would it be sensible for us to cheat and use the air conditioner? Most likely, yes: our cheating is very unlikely to make the difference between blackout and continued service. Suppose further that if our air conditioning did bring down the system, we would have double discomfort: our television, elevator, lights, and so forth would be blacked out, and in addition we would continue to sweat. The costs of our double discomfort would have to be discounted, as my vote was above, by the exceedingly small probability that turning on our air conditioner would actually cause a blackout that would not otherwise have happened. By any reasonable guess, that probability must be far below 1 percent, so as far as our household alone is concerned, it is worth the risk of turning on our air conditioner every hot weekday, even though if everyone does so the probability of blackout may be high.

5

ASYMMETRIES IN
COLLECTIVE ACTION

In order to simplify technical analyses of collective action, it is often assumed, as in chapters 2, 3, and 4, that groups are *symmetric* in many respects. That is, it is assumed that all members have identical interest in the collective good: all place the same value on a given unit of the collective good supplied, and all place the same value on a unit of cost. Although in some actual collective actions these assumptions may be very nearly met, in many and perhaps in most others, they are not. For members of a particular union striking for higher wages, symmetry of costs and benefits may be a reasonable approximation. But one would not want to claim that all Americans value pollution control equally, or even that all environmentalists do.

Introducing substantial asymmetries complicates analysis, as did the asymmetric contributions in the step good collective action of chapter 4. Nevertheless, the effects of certain asymmetries can be systematically analyzed. The three asymmetries that seem to be most important are each discussed at length below, and a fourth, which is less important, is discussed briefly. They are (1) nonfungibility of goods, or asymmetry between costs and benefits (for example, our costs may be hours of organizational effort, while our benefit is government provision of better streets); (2) inequality of benefits, or asymmetry of demand for the collective good (you might be willing to pay much more for clean air than I am, just as you might be willing to pay more to attend a football game or an opera); (3) heterogeneity of benefits, or asymmetry in the content of the collective good (as part of its generally improved quality, our local school now offers music or sports education, which may interest you, but not me); and (4) hysteresis in valuations, or asymmetry between gains and losses (I may think the loss I suffer from a bad is greater than the gain I enjoy from an equivalent good).

These asymmetries do not constitute a typology of logically exclusive categories. Nor are they even categories over the same range. As noted below, nonfungibility (that is, being neither monetary nor readily exchangeable for money) often underlies inequality, although fungible goods can also involve extreme inequality of benefits—for example, the Jarvis-Gann tax reduction measure, Proposition 13, benefited Jarvis and Gann vastly more than it did typical California voters. All four asymmetries exist in the perceptions of the relevant group members, but nonfungibility and heterogeneity generally do have, and inequality may have, substantial objective bases. In the following discussion of all four types of asymmetry, the concern is with asymmetries *within groups* all of whose members generally value their own groups' collective goods.

Asymmetries may have expectable political effects because they have particular implications for collective action. In a group of n members with symmetric costs and benefits and a ratio r of benefits to costs of supplying itself a collective good, the minimal efficacious subgroup is of size k_s, where $(n/r) < k_s \leq (n/r) + 1$. Now consider a highly asymmetric n-member group in which the average member's evaluation of costs and benefits is the same as in this symmetric group, but in which some members have much higher evaluations of the benefit of the group's good. The minimal efficacious subgroup will be of size k_a, which will be smaller than k_s, indeed much smaller if k_s is much smaller than n. Hence, although in *average* valuations the two groups would be similar, the asymmetric group could have an efficacious subgroup that was essentially an intermediate group, while any efficacious subgroup of the symmetric group would be a large group (in terms of their respective k's). Other things being comparable, therefore, one would expect better prospects for successful collective action in the asymmetric than in the symmetric group.

Similarly, asymmetry in the content of a group's collective good may enhance prospects for cooperative action. Suppose that our neighborhood is organizing to campaign for a better public school. I might be inclined to take a free ride on the efforts of others, but if I particularly want music education to be included in the package of improvements, I might sooner join the group in order to influence that part of the outcome, thereby perhaps also influencing the larger outcome to the general benefit of the whole group.

Not all asymmetries will enhance prospects for collective action, but many will. Multiple asymmetries may more or less cancel out in their effects—or their effects may multiply. For example, an obvious asymmetry not discussed at length below is asymmetry in available resources to contribute to a collective action. Certain collective goods, including such recent qualitative goods as conservation and clean air, may be *superior goods,* that is to say, the well-off demand proportionately more of them than do the less well-off. The well-off also happen to have more resources and, as discussed in chapter 7, may be more inclined to donate money to public causes out of extrarational motives. Hence, despite polls that show broad consensus in favor of environmental protection, it is not surprising that collective action toward that end is predominantly the doing of the upper middle class, indeed the top decile of the population in income. If the top decile also happened asymmetrically to suffer a disproportionate share of industrial pollution, the environmental movement might be considerably more impressive.

After discussing the four asymmetries, I consider some of their implications for political actions and outcomes, which help explain certain biases in group activity and in political outcomes. Probably their most interesting political effect is to benefit groups that want nonfungible goods; generally these happen to be middle-class or upper-middle-class groups. Given asymmetry of demand for various superior goods, we can expect higher levels of strictly voluntary activity in efforts to obtain such goods than would be expected in efforts to obtain such symmetrically demanded fungible goods as wage increases. Since group effort to obtain government action can be very much cheaper than the value of the government action, by turning to government even relatively poorly organized groups can obtain benefits that justify their group actions. Hence, in the voluntary public interest group system, one may expect to see a bias both in group activity and in government action to favor the upper middle class. As argued especially in chapter 7, this bias is likely to be heightened when individual support of group action is based on moral motivations.

NONFUNGIBILITY: ASYMMETRY
BETWEEN COSTS AND BENEFITS

In the discussions of chapters 2 and 3, all the analyses and many of the examples of collective action problems could as well have been based on the assumption of a scale of utility on which benefits and costs could simply be added. It is easy to suppose that this could be done if costs and benefits were both in money or in expected money returns. If benefits or costs are not in money and are not readily exchangeable for money, we may say that the collective good and its costs are not fungible. More generally, we may refer to nonfungible costs or nonfungible benefits, meaning that they are not monetary or readily exchangeable for money.

Strictly speaking, these terms are wrong, since all that is required in chapters 2 and 3 is that costs and benefits be commensurable. A messiah who can convert individuals' loaves into larger, but limited, numbers of collective loaves presents followers with a conflict of group versus individual interest as severe as that of any labor union that wishes to convert members' dues into collective wage benefits. However, messiahs are not commonplace, and in commonplace contexts commensurable costs and benefits are likely to be fungible with money.

Of course, for many important classes of collectively provided goods, costs and benefits are fungible, so that approximate representation of them in simple monetary terms is not unreasonable. For example, oil industry effort to maintain or obtain tax concessions is money spent essentially to obtain money. Similarly, the costs of union activity may principally be dues plus wages forgone during strikes, and the benefits may principally be increased wages. And the benefits to a profession from its lobbying for exclusionary licensing are increased fees and incomes. The payoffs in such collective actions are well represented in Olson's simple additive equations, in usual game theory matrices, or in accountings such as those in table 3-1. The oil industry may be privileged if indeed Exxon reckons that its own expected return on a dollar invested in relevant lobbying, public relations, or campaign contributions well exceeds a dollar. The hapless union, however, will require side-payments, and probably coercive legal support or extra-rational behavior, in order to overcome latency.

But goods amounting to money in the pockets of those who benefit from them do not normally come to mind when one thinks of Samuelson's public goods, or even, more generally, of politics. Collective goods commonly cannot be converted either back into cash or into private goods. Once provided, they can merely be enjoyed or not enjoyed. For Samuelson's public goods, one can never appropriate one's share of the good. That is, one can enjoy it, but one cannot sell one's enjoyment of it or trade it to someone else for some private good. If the collective good is a higher wage rate, one does wholly appropriate one's share. Moreover, we have a far richer sense of what the higher wage rate means to any individual—we know how much money per hour the individual earns and how it is likely to affect spending. We can confidently expect that virtually all recipients will think their well-being has been increased. If the collective good is, say, cleaner air, we know very little about its impact on the individual. Some may think their well-being has been improved considerably, others not. In general, we would expect great asymmetry in the perception of benefits in the clean air case, relative symmetry in the wage increase case. When goods are obtained not through purchase but through activity, the activity may also not be readily converted into a cash equivalent or into desired private goods. The activity involves a trade-off: for instance, watching so many hours of television reruns versus spending those hours in meetings, letter writing, campaigning, or otherwise working for a collective benefit.

Note the parallel with private goods. If there were fungible private goods that sold below par (as some fungible collective goods do), one would require no sophisticated utility theory or knowledge of individual preferences to comprehend or predict behavior: anyone offered such a good would buy it. We would all trade five dollar bills for ten dollar bills one for one. For a nonfungible private good, however, one could not sensibly make a similar claim. One would have to know how much of the good and how much of other goods the individual had, and how the individual traded off all these against each other, in order to comprehend or predict the individual's behavior (unless, of course, there was a perfect market for the resale of the good, which is tantamount to saying it is fungible).

Suppose for a moment that we are a group of people with similar preference schedules and that we would like to have a particular collective good. If we are well endowed with whatever constitutes the costs of obtaining the good, but have none of the good, then the rate at which we will be willing to trade costs for benefits may be relatively high. That is to say, the size of k for our group with respect to initial provision of our good may be only a fraction of the group size. As we provide ourselves some of the good, the rate at which we will be willing to trade costs for benefits will probably decline, and k will increase for further units of supply. The more of the good we have, the less likely will we be able to cooperate (or individually act) to provide still more. If we all have identical assessments of the benefits against the costs of supplying the good, we can be said to be symmetrical in our demand for the good. Often, groups are asymmetrical, with some members valuing the group good more highly than others in the sense that they would be willing to pay more to see it provided or to see it provided at higher levels. Asymmetrical demand is particularly likely for collective goods that are not fungible, for example, for such qualitative goods as education, clean air, scenic conservation, and health care. Hence, asymmetry between costs and benefits will often underlie the asymmetry of demand for collective goods, as is discussed in the next section.

Before turning to consideration of asymmetry of demand, however, note a peculiar implication of nonfungibility of costs and benefits. Olson's logic of collective action is based on the simple relationship, $A_i = V_i - C$, in which recall that A_i is the net advantage to an individual group member i from providing a group good at cost C if the member's valuation of the good is V_i. If A_i is positive for some i, the group is privileged; if it is negative for every i, the group is latent. Note that in order to decide whether A_i is positive or negative, we would need to have substantial utility function information on i. To show that a latent group is latent, we would need such information on every member of the group—for example, on every member of the group of environmentalists.

The charm of Olson's result is that it seems to free us of the need for such information. For the actual groups he discusses, he is essentially concerned with answering the question, How many private dollars will an individual spend to get even more dollars allocated collectively? To answer this question requires little information—we can often answer it by doing little more than thinking about it. For many collective action problems, we must instead ask how many dollars (or how much time) individuals in a group would each be willing to spend in order to obtain a qualitative change in their lives. The answer may require a vast volume of information on all the members of the group, information that may not easily be collected.

To escape the need for such information, it is generally sufficient for both costs and benefits to be in money. Theoretically, if private market substitutes for a collectively provided good are available, the good can be roughly valued in monetary terms, even though it would not be appropriable or fungible if provided. Nevertheless, the distinction between goods that display asymmetry between costs and benefits and strictly fungible goods is clear enough, and is often meaningful in that it may make a difference in our expectation of the prospects for collective action, as the following sections should demonstrate.

INEQUALITY: ASYMMETRY OF DEMAND
FOR GROUP GOODS

When group members' intensities of demand for their group good are highly asymmetric, the results may be polar opposites: to enhance or to dissipate prospects for collective action. Regarding the possibility of enhancement, consider the distribution of the intensity that the asymmetry implies. If all members were as intense as the most intense demanders in fact are, k for the group would be smaller, perhaps considerably smaller than if all members were no more intense than the average member. The very intense demanders might be only a small fraction of the whole group, but might nevertheless constitute an efficacious k-subgroup in the sense defined in chapter 3. And k for the intense subgroup might be small enough to encourage some degree of cooperation, perhaps through solidary effects, through convention (as discussed in chapters 10 through 13), or even through some degree of extrarational behavior that might be less likely in a much larger group (chapter 7).

Regarding the possibility of dissipation, suppose that the benefit the group seeks could also be obtained privately rather than collectively, although perhaps at higher per capita cost. For example, clean air could be supplied collectively by reducing air pollution. Or it could be supplied privately by installing air-cleaning systems in private homes and cars. In this case there is a *private good substitute* for the group's collective good, and the intense demanders may opt for the relatively expensive private good instead of struggling to instigate collective action.

The difference between these two possibilities recalls Albert Hirschman's distinction between "exit" and "voice" as individual responses to declining organizations.[1] Exit is the market response of switching to a different product. Voice is the political response of trying to change the organization. In collective action, whether an acceptable substitute is available will be important in determining whether intense demanders organize a collective effort or opt for a private solution of their problem. In part, therefore, the prospects for successful collective action will turn on the "technology" of production of the desired benefit.

It is commonly noted that collective goods often have private good substitutes. For some lighthouses, the traditional example of a genuine public good, shipboard radar can be substituted. For public police protection, locks, dogs, and private guards can be substituted; for fire departments, private sprinkler systems; for public regulation of product quality, brand name advertising; and so forth. Private good substitution often may not be ideal, because substitutes often are not perfect, but collective provision also may not be ideal. In particular, collective provision implies a lesser degree of control over qualitative and quanti-

---

[1] Albert O. Hirschman, *Exit, Voice, and Loyalty.*

tative levels of supply. The principal advantage of collective provision over private good substitutes is likely to be relative price.

Consider two examples in quite different contexts. Relatively affluent Americans, who dearly want high-quality education for their children, exit from central cities to costlier suburbs instead of staying to campaign for better schools in the city, or they send their children to expensive private schools. To suppose that neither of these exit options was available would be too absurdly counterfactual to permit clear analysis of their effect. But when there are other amenities in particular sections of large cities, collective action in support of public school quality seems common, although it is still undercut by the development of private school systems.

For a second example, suppose U.S. Steel had had the foresight in the sixties to suspect that air pollution would become a national issue and had calculated that air pollution control might cost it an investment of billions of dollars, plus hundreds of millions of dollars in annual operating costs. Suppose it had therefore developed and put into production a home depollution device that could be added onto typical central air conditioning and heating systems at an installation cost of perhaps a thousand dollars and operating costs of a hundred or a few hundred dollars per year. Many institutions would surely have installed large versions of the device, new luxury homes would have been equipped with it, and retailers would soon have marketed it. By 1970 the majority of upper-middle-class Americans might have been living in pollution-free homes, working in pollution-free offices, shopping in pollution-free malls, and perhaps even beginning to ride in cars with pollution-free passenger compartments. The cost of installing and operating home, commercial, and automotive units might greatly have exceeded current outlays to prevent pollution at its source. But the benefits from the private installations would go almost entirely to the upper middle class, who could generally escape air pollution—except when they chose to take to the fresh air of golf courses, tennis courts, and beaches. The poor and the working classes would largely be left out of the system.

How would collective action over air pollution have been affected? Quite possibly, the motivation of many people to do something about pollution would instead have become a motivation to monitor their filter systems. The public good of air pollution control would suffer from the availability of a private market substitute cheap enough for high demanders. Air pollution might not have become such a major political issue, because only the poor and the lower middle classes would still have suffered enormously from it. Even an entrepreneurial politician might have had little to gain from the issue. Not polluting in the first place might have been cheaper than the decentralized cleanup system, but the collective good of reduced monetary costs is less likely to provoke this very large group to collective action, because interest in the collective good of money savings will be relatively symmetric. Hence, as argued above, k will be relatively larger for the group with respect to the savings than with respect to air pollution.

Asymmetry of intensity of demand may shade into asymmetry of content of the collective good (discussed below), because the issues of qualitative or quantitative level of supply of a good can often be seen as distinguishing differences in content. Consider the following example. According to Samuel Popkin,[2] as technology intruded into parts of South Vietnam, peasants in some communities began to have two possible ways of watering their land. They could collectively maintain a communal irrigation system by helping to dredge and weed the ditches, or they could individually dig wells to water only their own holdings. A few peasants dissatisfied with the quality of a communal system might better be served by wells, but their opting out would either reduce the quality of the irrigation system or require greater efforts by others to maintain it at its previous level of quality. In either case, after a few began to use wells, a few more might also decide they would be better served by wells, and, in the end, the communal system might deteriorate enough that it would be almost entirely abandoned. Private watering might clearly be more laborious or costly than a well-maintained collective system, yet it might prevail. Asymmetric demand on the collective system means that if its quantity or quality is at the right level for some, it will be at the wrong level for others, who either will be receiving poorer benefits than they want or will be contributing more to the collective effort than their benefits justify. If it could be arranged for the more intense demanders to do a larger share of weeding and dredging, the most efficient outcome could be achieved, but the problems in working out such "fair" apportionment of costs are severe (see further, chapter 6). As with the private solution of the problem of air pollution, the private provision of water may be not only inefficient but also asymmetrically beneficial, serving the well-off peasants best and the poor peasants worst.

[2] Samuel Popkin, University of California, San Diego, Calif., personal communication, 1978.

HETEROGENEITY: ASYMMETRY
IN THE CONTENT OF GOODS

In the example of the peasants' irrigation problem, the "quality" of the collective system determined the quantity of water delivered to individual plots, because deeper dredging and more thorough weeding meant greater carrying capacity. The good of irrigation was not uniformly perceived, because some wanted a heavier flow of water than others did. But a good may be complex enough to have diverse attributes in a more striking sense. In Marshall's classical example of jointness in production (as distinct from Samuelson's jointness in consumption), the production of mutton and wool are connected, or "joint"—sheep are valued for both these products.[3] The members of a group may want a group good for various reasons, some of them especially valuing one attribute, others another. In such a case, there is asymmetry in the definition of the good rather than merely in the degree of valuation. Such asymmetry may enhance the prospects for voluntary cooperation in the provision of the good, especially if the jointness of the attributes of the good is not strictly necessary. For example, the lobbying efforts of a trade association could be directed at tariff legislation that would generally benefit an industry. But, as George Stigler argues, if the product mix of all firms in the industry is not identical, a carefully drawn tariff might easily benefit cooperative firms more than those attempting to free ride.[4] Hence, many (if not almost all) firms in the industry will receive direct benefits from their individual contributions to the lobbying effort.

It is often easy to see such asymmetry in contemporary group political goods. For example, the environmental movement is concerned with two quite different, though related, issues: pollution and conservation. And the issue of conservation itself involves a good whose content is unavoidably asymmetric: how much and what parts of Alaska should we conserve, and how much and what parts of California? Should we more readily yield up areas that are oil- or mineral-rich than those that are merely forested? And if the Rockefeller family has a very strong commitment to certain forms of conservation specifically in Alaska, should it put its resources directly into influencing Congress and the administration, or should it try to influence environmental interest groups? If it chooses to do the latter, environmental organizations will benefit, possibly at some cost in biasing their objectives, and those most likely to pursue Alaskan conservation may benefit most.

[3] Alfred Marshall, *Principles of Economics,* bk. 5, chap. 6, sec. 4.
[4] George J. Stigler, "Free Riders and Collective Action: An Appendix to Theories of Economic Regulation," p. 362.

This phenomenon can occur in groups of any kind. A neighborhood group may collectively maintain a playground. Since my child will be using it, I may be motivated to assist in the collective action in order to influence the outcome, for instance, to provide heavier-duty, safer equipment. If my academic department is recruiting a specialist in American politics, I may actively participate in the effort, which in the end will provide a largely collective benefit, in order to influence the chance that the eventual recruit will be an Americanist with methodological, historical, theoretical, or whatever leanings I prefer.

Earlier in American political history, the tariff may have been the single most important nationally provided asymmetric collective benefit—asymmetric in the present sense of differentially benefiting primary (industry) beneficiaries, rather than in the sense of implicitly taxing some to benefit others. But customs receipts fell from over 90 percent of total federal revenues to about half the total by 1910, and to only about 1 percent in the later 1960s.[5] The weight of politics naturally shifted elsewhere, and in contemporary national politics the corporation tax laws have become by far the most important source of asymmetric benefits (or burdens) as they have grown to generate many times the customs receipts. They generate less than they might, however, because of hundreds of special provisions that imply so-called tax expenditures, or forgone revenues. It is generally easy to see special interests behind any tax expenditure provision. For example, the mortgage interest deduction that benefits homeowners more specially benefits lending institutions and the construction industry. The Catholic Church and various other often de facto segregated church schools would be principal beneficiaries of proposed tax credits for private school tuition. The corporation tax code contains the largest number of, the most specialized, and the least transparent tax expenditure items. These provide the most straightforward and compelling examples of implicit influence by special interests.

The recent, extraordinary success of the publicity-shy Business Roundtable—it has brought the chief executive officers of diverse major firms into one very active lobbying organization—might partially be the result of the asymmetry of the tax code with its reams of special provisions to benefit specific industries and firms. If the only stake business had in tax reform efforts was to reduce or increase the corporate tax burden uniformly across all companies, by the logic of collective action we would expect little cooperative lobbying effort by business (beyond individual efforts by the largest taxpayers, who might expect to benefit or lose more from slight general changes than a lobbying effort would

[5] Congressional Quarterly, *Guide to Congress,* p. 113.

cost). Although some people think uniform taxes on businesses would be a worthy reform, it is not one to be considered seriously by Congress, which finds greater challenge in phrasing in general terms laws whose purpose is to benefit specific individuals, firms, or industries.

Consider an extreme example of a general law to benefit an unnamed individual. While writing tax revisions in 1975, the House Ways and Means Committee quickly voted a provision that would have given wealthy Texan Ross Perot (the unnamed individual) a windfall rebate from the Treasury. But for the special competence of *Wall Street Journal* reporter Albert Hunt, no one besides Perot, his tax lawyer (former commissioner of the Internal Revenue Service Sheldon Cohen, who apparently wrote the Perot provision), and no doubt certain members of Ways and Means might have known that the measure, permitting retroactive carryback to 1974 of personal capital losses greater than $30,000 to offset capital gains, meant paying Perot as much as $15 million.[6] (A similar provision had passed Ways and Means in 1974, but had gone no further.[7] In the interim, mostly in late December, Perot contributed over $27,000 to whatever future campaigns twelve of the committee members might wage. Six of these finished their 1976 reelection campaigns with surpluses well in excess of Perot's late-1974 gifts to them.[8] Under the 1974 campaign finance law, they could use the excess funds for any lawful purpose, including personal expenses or investments.[9] Two of them could reasonably have seen their $5,000 donations as personal gifts, since they could expect, as usual, to have large surpluses while running virtually unopposed. Ten of the twelve beneficiaries voted for the Perot provision in the 20 to 14 committee vote.) After Hunt's instant reporting of the various levels of venality involved in the Perot provision, Al Ullman, chairman of Ways and Means, who had not voted for the provision in committee, recommended to the Rules Committee that the provision be reconsidered on the floor of the House. By a vote of 379 to 27, the provision was deleted a month after it had been hurriedly adopted in committee.[10]

Odd as it may seem, the Perot provision was genuinely a collective good, since in addition to giving him about $15 million from the

[6] *Wall Street Journal*, Nov. 7, 1975, p. 1.

[7] *CQ Almanac 1974*, pp. 190–193.

[8] *CQ Almanac 1977*, pp. 37A–43A.

[9] Ibid., p. 33A.

[10] *Wall Street Journal*, Nov. 7, 1975, p. 1; *CQ Almanac 1975*, pp. 147, 152. Perot had personal capital losses in 1974 estimated to have been enormous. With one-year retroactivity, the Perot provision would have allowed him to carry back those losses to 1971 when, alas, he must have paid more than $20 million in capital gains taxes.

Treasury, it would have given an estimated $150 million more to many others. The "closed rule" under which Ways and Means measures are generally considered on the floor protects members from having to take a public stand on such sleazy measures, because amendments to add or cut special provisions are prohibited—the House as a body must swallow a new tax package whole or reject it whole. Hence, Ullman's recommendation that the Rules Committee allow a floor vote on an amendment against the Perot provision was an unusual move to undo what Ways and Means had done. Senators seem to have tougher skins, and they regularly introduce their special provisions in recorded votes of the whole Senate.[11] Hence, despite the openness of the Senate, examples of provisions offering asymmetric benefits that entice participation in collective actions are legion. The Perot measure would have been, perhaps uniquely, a special provision for a single person written into the individual income tax code—most such provisions are in the corporation tax code. It is instructive to consider a handful of these.

When the perversely named tax reform bill of 1976, which the House had finished at the end of 1975, came before the Senate, a group of liberal senators forced reconsideration of seventy-three special-interest provisions, of which only twenty were eventually dropped. The liberals suffered insult to aggravate their losses when, in a complicated parliamentary sequence, a vote of 42 to 20 carried a motion to table a previous motion to reconsider the vote by which an amendment to delete the word "reform" from the title of the bill was tabled.[12]

[11] As noted in the discussion of collective bads in chapter 4, a specific outcome that will happen in the absence of activity can focus and coordinate action. The tax laws that pass through Congress every year provide examples of a similar focus, although the examples do not involve bads for the relevant groups. The House Committee on Ways and Means has the constitutional prerogative of initiating all revenue bills, and the Senate Finance Committee can only amend the House bills. Richard Fenno argues that, since "Ways and Means always acts first, every disappointed clientele group descends on the Senate Committee seeking last resort redress. Thus the intractable legislative sequence concentrates a heavier and more intense volume of clientele activity on Finance." He adds, "This concentration is further insured by the Ways and Means practice of drafting its own bill from a rather general administration message, which means that clientele groups cannot know in advance the specific provisions on which the Committee will act" (Richard F. Fenno, Jr., *Congressmen in Committees,* pp. 153–154). Perot's near-success suggests, on the contrary, that clientele groups *can* know in advance, indeed, can themselves have drafted "the specific provisions on which the Committee will act."

[12] *CQ Almanac 1976,* pp. 51, 69S. If corporate taxes were on income (gross receipts) or on value added rather than on profits, such special provisions would have little point. Hence, business involvement in American politics might be substantially lessened.

Not surprisingly, the pattern of legislative sponsorship of special provisions correlates well with patterns of campaign contributions. In 1976, Senators Lloyd Bentsen of Texas and Clifford Hansen of Wyoming sponsored tax measures to benefit oil firms; Representatives Joseph Karth and Bill Frenzel of Minnesota sponsored a measure to benefit Cargill, Inc.; Senator Abraham Ribicoff of Connecticut sponsored benefits to various insurance companies, and so forth.[13] Some benefits are more systematic and more enduring, as in the case of oil and paper industry tax expenditures. What is technically impressive in the measures is just how special the fine print can be. Which firms in an industry benefit may turn on whether a provision is retroactive to 1973 or 1974, on where potentially taxable profits were earned, and so forth. The final content of a measure often depends on which firms participate in the influence effort. In some cases, successful influence may require expanding the coalition of potential beneficiaries. Representative James Burke of Massachusetts sponsored a measure in 1975 to allow businesses to carry back losses eight years (rather than merely three as already permitted). The number of backers was dramatically increased by making the provision retroactive to 1970. Again, Hunt's reporting may have helped to derail the effort. He noted that "the retroactivity would give a maximum benefit for some large companies, notably Lockheed Aircraft Corp., as well as some smaller New England shoe companies, which are Mr. Burke's chief concern."[14]

From the groups' and their members' perspectives, asymmetric goods such as those exemplified here come perilously close to being straight private goods, sometimes sought from government. But that is not the whole story in any of these cases, except probably for the Perot tax break. The benefits sought by environmental groups are, for the most part, collective in quality, even though many of the potential beneficiaries may be geographically determined. The neighborhood playground and departmental recruitment are likely to be seen by all or nearly all members of the relevant groups as providing genuinely collective benefits. Even the tax and tariff issues often are primarily general with respect to a given industry or across industries, and special only in certain details. Often the magnitude of the general benefit may dwarf that of the correlative special benefits, just as the eight-year carryback provision would have been enormously beneficial to many firms later on,

[13] *Wall Street Journal*, June 11, 1976, p. 2; July 20, 1976, p. 4.
[14] *Wall Street Journal*, Oct. 28, 1975, p. 3. It would have been unseemly for Lockheed, two major airlines, Chrysler Corporation, and the W. T. Grant Company to lobby too openly for the measure, because it would have netted them half a billion dollars in immediate tax rebates. Hence, they may have used smaller firms to front for them.

even if not at the time of passage. The expected value of the special benefit to certain firms or individuals may nevertheless be large in comparison with the costs of participation in the group effort to secure the whole package. Hence, for action with a very large collective return on the group effort distributed over a very large group, a bit of asymmetry in the collective good may facilitate spontaneous voluntary effort by individual group members. Such effort may be generated in the absence of the ongoing organization assumed in the by-product theory to be built on supplying selective incentives. And, as the tax expenditure provisions suggest, asymmetry in content of a good need not be associated with asymmetry between costs and benefits. Firms spend money to influence legislation that will give them money benefits.

The implication of this analysis and of the examples given is that, other things being comparable, asymmetric goods provoke higher levels of collective action than do symmetric goods. Hence, general regulations on pollution should be less actively supported than should a package of many conservation projects. This is similar to the traditional claim that rivers and harbors bills or, more generally, pieces of pork barrel legislation are more intensely supported than comparably beneficial general legislation. The principal difference is the concern here with motivations of interest groups and of group members rather than with those of legislators, although the former presumably heavily influence the latter.

The possible impact of such asymmetrically stimulated efforts by groups to influence wider aspects of congressional behavior are discussed briefly in chapter 14. Members of Congress are commonly said to treat other members' special-interest bills more kindly than might seem to make sense because there has developed in Congress a "norm of reciprocity," under which "I do not object to your measure if you do not object to mine." Such a "norm" can profitably be seen as a fairly obvious convention, in the sense defined in chapter 10.

Another aspect of congressional behavior that merits an aside is the commonplace assertion that public financing of congressional elections would be nothing more than a raid on the federal Treasury. Although true, the assertion is pointless, since net costs or savings are at issue. If special-interest influence were reduced, public financing could far more than pay for itself—it could be a powerful revenue generator. The relatively cheap Perot provision alone would have caused the Treasury to pay out about $60 million a year through 1980, almost all to wealthy individuals. All of the 1976 congressional campaigning cost only about $100 million.[15]

---

[15] *CQ Almanac 1974*, p. 191; and *CQ Almanac 1977*, p. 35A.

HYSTERESIS: ASYMMETRY BETWEEN GAINS AND LOSSES

Recall the discussion of pollution control earlier in this chapter. It may happen that there is no reasonable private good substitute for pollution control, which is to say that the public bad of pollution cannot be rejected if it is provided. In this case, the asymmetries discussed above might increase the prospects for some level of activity by environmental groups to obtain pollution control. Indeed, their level of activity might also be enhanced by the fact that their "good" is the prevention of a bad.

Psychologically, utility assessments often seem to suffer from *hysteresis:* that is, we sense that the utility gained in moving from one indifference surface to a higher one is in some sense less than the utility that is lost in subsequently retreating to the lower surface. Hume states the issue with characteristic force: "Men generally fix their affections more on what they are possess'd of, than on what they never enjoy'd: For this reason, it would be greater cruelty to dispossess a man of any thing than not to give it him."[16] From even strong opponents of Nixon, the commonplace remark that by loss of office he had suffered enough for his illegal actions to need no further punishment may have been an expression of the hysteresis effect. (By inference, had he been unemployed in the first place, he should have been remorselessly sent to jail.)

This is an issue that arises in utility theory: in many choice situations, what happened in the past matters in a fundamental way. As many besides Thomas Wolfe have realized, "You can't go home again." In economics, the problem is expressed more drily in various relationships. For example, one's spending depends not only upon one's current real

---

[16] David Hume, *A Treatise of Human Nature,* bk. 3, pt. 2, sec. 1, p. 482. The notion of hysteresis has been widely grasped. For example, Blum and Kalven use it as an objection to one egalitarian principle of taxation. (Walter J. Blum and Harry Kalven, Jr., *The Uneasy Case for Progressive Taxation,* p. 53.) Kahneman and Tversky make hysteresis a part of their "prospect theory" of choice under risk. They report numerous studies: "With a single exception [out of thirty business decision makers], utility functions were considerably steeper for losses than for gains" (Daniel Kahneman and Amos Tversky, "Prospect Theory: An Analysis of Decision Under Risk," p. 280). Bentham characteristically thought it self-evident that our valuations are subject to hysteresis. *"It is worse to lose than simply not to gain"* was one of a class of propositions that "have the claim to the appellation of axioms . . . ; since, referring to universal experience as their immediate basis, they are incapable of demonstration, and require only to be developed and illustrated, in order to be recognised as incontestable" (Jeremy Bentham, *An Introduction to the Principles of Morals and Legislation,* n. beginning on p. xxv).

income, but also on one's highest real income in the past, not only because one may be stuck with a past mortgage, but more importantly because life at an earlier time under a higher income may have changed one's tastes.[17]

If hysteresis is important, we should expend more to prevent a quality deterioration than we would have expended to achieve a quality improvement over exactly the same range. We should expect that in some sense individual responses to impending public bads will be more intense than to potential collective goods. If the bads cannot be rejected, group-oriented activity may be surprisingly extensive and intense, as in various contemporary attempts by local American populations to prevent installation of refineries and offshore unloading facilities for supertankers. For example, Durham, New Hampshire, is a community of unusual attractions. The loss of welfare that would have been occasioned by an oil refinery there, with its threat of a supertanker-unloading facility at the nearby Isles of Shoals, may have been heightened by hysteresis to help stimulate extraordinary group-oriented activity.[18]

POLITICAL EFFECTS OF ASYMMETRIES

The principal issue in the politics of collective action is that perverse asymmetry in which some benefit to the detriment of others. Environmentalists do not want to buy clean air; they want others to stop fouling it. The others would no doubt be happy to stop, except that stopping would be expensive. If environmental collective action succeeds politically, the others will effectively have to buy clean air. The people of New Orleans would like to have the people of Chicago, St. Louis, and most communities in the Mississippi River watershed stop fouling the Mississippi. But the people of Chicago would benefit very little from keeping their sewage out of the Mississippi—indeed, they chose to put

[17] Nicholas Georgescu-Roegen, *Analytical Economics,* pp. 173–177, 65.

[18] Although the notion of hysteresis seems consonant with adaptation-level theory, the latter might be seen to counter the hysteresis argument in some contexts. For example, if the current level of pollution developed slowly over many years, we may have adapted to it, so that it has become the "normal" level we expect. However, our antipollution reaction may not be due to a change in the pollution level, but to a change in our knowledge or understanding of how great the pollution is and what it does to us. Such knowledge and understanding may have come suddenly, concomitantly with the "creation" of the pollution issue, so that a sudden growth in activism over pollution may be consistent with both adaptation-level and hysteresis explanations.

it there by reversing the flow of the Chicago River in order to clean up Lake Michigan, whose cleanliness is of greater interest to them.

The asymmetries discussed in the foregoing sections involve varied weightings of what are generally consonant interests. The asymmetry that makes collective actions political involves a conflict of interests. The effort by a neighborhood group to eliminate a local source of pollution is not profoundly political if the group effort is directed at raising among its members the requisite funds, say, to contract with the polluter to clean up. It can become political in the usual strong sense if it is directed at getting government to act. There are at least three important things the group might ask government to do: first, to provide the funds to end the pollution; second, merely to enforce a Baumol solution (as discussed in chapter 4), to give effect to the group's desire to concert its action by taxing the members of the group to secure their effort to pay the polluter to stop; and third, to compel the polluter to stop, with whatever cost that might involve to be borne by the polluter.

Which of these actions the group takes will depend in part on extant institutions or precedents and in part on the relative benefits and costs of the actions. A large group (in terms of k—that is, a group whose smallest efficacious subgroup is large) cannot easily solve such a problem through mutual cooperation in contracting with the polluter. If precedents suggest no prospect of government intervention in one of the three ways mentioned above, then government intervention may be out, because inducing government to work a new precedent would probably be costly. In many realms, government can be induced simply to provide collective benefits such as schools, roads, parks, and playgrounds directly through taxes, which need not be borne by the beneficiaries of the collective goods. In some realms, government is prepared to effectuate collective action by helping groups concert their own actions, as with union shop laws. In other areas, notably air and water pollution and, at less expense, in certain other regulatory fields, government is prone to compel other parties to provide benefits to particular groups. In all these spheres, the role of government is often substantially to lower the barriers to successful collective action, so that relatively low-cost collective actions can be leveraged into massive collective benefits. For example, the political budget of environmental groups may be perhaps $10 million a year, and the return may be more than 2,000 times that in environmental and conservation expenditures.[19] Ross

[19] Rough estimates from data in Robert Cameron Mitchell, "National Environmental Lobbies and the Apparent Illogic of Collective Action," and Council on Environmental Quality, *Environmental Quality 1978*, p. 424.

Perot spent a few tens of thousands of dollars and nearly received $15 million in return.[20]

If certain of the intragroup asymmetries discussed above are multiplied together and then leveraged through government intervention, the prospects for collective action can be seen to be far better than an account of the average person's interests would suggest; if it is true that there is a substantial multiplier effect of certain kinds of activity to provide the benefits, then it follows that the k-subgroups for relevant groups may be far smaller than the groups. One of these asymmetries can involve strictly fungible costs and benefits: the asymmetry in content, as with the good of corporate tax benefits. The others largely involve nonfungible goods. Recent American regulatory legislation and policy have predominantly been directed at nonfungible goods such as air quality, safety in the work place, and so forth. These often essentially involve the elimination of collective bads through severe regulation of particular industries. Politics over such goods is typically a conflict between large groups of individuals who want severe regulation and small groups of organizations that oppose regulation. Even if they remain latent, the former groups can be expected occasionally to win in the legislative arena through the activities of political entrepreneurs, as discussed in chapter 2.

Experience suggests that once regulatory legislation is enacted, the small groups of regulated organizations have substantial advantages over the large groups of individuals, whose motivations may shift, as Edelman and others have argued for past regulatory efforts.[21] But experience may be a poor indicator of the potential success of groups of individuals whose costs and benefits are asymmetric (because the benefits are qualitative), whose demand for their goods is asymmetric and for whose goods there are no reasonable substitutes, and whose evaluations of their goods may even exhibit substantial hysteresis.

Traditional regulatory agencies have largely regulated either intra-industry conflicts or conflicts between the public and natural monopolies (railroads and utilities). The latter conflicts are in many respects similar to the conflicts between, say, opponents of pollution and an

---

[20] Milk producers contributed $300,000 to Nixon's 1972 reelection campaign in return for his administration's increasing price supports for milk by twenty-six cents per hundredweight. According to *New York Times* reporter William Shannon, "that meant $500 million to $700 million more for dairy farmers in the new marketing year" (Norman Frohlich and Joe A. Oppenheimer, *Modern Political Economy*, p. 40). Dollar for dollar, it is evidently worth more to buy a president than to buy the Ways and Means Committee.

[21] Murray Edelman, *The Symbolic Uses of Politics*.

industrial polluter, because they involve collective benefits. But the principal interest in regulating natural monopolies is to prevent them from charging excessive user fees, as their locally monopolistic positions would allow them to do. Hence, in the conflict between "the public" and a natural monopoly, the public admirably fits the analysis of latent groups in chapter 2, because its good is strictly monetary and commensurate with its costs. The politics of contemporary regulation of certain public bads differs considerably from the politics of regulation of natural monopolies, because, as discussed above, at issue now are public bads that cannot readily be rejected—there are no attractive private good substitutes—for whose regulation demand is highly asymmetric.

Analytically, there are more general effects that asymmetries imply. If our group is interested in obtaining several collective goods, and if our demands for them are strongly asymmetric, we may well supply ourselves with substantial levels of all the goods through the activities of a different k-subgroup for each good. Without the strong asymmetry, the k-subgroup for provision of a given level of each good would be much larger, and we might fail to provide much of any of our goods. Although a symmetric and an asymmetric community might collectively choose similar levels of supply of a host of collective goods, the asymmetric community might be far more successful in generating the political activity to bring about supply. The community with the higher level of consensus would achieve less of its collective ends through voluntary collective action.[22]

There is another broad conclusion about political activity to be drawn from the analysis of asymmetries. As noted at the outset of this chapter, many of the qualitative goods collectively sought today may be superior goods—the well-off would spend a larger proportion of their incomes for them than would the less well-off. Asymmetry of demand for these goods may correlate, therefore, with asymmetry of ability to pay. Robert Dorfman suggests that environmental protection is a superior good,[23] and there is evidence that the quite well-off pay for a very large share of the collective action in favor of conservation and environmental regulation.[24]

Burton Weisbrod notes that, because of lessened individual control over quality of a collective good, higher-income classes may tend to opt

[22] Even in the asymmetric community, if private good substitutes were available for all the collective goods, the average level of supply of all benefits might be very low.

[23] Robert Dorfman, "Incidence of the Benefits and Costs of Environmental Programs," p. 336.

[24] Don Coombs, "The Club Looks at Itself."

for private good substitutes. Hence, he argues, the relationship between
the level of per capita income and the relative size of the government
sector is likely to be curvilinear (it will be an inverted U). As an
example, he suggests that higher income should reduce the demand for
library services of lending out best-sellers.[25] The shift from public to
private school education as income rises may be a more compelling
example. Nevertheless, this conclusion is rather too easy, since, for
example, at the financially trivial level of his best-sellers, demand for
public-supported opera seems to rise with income. And, as Weisbrod
himself has shown, demand for public-supported higher education also
seems to rise with income.[26] Hence, the issue turns on which goods
weigh more heavily in the balance of government provision, and an a
priori account will not carry us far.

Against Weisbrod's thesis, note that many goods roughly approximat-
ing Samuelson's public goods seem to be superior goods (clean air and
conservation perhaps being the economically most important examples),
or at least not inferior goods, so that demand for them rises absolutely
and perhaps even relatively as income rises. For some of these, there
are presently no attractive private good substitutes available for any
but the extremely wealthy (the Rockefellers can buy a large chunk of
Maine, Idaho, or Alaska and thereby achieve private conservation, but
few of us can emulate them). Hence, whether the government sector
will grow or shrink as income rises depends on how commonly superior
collective goods will have attractive substitutes. It also depends,
obviously, on how we count the use of government to force "market"
provision of various goods (Should we include some part of government-
mandated expenditures by industry in the public sector?), as well as on
whether those things that produce rising incomes also produce collective
bads.

At a time when a relatively smaller fraction of federal expenditures
in the United States was for welfare programs, Aaron Director noted
that a disproportionate number of benefits provided by government
seemed predominantly to serve the middle, indeed, the upper middle
class. For example, while wintering in the Southwest, he noticed that,

[25] Burton A. Weisbrod, "Toward a Theory of the Voluntary Non-Profit Sector
in a Three-Sector Economy," pp. 184–185.

[26] W. Lee Hansen and Burton A. Weisbrod, "The Distribution of Costs and
Benefits of Public Higher Education: The Case of California." See also Douglas M.
Windham, *Education, Equality and Income Distribution,* which is a study of state-
supported higher education in Florida. In both California and Florida, the well-off
seem to benefit more from such education than their share of relevant taxes would
justify, so that the provision of that education is redistributive upwards.

on average, cars in the national parks were conspicuously more expensive than those on the streets of Chicago. His general observation has been canonized as "Director's law," and various explanations have been proposed.[27] Director's explanation is that many government provisions are complementary goods—to enjoy them one must have other goods. To enjoy national parks, one must have a car, extended leisure time, and other resources.[28] One may still wonder why a supposedly democratic government would use its resources so heavily to benefit the upper middle class. The usual Downsian argument that winning politicians will locate their policies at the median elector's demand would yield a slight upward bias in the United States, since voting turnouts have an upward bias, with the poor generally less likely to vote than others. But many policies, including environmental regulation[29] and national parks, have a considerably more substantial upward bias. Political effects of asymmetries in collective action fit many of these policies very well.

Director's "law" does not account for government policy in general, but it seems to cover two categories of government provisions that often merge: (1) provisions that are like older national parks in that they were sought as public goods in Schattschneider's sense (for example, of the public interest group that seeks to end capital punishment as opposed to the special interest group that seeks a specific tax benefit for its members); and (2) provisions that are sought by upper-middle-class groups such as the Sierra Club. Provisions in the first category often just happen to benefit the upper middle class more than others because, as Director notes, they are complementary goods. John Muir, Gifford Pinchot, and many of the American elite at the turn of the century wanted government protection for such areas as Grand Canyon and Yosemite on principle—not merely for their personal benefit. Yet there appears to be a strong upward bias in the class of those who actually enjoy visiting these areas. (For fuller discussion, see chapter 7.)

The second category includes many goods in highly asymmetric demand: some of the upper middle class want them intensely. They are generally superior goods. (In this respect they are sometimes similar to the first category, because the best explanation of why certain goods are superior is that they are complementary goods.) Hence, they are

[27] George J. Stigler, "Director's Law of Public Income Redistribution."

[28] Aaron Director, Hoover Institution, Stanford, Calif., personal communication, 1975.

[29] Dorfman, "Incidence of the Benefits and Costs," esp. p. 336; and William J. Baumol, "Environmental Protection and Income Distribution," esp. pp. 99–103, 110–111. For a purple view, see William Tucker, "Environmentalism and the Leisure Class: Protecting Birds, Fishes, and Above All, Social Privilege."

more likely to stimulate group activity. As a special case, moral *action* may generally be a superior good. But the particular moral issues that dominate one's concern might tend to be those that affect one's interests. Workers may concentrate on the immorality of capitalists for paying them too little; the upper middle class may more readily be concerned with the immorality of pollution. Because of the much greater asymmetry of the latter concern, and also perhaps because moral action is a superior good, pollution may stimulate far more group action of a strictly voluntary nature than do wage demands.

Some of the most expensive goods in this second category are provided in part through qualitative regulation of industry. Most costs of such regulation are not borne by taxpayers through government, but by consumers through a generally higher level of prices paid for private consumption goods. Hence, one whose utility is increased by the provision of these collective consumption goods (reduced noise, reduced pollution, and so forth) has transferred part of the cost to those who are more nearly indifferent to the particular collective good, but who nevertheless pay higher prices for their private consumption goods. As the general level of prices rises, people of low income may see their utility lessened because they value the collective goods produced through regulation relatively little, if at all, while their consumption of private goods falls off. Director's law may hit with a vengeance here when, for example, reduction of pollution leads to more expensive cars and gasoline, which make enjoyment of other government-provided collective goods such as national parks still harder to obtain for the less well-off.

6

CONTRACTARIAN PROVISIONS

In previous chapters, it has generally been assumed that group members are possessive individualists, that they act wholly from their own interest. Since not everyone is always a possessive individualist (Homo economicus, or rational man), it is interesting to consider what happens if this assumption is violated in some degree. There may be collective action problems even when members of a group are not only possessive individualists, but also *contractarians,* that is, people who play fair, who try to cooperate if others do. For such a group, success depends in part on whether there is a clear or, in Schelling's term, a "prominent" notion of what is fair.[1] Unfortunately, it seems that there can be no generally compelling notion of fairness, that even in some very simple contractarian situations, substantial disagreement may balk cooperation.

A portion of this chapter has appeared in an article by the author, "The Contractarian Provision of Group Goods," in *The Papers of the Peace Science Society (International)* vol. 27 (1977).

[1] When two or more people try to coordinate their efforts for some joint purpose, they may often find coordination easier if there is some unique point, or method, or idea that stands out prominently from among various alternatives. For example, in the terminal hours of a contract negotiation, to "split the difference" might seem to both parties to be the prominent resolution of remaining issues. (Thomas C. Schelling, *The Strategy of Conflict,* pp. 57–58.)

Assume a group of contractarians who wish to supply themselves with a group good. In general, the group faces two decisions:

1. Concerning the level of supply of the group good if it can be supplied at various levels;
2. Concerning a scheme for sharing costs of supply if individual members can contribute at various levels; or, in short, a tax rule.

These are the concerns of the public finance literature—the optimum level of supply and the equitability of tax or cost-sharing schemes.

The two decisions the group faces will be subject to two constraints:

1. The final outcome should be Pareto-optimal, which, it will be remembered, means that no one can be made better off without making someone else worse off.
2. The final outcome should be realizable, that is, no member should be worse off after the collective action than without it (this condition may be complicated if the tax rule calls for incremental provision of the group good, in which case each incremental outcome should be realizable).

The set of Pareto outcomes and the set of realizable outcomes might each be considerably larger than their intersection, but their intersection will never be empty (unless there is no realizable outcome, in which case there is no point in collective action, since its cost would outweigh its benefits).

In some respects, it might seem that the level of supply should be the first issue decided by a group. But, as noted below, when utility is not transferable, this may not be possible in principle. Furthermore, if a contractarian group is to succeed in its cooperative venture, it must achieve a sense of equality or fairness, and it must avoid the creation of invidious zero-sum (or constant-sum) conflicts. If the group first decides on a level of supply and then turns to deciding on the division of costs, it will enter into a constant-sum game in which some members may feel that others gain what they lose. The solutions to *n*-person constant-sum games are relatively unappealing and inequitable. Consequently, a preliminary agreement on the division of costs may improve the prospects for group cohesion. Agreement need not be explicit so long as the group deems a particular scheme to be compelling or natural. For a contractarian group, a compelling scheme is likely to be a prominent solution that the members all consider equitable. Whatever principle seems to underlie that scheme should not, when applied generally to their collective action, lead to disagreement over the level of provision of their good.

The simple case for analysis is that in which utility is transferable, as we can assume for goods whose costs and benefits are monetary or can be properly evaluated in monetary terms. In this case there is a Pareto level of provision, and a contractarian group need only agree to a fair division of costs. A group may easily agree on a rule of fairness if the group is symmetric, that is, if all members value the good equally (in units of the cost of providing the good) at all levels of provision. If the group is asymmetric, however, it is not likely that any general cost-sharing rule would invariably seem fair. In other words, there is no a priori cost-sharing rule that an asymmetric contractarian group would find agreeable post hoc in diverse collective actions. No matter what rule was adopted in the abstract, it might lead to conflict in actual application. In principle, fairness cannot be well defined. To complicate matters, when utility is not transferable, it may not be possible for contractarians to reach agreement even on the level of provision.

FOUR COST-SHARING RULES

Assume a group of n members and a continuous good, a good that can be provided to the group at various levels at cost C_q for provision at level q. Further assume that each member of the group may contribute any proportion of the total cost of the good's provision (hence, members do not face a binary choice of contributing or not contributing). Finally, assume that there is an underlying unit in which each individual member can measure the difference between the benefit of receiving the good and the contribution toward its cost, so that utility is transferable, as would be true if the good and its cost were monetary.

Let r_{iq} be the ratio of group benefit to cost *if* all members had valuations of the good similar to individual i's (in fact, of course, they might not, so that r_{iq} need not equal r_{jq} if i is different from j). If

$$\frac{1}{n} \sum_i r_{iq} > 1 \tag{1}$$

there is value in providing the good at level q. The collective value V_q of the good to the group is

$$V_q = \frac{1}{n} \sum_i r_{iq} C_q$$

Hence, condition (1) is equivalent to $V_q > C_q$, which is a necessary condition for provision of the good at level q. The Pareto level p of the good is the lowest level for which $(V_p - C_p)$ is maximum.

An outcome of a collective action is a combination of a level of supply of the group good and a scheme for apportioning its cost at that level. An outcome is not realizable if it makes some member worse off than the member would be without group cooperative action. For example, the outcome in which one member bears the full cost of supplying a group good is not realizable unless the member derives a net benefit despite bearing the full cost (in which case the group is, in Olson's term, a privileged group). Obviously, if $V_q < C_q$, no outcome at level q is realizable. If $V_q > C_q$, there is a realizable outcome at level q.

If an outcome is to be selected by a group, a necessary condition on the *outcome* is that it be realizable. If utility is transferable, for a *given level of provision* to be selected, it is sufficient that the level be Pareto-optimal, that is, that net benefits be maximum, given that costs and benefits are all in money. At a given level, however, there may be numerous outcomes, each corresponding to a particular tax rule. Since the outcome chosen by a contractarian group must be both realizable and Pareto-optimal, any a priori rule of fairness for cost sharing must produce an outcome subject to both these conditions. It is easily shown that many particular a priori rules would fail to meet both these conditions in general.

For example, equal cost sharing would clearly work in a symmetric group. Indeed, it might even be the prominently fair rule for such a group (although see Luce and Raiffa's game of fair division between a pauper and a millionaire[2]). If in an asymmetric group some member's valuation of the Pareto level of provision were $r_{ip} < 1$, then that member's equal share, C_p/n, of the cost would be more than the member's benefit, $r_{ip}C_p/n$. Hence, the Pareto level would be unrealizable under this tax rule.

Three standard rules that would invariably work, in the sense that at Pareto levels of provision they would yield realizable outcomes, are proportional benefits taxation, marginal rate of substitution taxation,

[2] R. Duncan Luce and Howard Raiffa, *Games and Decisions,* p. 364. The authors suppose that "a wealthy man and a pauper" together come upon $100 and must split it "fairly." One way to achieve a fair division is that used to let two children split a piece of cake: one slices it into two pieces and the other chooses first. The slicer thus has incentive to make an appropriate slice. In our case, "The rich man may prefer to give a larger share to the pauper, and therefore as divider he may make a 60-40 split. Even with their roles reversed, the pauper, in an obvious appeal to the conscience of the rich man, might also elect the 60-40 rather than the 50-50 split" (Ibid.). Of course, ruder souls might take advantage of the pauper's division and take the $60 share. They might even think it fair to do so on an argument that $60 would give them less pleasure than $40 would give a pauper.

and proportional incremental benefits taxation. These may produce divergent results, however, so that there may be disagreement over their prominence and fairness. (They need not produce divergent results, of course. In a symmetric group, all three rules reduce to equal cost sharing.)

Although it might seem the most natural or prominent scheme to anyone other than an economist, the proportional benefits rule [3] may be objectionable in its own right, because, under it, individuals' net benefits might not all be simultaneously maximized at a single level of supply. Group members who are relatively easily satisfied will pay more in order to benefit others who are less easily satisfied, i.e., they will subsidize the higher level of demand of others. This can be seen from a small-scale numerical example. Assume a three-member group, of members A, B, and C. A is equally satisfied at 1 or 2 units of the good; B and C are twice as satisfied at 2 units as at 1 unit. A, B, and C value 1 unit of the good at $r_{A1} = r_{B1} = r_{C1} = 2$ (hence, if 1 unit of the good is supplied, tax shares are equal at 0.333 under the proportional benefits tax, and *net* benefits are equal at 0.333). But A values 2 units at $r_{A2} = 2$, while B and C value two units at $r_{B2} = r_{C2} = 4$. Tax shares at 2 units are $t_{A2} = r_{A2} (2/\sum r_{i2}) = 0.4$, and $t_{B2} = t_{C2} = 0.8$. Net benefits, $a._2$, are $a_{A2} = 0.267$ and $a_{B2} = a_{C2} = 0.533$. Under this tax rule, A is worse off at 2 units of the good than at 1 unit. Hence, there would not be unanimous agreement on supplying the good at a Pareto level. The proportional benefits tax rule is therefore generally objectionable on a priori grounds, although it might be quite acceptable in a particular case (again, for example, in a symmetric group). Nevertheless, any rule that too severely violated the proportional benefits rule might seem unfair.

Consider now the marginal rate of substitution tax rule. In the numerical example above, A would pay nothing if the good were provided at 2 units, because A values the second (marginal) unit at 0. Under this rule, a member who is relatively easily satisfied would contribute nothing. Worse still, the net benefits at 2 units would be $a_{A2} = 0.667$ and $a_{B2} = a_{C2} = 0.333$, so that the noncontributor would reap the greatest net benefit from the group effort. Such an outcome would probably not seem fair to many people.

[3] It is the counterpart of Homans's "general rule of distributive justice": that one's net rewards in an exchange relation be proportional to one's investments. (George C. Homans, *Social Behavior: Its Elementary Forms*, p. 75.) It is also the counterpart of Gamson's "parity norm": the belief that one "ought to get from an agreement an amount proportional to what [one] brings into it" (William A. Gamson, "Experimental Studies in Coalition Formation," p. 88).

The incremental net benefits rule would overcome the problems of both the other rules applied to the example above. Under it, the ratios of benefits to costs of the first increment would be $r_{A(1)} = r_{B(1)} = r_{C(1)} = 2$, and the taxes would be $t_{\cdot(1)} = 0.333$. For the second increment, these would be $r_{A(2)} = 0$ and $r_{B(2)} = r_{C(2)} = 2$; and $t_{A(2)} = 0$ and $t_{B(2)} = t_{C(2)} = 0.5$. The net benefits summed over both increments would be $a_{A(1+2)} = 0.333$ and $a_{B(1+2)} = a_{C(1+2)} = 0.5$. This result should not seem perverse; indeed, one might be surprised if any of the group members considered it unfair.

Unfortunately, the incremental benefits rule can produce perverse results in other cases. Consider, for example, another simple three-member group in which A values the first unit of the group's good at $r_{A(1)} = 3.3$, and B and C value it at $r_{B(1)} = r_{C(1)} = 0$, whereas the valuations of the second unit are reversed. For the first increment we have tax shares at $t_{A(1)} = 1$ and the others 0, and we have net benefits $a_{A(1)} = 0.1$ and the others 0. For the second increment we have tax shares $t_{A(2)} = 0$ and $t_{B(2)} = t_{C(2)} = 0.5$, and net benefits $a_{A(2)} = 0$ and $a_{B(2)} = a_{C(2)} = 0.6$. Total tax shares would be $t_{A(1+2)} = 1$ and $t_{B(1+2)} = t_{C(1+2)} = 0.5$, and total net benefits would be $a_{A(1+2)} = 0.1$ and $a_{B(1+2)} = a_{C(1+2)} = 0.6$. In this case, A pays heavily just because A is more easily satisfied than B and C. This is the opposite of what could occur in the market for private goods, as well as, of course, under the marginal rates of substitution tax rule. The rule one might expect to seem most prominently fair in this case would be the proportional benefits rule, under which individual tax shares and net benefits would be equal at 0.667 and 0.433, respectively.

(In economic contexts, the increasing valuation of players B and C might seem to be ruled out as an ill-behaved utility function. The desire for an additional fix of heroin might increase the more fixes one has had already, although that is part of the proof of the pernicious quality of heroin. But there are cases that sound more reputable. For example, the three-member group above may have joined to build a common tennis court. Two very good players in the group might not wish to play on a mediocre court, preferring a doubly expensive quality court. The duffer in the group might be able to notice little difference between a quality and a mediocre court.)

The examples above appear to rule out the a priori adoption of any of the three tax rules (proportional benefits, marginal benefits, and incremental benefits taxation) as clearly fair in general. Contractarians might successfully reach agreement on both a level of supply and a fair cost-sharing scheme in providing themselves a group good, but there does not appear to be a prominent general rule for doing so. A tax scheme based on individual total benefits might lead to disagreement over the level of provision. A scheme that guaranteed Pareto agreement on the level of provision might seem to yield an unfair distribution of total benefits.

If a level of supply is first decided, then cost sharing is a constant-sum game. It is subject to the constraint that no member will contribute more than the member benefits, so that if the net benefit to the group from collective action is small relative to cost, there will be a narrow range of possible cost-sharing schemes. If the net benefit is large, however, there will be great leeway for diverse cost-sharing schemes and consequent leeway for severe disagreement. A constant-sum game whose total payoff is small will not provoke the interest or potential antagonism of one whose total payoff is large.

GENERAL CONSIDERATIONS

The foregoing discussion necessarily is unrealistic for many actual group activities. Various modifications in the relationship between costs and benefits of supplying a group good suggest that the prospects for contractarian agreement will often be even worse, and sometimes better, than in the cases above. If there are dynamic relationships between individual tax shares and demand for higher-level provision, or if utility is not transferable, the task of agreement may be much harder. On the other hand, there may be such prominent notions of fairness in some collective actions that agreement by contractarians should be quite easy, as in symmetric valuation of binary-choice cases.

If the members of a group have alternative ways to use their limited resources (as is generally the case), their valuation of the qth increment of the good may not be static, but may depend on how much they have already spent in providing earlier increments. Consequently, the Pareto level may depend on the tax scheme. The group decision becomes more complicated in that neither the tax scheme nor the level of supply can be determined a priori, as at least one of them could be in the static-demand case considered above. For many collective actions that interest us, of course, limited resources need not be a serious problem over the likely ranges of provision of group goods. Only very substantial undertakings would necessitate our taking demand shifts into consideration.

In the discussion of the arithmetic examples above, saying that an outcome was Pareto-optimal meant that it yielded maximum net benefit. However, if utility in the group is not transferable and not interpersonally comparable, it is not meaningful to claim that an outcome maximizes net benefit. Nor is it possible in general to say that there will be a unique Pareto *level* of provision of the group good. There will be numerous Pareto *outcomes* which may involve provisions at various levels. In this case, the group will be faced with simultaneous decisions over level of supply and tax scheme, with neither resolvable a priori. Clearly, in many contexts it would be unrealistic to assume transferable or interpersonally comparable utility, and in these contexts groups would face conflicted decisions. They would be forced to choose among a wide array of Pareto outcomes, knowing that the choice between two such outcomes would disadvantage some in the group and advantage others.

Not all contractarian collective actions need be so conflicted as most of those discussed above. If a group's good is the product of binary choices (such as cooperate versus defect, or vote for A versus vote for B) by the members, then there may be a uniquely prominent contractarian choice. For example, in a binary-choice *n*-person Prisoner's Dilemma [4] the contractarian fair choice is clearly to cooperate. Similarly, in many of the binary-choice generalized Prisoner's Dilemma games discussed by Schelling, cooperation is the prominently fair choice.[5] Even if choice is not binary but the group is symmetric, there may be a prominent fair choice at equal cost shares. (Indeed, if individuals can choose among numerous clubs that provide equivalent benefits and can exclude noncontributors, the symmetrically fair payoff to all may be enforceable even among noncontractarians.[6])

Although this is not the context in which to argue the factual point, a contractarian group might be extremely large. If so, it will be important that the members of the group see a uniquely prominent, relatively fair solution for cost sharing. Public television stations in the United States solve the problem of reaching consensus on cost sharing by stipulating a set cost of "membership." For many activities that generate collective bads, the prominent, fair solution is for each potential contributor to the bad not to contribute—for example, by not littering. Given the difference in the ease of agreeing on a notion of prominence in many collective good and bad games, it would seem that anarchic cooperation may be easier in preventing many internally generated bads than in providing a non-binary-choice good. On the other hand, the proportion

[4] Such as those in chap. 2.

[5] Thomas C. Schelling, "Hockey Helmets, Concealed Weapons, and Daylight Savings"; Schelling, *Micromotives and Macrobehavior,* pp. 213–243. In Schelling's generalized Prisoner's Dilemma games, the "right" choice generally is to cooperate, the "left" choice to defect.

[6] Mark V. Pauly, "Clubs, Commonality, and the Core: An Integration of Game Theory and the Theory of Public Goods."

of group members required to form an efficacious subgroup may be larger for typical internally generated bads than for goods. If contractarians constitute too small a fraction of the set of potential contributors to a collective bad, they may not benefit noticeably from their collective abstention. While 17 percent of viewership may be sufficient to fund a public television station so that all may benefit, if only 17 percent of the users of a beach are nonlitterers, their impact on the quality of the beach may go unnoticed.

If group members are possessive individualists, then, under the logic of collective action, free riders impair the prospects for success in group endeavors. But even if members are contractarians, the structure of their individual utility functions may still impede their agreeing on the fairness of various schemes for providing themselves a group good. In particular, asymmetry of valuations of the group good by individual members in cases of goods that can be provided over a range of levels may lead to conflict over the relative fairness of possible tax rules even when the arithmetic of benefits and costs is simplified by the assumption of transferable utility. If utility is not transferable, conflict may arise over both the choice of tax rule and the choice of level of supply. Of course, there are cases, including many binary-choice and symmetric-group problems, in which contractarians (unlike possessive individualists) need not suffer conflict in providing themselves group goods. Hence, one cannot generalize from one class of interaction to others. Taylor's argument for cooperation in a state of anarchy,[7] for example, does not generalize from his binary-choice interactions to other classes of problems. The strategic prospects for anarchic cooperation in asymmetric nonbinary cases will in general be enormously more problematic.

Generally, one would not expect these problems to afflict genuine friendship groups—which are necessarily likely to be very small—because such groups might be relatively symmetric in their evaluation of relevant group goods. Even if their valuations were not symmetric, however, members of a friendship group might still succeed. I have considered allocation *rules,* but there might be *procedures* that would work for such groups. For example, Guttman's matching game, as discussed in chapter 8, should work well enough for a genuinely contractarian group of trusting friends in a position to work through the game. But for groups less given to trusting one another or less able to meet and discuss what constitute fair tax shares, the problems discussed here may be insurmountable. Hence, even if the contractarian attitude is widespread among the members of a large group, they may still have

---

[7] Michael Taylor, *Anarchy and Cooperation.*

difficulty coordinating their cooperative actions (see further, the discussions of chapters 10 through 13). The general problem is reminiscent of the problem of devising a priori arbitration schemes for certain classes of games.[8] There are numerous possible a priori schemes, each of which would be objectionable on some ground.

Even more generally one should not expect most people to treat such problems so technically. It would be surprising if the general populace happened upon marginal rate of substitution or proportional incremental benefits cost sharing. Even proportional benefits cost sharing might seem difficult, but one can imagine its use. For example, San Francisco Bay Area hikers might expect to benefit far more from the conservation of a bit of the Sierra Nevadas than I would, and they might also in part therefore think it fair that they contribute proportionately more to the cause. For many issues, however, the only tacitly acceptable rule would be equal cost sharing for most members of any relevant group. Hence, groups commonly ask for a "fair share" contribution of a specific amount. When a group is dispersed, rather than being a tightly knit friendship group, the workable rules must generally be simple, widely accepted in the culture in other contexts, and somehow generalizable to the group issue. The notion of "fair play" is extraordinarily complex— because it has its particular meaning in each of the countless contexts.[9] Doing one's fair share in a cooperative group effort may be a notion of relatively late development and may not be readily amenable to application in commonplace asymmetric cases. Hence, a dispersed group's success in tapping contractarian urges may depend on its ability to define relevantly different fair shares for members of varying intensities and on its capacity to keep the classes of members separate in its appeals.

Finally, consider how the contractarian urge might be fitted to the usual rational analysis of choice. Howard Margolis, in a clever scheme, proposes that a person's—say, Smith's—choice function be derived from two separate utility functions, as though Smith were two different people in one package.[10] G-Smith responds to group interests; S-Smith is strictly a self-interested Homo economicus. The more S-Smith has already been satisfied, the more Smith's resources in the present will go to satisfy G-Smith, and vice versa. Of course, G-Smith can never be satisfied, since Smith's contributions to G-Smith's causes will be of small to negligible effect. As Smith's income rises, assuming that S-Smith's

---

[8] See Luce and Raiffa, *Games*, pp. 121–124, for discussion of the latter problem.

[9] Friedrich A. Hayek sensibly doubts "whether anyone has yet succeeded in articulating all the rules which constitute 'fair play' " (Hayek, *Law, Legislation, and Liberty* vol. 1 *Rules and Order*, p. 76).

[10] Howard Margolis, "A New Model of Rational Choice."

tastes do not change as a result, we may expect to see G-Smith get an increasing share of Smith's resources. Other things being equal, therefore, a group wanting to build on contractarians should direct its appeal to quite well-off Smiths first. If it is successful at this stage, it then will have the infrastructure with which to direct a much broader appeal for individually smaller-scale contributions from the middling well-off. For the small number of very well-off contributors, one might expect something like proportional benefits cost sharing; for the wider class of members, equal shares might be more acceptable.

7

EXTRARATIONAL MOTIVATIONS

Under the logic of collective action, we should expect to see very little large-scale collective action motivated by narrow self-interest. There can be exceptions to this conclusion—for example, when the by-product theory applies. Exceptions might include business and farmers' organizations, which can be centralized suppliers of valuable information to their members, labor unions once they have the power of the state behind them to compel membership, and various other organizations; but most large-scale interests cannot readily be included. Yet we know that many large-scale interests are organized. Most notably in recent times, the civil rights, antiwar, environmental, and women's movements have achieved impressive levels of sustained organization and activity on behalf of the interests of large segments of the population.

In part, their organizations have represented *public* interests in the sense emphasized by Schattschneider (see further, "Moral Motivations," below). For example, the early movement for conservation in the United States may not have been self-interested, but public-interested in the grandest sense of the term. John Muir, Gifford Pinchot, and others may have been concerned with conserving certain areas, not because they personally wanted to be able to enjoy those areas, but because they thought it wrong of the nation not to conserve such monuments of nature, and because they thought others, especially future generations, should be privileged to experience them. Contemporary environmental concern is probably a mixture of economic and extraeconomic concerns:

101

one might say, "It is worth X dollars to me to clean the air or to preserve a certain stand of redwoods," much as one would evaluate buying an economic good (such as a trip to the Grand Canyon). One might also say, "It is immoral to foul the air or not to preserve the redwoods," much as one would think it immoral to torture cats.

Contractarian provision, as discussed in chapter 6, is merely one of a class of extrarational intrusions into the analysis of collective action (although, as is argued in chapters 10 through 13, contractarian provision may be achieved by strictly rational motivations when a group faces its collective action problem repeatedly). Three extrarational intrusions are discussed here: moral motivations, the desire for self-development through participation, and ignorance and misunderstanding. These categories may not be exhaustive, but they may be fundamentally important in explaining the existence of many contemporary organizations representing very large groups. In general, it appears that rational incentives can induce cooperation by a large fraction, even a large majority, of the members of a relevant group. The three categories discussed here, however, seem to motivate only a very small fraction of many important groups (on one account, discussed below, misunderstanding may stimulate participation by perhaps a third of the large group of Minnesota farmers). Little more than 1 percent each of blacks, women, and professed environmentalists have contributed to their group's cause in any year.

In general, as discussed in chapter 5, when costs and benefits are not commensurable, it is not a simple matter to determine whether individual actions are rational in narrow self-interest terms. Rational action is intentional action par excellence. Hence, direct behavioral data are sufficient to judge an action only if the relationship between means and ends and the evaluation of more and less can be assumed to be clear to the judge. If the goal of an individual's actions is monetary gain, academic judges can safely enough assume they know what constitutes more or less. But if an individual's goal is to select the most-preferred bundle from a large set of bundles of goods, then the judges usually have to turn to the individual to discover what constitutes more or less.

When moral concerns are involved, one cannot avoid recognizing that costs and benefits are not readily fungible or commensurable. Hence, many of the implications of inequality, or asymmetry of demand, discussed in chapter 5, apply to collective actions, some or all of whose participants act from moral concern or from the desire to participate in their history. In particular, when such motivations enter, the prospects for successful collective action are often enhanced, because asymmetry reduces the size of the relevant k-subgroup. For several recent broad-scale social movements, k-subgroups do not seem to have exceeded 1 percent of the relevant larger groups. As with individuals' tastes for various goods, whether people have the moral or participatory commitment to act cannot be determined a priori, but only by massive observation of more than behavior: observation of intentions is also required.

MORAL MOTIVATIONS

One of the best-known passages in American political science is Schattschneider's defense of the notion of public interest groups:

> Is it possible to distinguish between the "interest" of the members of the National Association of Manufacturers and the members of the American League to Abolish Capital Punishment? The facts in the two cases are not identical. First, *the members of the A.L.A.C.P. obviously do not expect to be hanged.* The membership of the A.L.A.C.P. is not restricted to persons under indictment for murder or in jeopardy of the extreme penalty. *Anybody* can join A.L.A.C.P. Its members oppose capital punishment although they are not personally likely to benefit by the policy they advocate. The inference is therefore that the interest of the A.L.A.C.P. is not adverse, exclusive or special. It is not like the interest of the [American] Petroleum Institute in depletion allowances.[1]

At Schattschneider's writing (about 1960), there were 720 members of the American League to Abolish Capital Punishment. There were a few thousand members of each of various other public interest organizations. The federal structure of the League of Women Voters of the United States (as discussed in chapter 2 under "The By-Product Theory") probably accounted for that organization's impressive 106,000 members.[2]

Although Schattschneider was concerned with demolishing an apparent misconception in much of traditional group theory (that there are no public, only special, interests), there is presumably no doubt in most circles that people are often public-spirited. What is in doubt is that public-spiritedness motivates much large-scale activity other than possibly wartime and emergency efforts. For example, Titmuss argues in favor of a voluntary blood collection system, as opposed to the contractual and commercial (paid donor) systems that generate most blood for transfusions in the United States.[3] It may be that his argument is

---

[1] E. E. Schattschneider, *The Semi-Sovereign People,* p. 26.
[2] Ibid., p. 48.
[3] Richard M. Titmuss, *The Gift Relationship.*

tenable at all only because the system would require voluntary donations from just a few percent of the population. If substantially greater supplies were needed on a regular basis, voluntarism might be woefully inadequate to the task. The interesting issue for moral motivations is not whether they underlie any actions—surely they do—but whether they underlie any large-scale actions where narrow self-interest could not motivate cooperation. Hence, whereas the analyses of this book more generally cover motivations for all levels of collective action, from very small to very large scale, discussion here focuses on large-scale collective action.

Consider what is probably, on a count of dues-paying members of active organizations over a period of many years, the most organized public interest group in American history: that concerned with environmental protection. Among the largest, politically most active, and most influential of the environmental (indeed, of all contemporary public interest) organizations is the Sierra Club. In 1977 it had 178,000 members and a budget of $7.2 million. Most of the budget went to outdoor activities, publications, and organizational functions. But $1,918,000 went for "studying and influencing public policy."[4] However, it would be wrong to suppose from these figures that political activity by the club is strictly a by-product of club functions that actually generate the funds.

From surveys of its membership, it appears that only about 60 percent of the members of the Sierra Club are active—40 percent do no more than receive the club magazine, *Sierra,* in return for their annual dues,[5] which as of 1981 were $25, of which $3 was for the magazine. On the basis of the club's published financial statements, it appears that the costs of servicing the active members exceed *their* dues, so that nonactive members, who may think they are contributing to the cause of environmental politics, are partly perhaps only subsidizing active members. The full cost of club politicking appears to be no more than the sum of voluntary contributions beyond dues ($1,947,000 in 1977).[6] If most voluntary contributions and much of the dues of nonactive members are motivated by concern for the environment and for conservation, then some of this politically intended money may in fact service the active members' individual pleasures. Those members who think the club

[4] *Sierra* (May 1978) pp. 22–25.

[5] Reported in Don Coombs, "The Club Looks at Itself."

[6] Club financial data for 1977, from *Sierra* (May 1978) pp. 22–25, are reported here for comparability with Mitchell's data on the largest national environmental organizations (see below at nn. 8–10). In 1979 the club had 700 fewer members; contributions above dues were up to $2,233,230, and political expenditures were up to $2,307,797. (*Sierra* [March/April 1980] p. 42.)

should stick to outdoor activities and leave politics to others should perhaps instead be grateful for the recreational benefits of politics. (If committed environmentalists in the club recognize this, they face a difficult problem. They could argue for increased dues on the ground that dues are insufficient to cover the individual pleasures of membership—which pleasures therefore cut into contributions beyond dues. But that argument might bother those who contribute beyond dues or whose dues are intended as contributions, just as news that certain major charities were spending most of what they collected on organizational costs may have deterred contributions. Hence, the club might lose more political funds than it gained if it tried too forthrightly to argue for an increase.[7])

It appears that the bulk of the Sierra Club's political activity is supported by public-spirited donations that are not tied to reciprocal exclusive rewards to the donors. Contemporary labor union political activities may be a by-product; the Sierra Club's generally are not. Nor can one sensibly construct rational arguments for individual contributions to Sierra Club political activities, at least not rational in the sense of narrowly self-interested (for an account of relevant data, see further, chapter 8, section on "Applications to Large Groups").

But if one cannot explain contributions to Sierra Club politics in self-interested rational terms, neither can one conclude that environmentalists are highly irrational. Robert Mitchell estimates nonoverlapping membership in fifteen environmental groups, including the biggest and best-known groups, at 1 million in 1977. He says certain self-report survey data suggest that as many as 5 million adult Americans may belong to environmental organizations such as the Sierra Club, Friends of the Earth, and the National Audubon Society,[8] although this figure seems quite improbable unless it includes members of sports clubs such as the National Rifle Association and those affiliated with the National Wildlife Federation (servicing these affiliates costs the national federation more than it receives from them[9]). Since the biggest organizations are included in Mitchell's tabulation, a million members, well under 1 percent of adult Americans, seems unlikely to be substantially wrong.

[7] In its board members' editorials for and against a 1979 dues increase from $20 to $25, this was not a stated issue. Membership peaked in 1978 and apparently stayed flat throughout the period of the increase despite a high ongoing drop rate (22 percent in 1978). (*Sierra* [Oct./Nov./Dec. 1978] p. 36.) Nevertheless, most of the increase in political expenditures has come from increased contributions, not from higher dues (see n. 6 above).

[8] Robert Cameron Mitchell, "National Environmental Lobbies and the Apparent Illogic of Collective Action," pp. 96–98.

[9] Ibid., n. 12, p. 93.

How much do these groups spend on collective action? Calculated on
the basis of the thirteen organizations for which Mitchell reports membership and dues, the total collected must have been something less than
$20 million in 1977.[10] Unless other organizations convert substantially
more of their funds into political action, or take in substantially more
contributions and grants above dues than the Sierra Club, a total environmental organization political budget of under $20 million, perhaps
nearer $10 million, per year also seems likely. (To put this sum in
perspective, *Time* magazine estimated in 1978 that $2 billion a year is
spent on lobbying American government.[11]) Polls regularly report that
the number of Americans concerned with environmental issues may
exceed 100 million.[12] And the value that even the 1 million active
contributors should expect to get from massive political actions should
dwarf the $10 million to $20 million of the total political action budgets
of the environmental organizations. All of the activity and contributions are little more than a token of the latent interest. Hence, environmentalists generally act as the logic of collective action suggests they
should, and the few million dollars of politics to be explained is a relatively small residual.

To explain the residual, one presumably would invoke such moral or
psychological motives as altruism, guilt, or a sense of injustice at having
to suffer collective bads in order to profit others. A modest percentage
of Americans are likely to be contractarians, people (not quite Kantian)
who play fair if enough others do, as assumed in the analysis of chapter 6. Even among the strictly amoral self-interested there may be a few
who contribute to collective actions out of misunderstanding of causal
relations, as discussed below under "Ignorance and Misunderstanding."

To find strictly rational, that is, narrowly self-interested, actors in
environmental politics one must look beyond environmental organizations—to industry groups and to certain politicians. The antienviron-
mental political expenditures of the major oil companies alone must
swamp all political expenditures by environmental groups. According
to a company executive in 1978, Mobil Oil had been spending $1 million
annually just on weekly op-ed-page environmental advertisements in

[10] Figured from ibid., tables 6 and 8. The total would have been $21 million if
all members paid full dues. The Sierra Club collected nearly a million dollars less
in dues than Mitchell's data imply, presumably because many members have
reduced rates. The same is likely to be true of other organizations in Mitchell's
tables.

[11] *Sierra* (Oct./Nov./Dec. 1979) p. 54.

[12] For example, see a Resources for the Future poll, from which some data on
the general public (and many more on Sierra Club members) are reported in
Sierra (March/April 1979) p. 15.

seven news outlets.[13] There remain the steel, electric utility, chemical, paper, and auto industries, all of which appear to be big spenders. Included in their political action budgets are enormous legal expenditures to defend against both rules and rulings of the U.S. Environmental Protection Agency and its state-level equivalents. Vis-à-vis industry interests, environmentalists are pikers. A comparison of the two sides in this issue confirms Schattschneider, Olson, Lindblom, and others in their view that group activity is dominated by business interests.

As for politicians, note that in an affluent society a residual of extrarational activity may generate enough money to have great impact, especially if astute political entrepreneurs sense the implications of the logic of collective action and believe that a little activity implies a lot of sympathy. In these circumstances, Olson's claim that larger groups are more likely to fail than smaller ones may be false. The cost of achieving some political goals may not rise as (or at least not as fast as) the numbers of supporters for the goals increase. But the likelihood that more morally motivated individuals will be counted among a group of supporters of a goal may well increase as the group grows. Of course, perceptive entrepreneurs should respond more favorably to large than to small numbers of unorganized people.

Return to the data on environmentalists. Only about 1 percent of those who profess concern for the environment actually contribute to a relevant organization each year. And those who do contribute only count for about ten dollars' worth of politics each. Perhaps it is their good fortune that environmental action is like blood donation: it takes only a very small percentage of the population to make it succeed on voluntarism.

In other contexts, I have noted that some successful collective actions depended on dedicated leaders, many of whom could not convincingly be called self-seeking. Comte comments that "if society is in need of any great resource of devotedness, the want cannot be supplied by accumulating any amount of moderate zeal furnished by individuals. The only use of a multitude in such a case is that it improves the chance of finding the *unique* organ of the proposed function. . . ."[14] Creating an organization, however, allows the accumulation of substantial amounts of "moderate zeal." A person moderately zealous in moral commitment to environmental protection can send a small check to the Sierra Club or to the Environmental Defense Fund. It is therefore only to the

[13] Herbert Schmertz, Letter to the editor, *New York Times,* Jan. 15, 1978, sec. 3, p. 14.

[14] Auguste Comte, *Auguste Comte and Positivism,* p. 276.

creation of such an organization that Comte's remark applies: at some point an extremely zealous person may have been required.

Once a group is successfully organized, however, one should often be more skeptical of its leaders, because motivations not unlike those of the political or corporate entrepreneur may come to the fore. For the leaders of many successful public interest organizations, one might paraphrase the characterization of the Quakers: they came to do good, and they did well. Given the uses they are privileged to make of certain of the capital assets of their organizations, leaders are de facto owners of those assets while they lead, just as the salaried managers of firms are the de facto owners of assets such as company golf courses and box seats in symphony halls and football stadiums, and as the president of the United States is de facto owner of Camp David. Similarly, the leaders of some public interest organizations can afford themselves a life-style —on organizational expense accounts—rivaling that of the relatively wealthy. Hence, leadership of an ongoing organization may be a very attractive position. Self-interest in leading an organization, however, may be congruent with the public interest purposes of the organization, because, as argued below under "Political Effects," organizations that depend on moral contributions must pursue relevant goals; leaders wanting the pleasures of leadership must convince contributors that their leadership is effective, or lose the contributions.

PARTICIPATION

There is another motivation which some would class as narrowly self-interested and some as moral. It has some affinity with Bradley's moral notion of self-realization, but without the Hegelian force.[15] It is the desire to be there, to take part in history, to have oneself develop through participation in significant, even world-shaping historical events and movements. For example, in the civil rights movement, whites like Viola Liuzzo, the Detroit housewife and civil rights volunteer who was murdered in Alabama in 1965, and blacks who had long since made it on their own seemed to find this a compelling urge—the civil rights movement at its height was an experience not to be missed.

Consider some disparate examples. Political scientists probably vote as often as others of their social status even though they generally know better. Are they merely irrational or oversocialized? Probably not. Many of them may simply realize that elections are among the few political experiences in which they can ever participate. Are Iranians

15 F. H. Bradley, *Ethical Studies,* esp. essay 6.

a loonier race than most? More likely they are merely further proof of economists' claim that the marginal value of an experience or good is, other things being equal, greater, the rarer its enjoyment. Iranians suddenly had the opportunity to participate in their nation's history during the late seventies, and they would not have missed it for the world.

More compelling than his theory of history in *War and Peace* is Tolstoy's grasp of how intensely people want to participate in the history, to share the experiences of their time and place. A twenty-year-old American male in 1943 might have joined the armed forces because going to war was likely to be the most important experience of his generation of males. We need not assess the costs and benefits of his choice—it is too fundamental to be a matter of costs and benefits (unless these were egregious); it is instead a matter of being a male of that generation. Even an Iranian who dreaded what rule by ayatollahs and mullahs would imply in the long run might have participated in the politics of 1978–79. The logic of collective action might even have eased the decision for many Iranians because, for example, a woman who could not expect to affect the outcome one way or the other certainly had no political reason not to participate in the revolution of the ayatollahs. She could therefore participate for the sake of living her people's history with them without fear that she might be effecting her own future illfare.

Note that the issue here is not merely the claim that one participates in a collective action because it is fun, or even profitable, as discussed in Edward Banfield's essay, "Rioting Mainly for Fun and Profit," on the urban ghetto riots.[16] Presumably there were, for instance, peace marchers who marched in order to hear Joan Baez sing for free. But there were also people who camped in the mud of Washington's Mall, marched in sleet and wind while Nixon watched football, took leave from their jobs to demonstrate for women's liberation, or even took extended leave in order to march and demonstrate in Teheran. Those were relatively costly undertakings. Participation in them may partly have been motivated by moral concern, partly by the desire to experience one's history.

At the peak of the civil rights movement in the early sixties, the chief civil rights organization, the National Association for the Advancement of Colored People (NAACP), had fewer than half a million members, and its national income was little more than $1 million[17]—less than

[16] Edward C. Banfield, *The Unheavenly City Revisited,* chap. 9.

[17] Specifically, at the end of 1964, only months before passage of the Civil Rights Act, NAACP membership was reported as 455,839, and its income for the year as $1,116,565.68. Kenneth B. Clark, "The Civil Rights Movement: Momentum and Organization," p. 262.

$3 per member, or about one nickel per black American. There were other organizations—especially the Southern Christian Leadership Conference (SCLC), the Urban League, the Congress on Racial Equality (CORE), and the Student Nonviolent Coordinating Committee (SNCC) —which added to these resources, although the total available funds must still have been very small. Yet, for that pittance, these organizations surely had substantial impact. Why?

In chapter 5, I noted that group politics is often worthwhile only because a relatively small effort is leveraged through government into a large effect. In spending a few million dollars a year on political action, environmentalists are probably responsible for a substantial part of the tens of billions of dollars a year currently spent on pollution control and for the great opportunity for production forgone in conserving many areas. Civil rights organizations spent minuscule amounts per year per black American during the sixties, and yet most observers would think the value of their effort was vastly greater than the expenditure.

But there are considerable differences in how these two movements have accomplished a large part of their goals. Environmental organizations educate, petition, lobby, and litigate—all of which mainly require paid skills. Civil rights organizations primarily litigate and demonstrate. Demonstration requires relatively little organizational expenditure of money, but very intensive individual participation, even expenditure of individuals' money for travel. Apart from increasing income, the principal advantage to environmental organizations of having large numbers of active members may be to show voting strength and the intensity of popular opinion, both of which could be shown by polls. The principal achievement of the civil rights movement was to *gain* voting strength, and the advantage of large numbers of activists was to make civil disobedience effective. Action per se was crucial to the civil rights movement at its height, when the movement was visual—its scenes of confrontation, marching, and demonstration are vivid memories even today. The phrase "I have a dream" calls forth, as though by Proust's involuntary memory, one of the most dramatic *scenes* of American political history. The chief visual content of the environmental movement is the natural beauty—redwoods, wilderness, lakes, and so forth— that environmentalists wish to conserve, and the man-made ugliness— smog, litter, and smoking chimneys—that they wish to clean up.

In California, especially around the San Francisco Bay, one can imagine that many environmentalists include among their motivations the desire to live the experiences of the environmental movement. However, participation in that movement need not so clearly contribute to the achievement of its goals as participation in the civil rights, antiwar, antishah, and perhaps even the women's movements contributed to the achievement of their goals. Although there is some participatory activity that serves environmental goals, especially in "service trips,"[18] the goals of the movement are achieved far more through paid skills—especially of lawyers—than through participatory politics. Therefore, the chief participatory incentive is probably the one that moves certain lawyers to work for the Sierra Club, for instance, at lower pay than they could get for working in traditional firms.

(The role of public interest lawyers calls up a point taken trivially for granted in traditional political analysis, but often neglected in voluntaristic rational explanations. One person's dollar is equal to any other person's, but one person's hour of organizational effort may be enormously more efficacious than another person's. In classical interest groups, such as those analyzed by Olson,[19] one member's resources might be much greater than other members'. But if benefits are symmetric, the "wealthy" member will not be inclined to contribute a disproportionate amount unless the ratio of group benefits to costs is very high. However, when benefits and costs are not commensurate—for example, when costs are time spent in skilled activity—asymmetry of resources may enhance the prospects for individual action and for group success.)

What is the scope of the desire to grow by taking part in one's history? It appears that it can motivate people to participate in broad social movements, great events, and probably in certain activities that are relatively more commonplace, but somehow central or important, in the life of a people—for example, in electoral politics. For small-scale activities, particularly when undertaken with people with whom one normally associates, the desire for growth through participation shades into solidarity and may be hard to separate, even in one's own mind, from reciprocity or contract by convention (as discussed in chapters 10 through 13). It does not appear to be a sufficient motivator for a large percentage of any relevant group except under extraordinary circumstances—for example, perhaps in the United States in World War II, in many European nations in World War I, and in a handful of revolutionary political movements. But it may be a—or even the—

---

[18] The "service trips are essentially organized work parties in the wilderness. Participants restore fragile wild areas, remove litter, and build and maintain trails. [The outings offer] the reward of doing something tangible for the environment" (*Sierra* [Jan./Feb. 1980] p. 67).

[19] Mancur Olson, Jr., *The Logic of Collective Action*.

principal motivator for numerous less-pervasive political movements, such as the civil rights, black power, antiwar, women's, and antishah movements.

That we are social creatures is not only a philosophical thesis; it is also a commonsense realization. We become more than we are by reading Shakespeare and the Greeks, by listening to Bach, Beethoven, and Bartok—and by participating in certain events and movements, for example, by going to war or refusing to go to war. Whether it is called moral or self-interested, the urge to participate is a fundamental motivation. For those collective actions built at least in part out of active personal participation, it might override all other motivations in importance for many individuals—perhaps for enough to make a collective action succeed against the narrower self-interest of the active individuals.

IGNORANCE AND MISUNDERSTANDING

Studies of voting and decision making in organizations have long since accustomed us to the realization that people regularly make choices in a state of essential ignorance. It is useful to break this problem into two parts: simple ignorance, or lack of information, and misunderstanding. The former is perhaps more commonly cited, especially under the rubric of the costs of information, in both voting and other decision contexts. But the latter, which is a problem of poor theory of the relevant causal relations, may often be more important, and it is discussed at greater length below. The problems of ignorance and misunderstanding often run together. If I have a clear grasp of the causal relations over some realm, I may be more likely to know the facts just because I am better able to put them into usable order. Or I might be said merely to be ignorant of causal relations that are widely known or could be easily accessible, just as Freud knew that tobacco was associated with cancer in 1923, while many Americans did not begin even to suspect it until the fifties.[20] Consider examples of each of these problems.

According to an extensive poll, in 1969 the average American would have been willing to incur more than a $40-per-year "increase in [his or her] family's total expenses for the cleanup of the natural environment."[21]

---

[20] The great man died victim of his favorite phallic symbol, the cigar. For an account of Freud's knowledge about tobacco and cancer in 1923, see Max Schur, *Freud: Living and Dying*, pp. 348, 350.

[21] Robert Dorfman, "Incidence of the Benefits and Costs of Environmental Programs," pp. 334–336.

The costs of environmental protection were then about five times and are now about twenty times this figure,[22] and it is commonly assumed that the costs are largely distributed across families as consumers and tax-payers even though they may often be borne in the first instance by firms. Yet polls commonly report that large percentages of Americans think more should be spent. Although there may be problems of ecological fallacy in deducing anything from such data, it is conceivable that people do not know what they are talking about and do not know what they want. Presumably, at some point they would begin to know better—say, when the cleanup cost $4,000 per family per year. In the meantime, people may be willing to vote for environmental measures whose costs, if known to those same voters, would amaze them. Or given better facts (and understanding) they might conclude that they were actually willing to spend much more than $40 per year in the implementation of such measures. (Presumably most people could easily be brought to realize that $40 was a laughable figure.)

Turn now to misunderstanding. Consider an obvious example. Many people no doubt support minimum wage laws out of self-interest, and many no doubt out of altruism. If the altruists and many of the frequently unemployed, lower-paid workers believed the large percentage of economists who insist that far more workers are severely hurt than are helped by minimum wage laws, the laws might not fare as well as they do in Congress. Clearly, either certain economists or certain supporters of the minimum wage laws misunderstand relevant relations. The complexity involved in understanding the causal effects of minimum wage laws is greater than that involved in understanding the logic of collective action, but academics should not slight the latter. After all, despite the elegant simplicity of its central argument, *The Logic of Collective Action* of Olson came as a revelation to many students of group activity.

Most people may intuitively comprehend the unarticulated logic of collective action, even though they might be struck by clear articulation of it. But there may be a part of the population that, when the logic is made explicit in a particular instance, does not consciously comprehend it. For example, once when I discussed the subject in an undergraduate class, a clear majority of the students thought I was crazy. Speaking of

[22] According to the Council on Environmental Quality, in 1977 dollars, the actual outlays in 1977 were $40 billion, and the estimated outlays for 1977–86 were to average $65 billion per year. (Council on Environmental Quality, *Environmental Quality 1978*, p. 446.) The 1970 expenditures, in 1971 dollars, were only $10 billion, or five times what the average family then was supposedly willing to pay. (CEQ, *Environmental Quality 1972*, pp. 276–277.)

labor union organizing, they insisted, against logic, that if you don't join, the union will fail. What I thought was merely a Kantian ethic they seemed to think was a causal relation. After half an hour they were not persuaded of my logic, but in a sense I began to be persuaded of theirs. Perhaps these people nevertheless understood the logic at an unarticulated level and therefore can be trusted not to contribute heavily to large public interest organizations, except in those unlucky moments when they are directly asked to contribute "in their own interest" to good causes. Under such pressure, the illogic of their conscious reasoning might then lead them, as in class they forcefully argued, to contribute. Such people taken together may experience enough unlucky moments to contribute a considerable part of the woefully slight political budgets of various public interests.

(It may also be that having to make a choice in the presence of others tends to lead people to act morally, especially when the choice is carefully defined as a conflict between personal and group interests. The relatively cooperative results found in a recent set of collective action experiments may be explainable in either of these ways—that is, as a result of muddled understanding at the conscious level or of pressure for morality in public. Gerald Marwell and Ruth E. Ames find that high school students in Madison, Wisconsin, are not entirely narrowly self-interested.[23] Their student subjects were given about 225 tokens each, which they could either redeem at 1 cent each, or "invest" in a collective good. The collective good in one experiment returned *to the group* about 2.2 cents for each token. Since subjects were told their group had eighty members, an individual's return on his or her token invested in the collective good was 0.0275 cent, so that investing in it was necessarily not self-interested.[24] Yet in various experiments, about half the tokens were invested in the collective good. After finding roughly similar results in experiments under four significantly variant conditions, Marwell and Ames conclude that "the power of the 'free-rider' hypothesis accurately to predict behavior remains severely limited."[25] Their conclusion is clearly valid for their experiments. It is also clearly invalid for the vast majority (99 percent) of the members of many large-scale interest groups. The responses of Marwell's and Ames's students may have been heavily influenced by the experimental setting (they had to make their investment decisions orally during a second telephone conversation with the experimenters), as my students' responses may have been by the

[23] Gerald Marwell and Ruth E. Ames, "Experiments on the Provision of Public Goods. II. Provision Points, Stakes, Experience, and the Free-Rider Problem."
[24] Ibid., pp. 930–931.
[25] Ibid., p. 937.

classroom setting. And they seem to have been far more contractarian in that setting than people normally are in spontaneous collective action settings.[26])

One need only read a bit of the philosophical "What if everybody did that?" debate to see how confused thoughtful people can be. As children, many of us must have been rebuked, after throwing a scrap of candy wrapper out a car window or on a sidewalk, with some such absurd claim as, "If you do that, everybody will, and the world will be a mess." Well, the world is a mess, but as an adult, I know that my dereliction was not sufficient to bring about the state of affairs, and only adults with delusions of grandeur laced with guilt could think otherwise of their own actions. But the adult logic and the childhood indoctrination may hold sway over different parts of our compartmentalized minds, and we may act sometimes by one, sometimes by the other understanding (we may also be moral on occasion, but that is not at issue here).

Perhaps the strongest claim for the importance of misunderstanding in explaining collective action has been made by Terry Moe. He argues that his "revised model [of interest groups] implies that anyone can have an incentive to contribute toward collective goods, depending upon his subjective estimates of the relevant quantities."[27] As an example, he notes that voters commonly overestimate the impact of their votes, apparently enough to make them think their efforts "will make a difference in bringing about net personal gains."[28] One can grant that anyone who suffered such a drastic misunderstanding should vote out of self-interest, but one must wonder whether such misunderstanding explains *many* votes. How many of those children who have heard their parents say democracy would collapse if they did not vote have also heard them say their votes were not worth a dime? More generally one may ask, Although misunderstanding may stimulate an occasional contribution, can it be a major source of large-scale group success?

Consider some remarkable data that seem to reveal impressive misunderstanding on the part of members of several traditional interest groups. Moe surveyed members of five Minnesota-based organizations including printers, retail merchants, hardware merchants, and two organizations of farmers. Their memberships range from 89 (printers) to 35,000 (Farm Bureau). "As a substitute for precisely measuring a member's perceived marginal impact on political success," Moe asked this question: "What effect do *your own* dues and contributions (and

[26] See also Marwell and Ames, "Experiments on the Provision of Public Goods. I. Resources, Interest, Group Size, and the Free-Rider Problem."

[27] Terry M. Moe, *The Organization of Interests,* p. 32.

[28] Ibid., pp. 32, 31. See also pp. 39–40, 79.

TABLE 7-1. MEMBERS' UNDERSTANDING OF EFFECT
OF INDIVIDUAL CONTRIBUTIONS ON THEIR OWN
GROUP'S POLITICAL SUCCESS OR FAILURE

Effect	Printers	Retail merchants	Hardware merchants	Farm Bureau members	Farmers Union members
Big effect	3%	4%	9%	6%	12%
Some effect	62	59	59	56	59
No effect	35	37	32	39	30
Total	100	100	100	101	101
(N)	63	336	375	559	537
Membership	89	600	900	35,000	23,000
Annual dues	n.a.	$50–$20,000	$25–$75	$40	$40

Source: Based on Terry M. Moe, *The Organization of Interests*: Effects from table 2, p. 207; Membership from p. 202; Annual dues from pp. 254–255.

only your own) have on the association's *success or failure* in achieving its lobbying goals?"[29] The three possible answers were, in short, a big effect, a noticeable effect, and no effect. The results, shown in table 7-1, are reported as percentages of each group giving each answer. The sample size (N), total membership, and dues are also given.

Subject these data to the powerful and renowned "interocular test of significance": Do they hit you between the eyes? Surely they do, although it may take a moment for the pain to register. The Farm Bureau is 400 times as large as the printers' organization, but there is negligible difference between their members' claimed perceptions of the effect of their individual contributions on their group's political success or failure. If one takes these data literally, one must conclude that members' subjective perceptions are unrelated to the objective facts. Moe concludes that "the uniformity across groups is intriguing because it suggests that perceptions of efficacy may be widespread among group members generally, throughout the group system, and that the average member does not view his contributions as a drop in the bucket."[30]

One might sooner conclude that Moe's thermometer is broken.[31] Perhaps his question is a proxy for asking about the effect his respond-

[29] Ibid., pp. 203–204. Note that the calculation here is still one step removed from the logic of collective action, under which one should consider the discounted effect of one's contribution not on the general provision of the group's good, but only the value to oneself of that provision.

[30] Ibid., p. 207.

[31] The broken thermometer image is borrowed from Brian Barry, "Is It Better To Be Powerful or Lucky?" p. 194.

ents think their organizations have, about their loyalty to them, about their team-spirited boosterism, about their childhood Kantianism, and so forth. Or one might suppose that cognitive dissonance or some other psychological theory gives a more credible explanation of these responses than does the assumption of misunderstanding. Perhaps, however, roughly a third of Minnesota's hundred thousand farmers are so weak in logic that they think their $40 each in annual dues out of a total of about $2 million has at least a "noticeable effect" on the success of lobbying for farmers' interests. One might sensibly express disbelief, with Edgeworth, on grounds of "a priori unverified probability," which is to say, "general experience and common sense."[32]

POLITICAL EFFECTS

What can we say of the moral sources of environmental and other large-group political activities? For the Sierra Club, presumably there would be no large organizational infrastructure for collecting and allocating funds for political action without nonmoral bases for the membership of many (perhaps the 60 percent of members, who, according to a survey in 1971, did not join only to support the club's conservation and environmental goals[33]). Hence, without the individual pleasures that membership offers, there would be no Sierra Club political efforts. But without morally motivated contributions, there would also be no—or very little—Sierra Club political program. It appears that a similar conclusion applies to the National Audubon Society, the Izaak Walton League, and perhaps a few other of the older environmental organizations. But the great majority of the memberships of all environmental organizations, especially of the newer groups, dates from the late sixties, and presumably is substantially motivated by political and moral commitments. (Many of the newer organizations got their starts with help from foundations, as did the Sierra Club litigation program. According to Frederic Sutherland, executive director of the Sierra Club Legal Defense Fund, "It's fair to say that there probably would be no Legal Defense Fund without the generosity of the Ford Foundation."[34])

Can one generalize from environmental to other interests? Perhaps not as readily as a social scientist might hope. The principal generaliza-

[32] Cited in George J. Stigler, *Essays in the History of Economics,* p. 376.

[33] Coombs, "The Club Looks at Itself."

[34] *Sierra* (Jan./Feb. 1980) p. 19. Foundations have now cut back their support (Ford in particular "no longer gives general support grants to organizations such as the Legal Defense Fund" [Ibid.]), and we may begin to see a more severe test of the strength of moral commitment to environmental protection and to public interest law more generally.

tion is the a priori logic of collective action: if correct calculation of self-interest was all that motivated action, there would be no environmental groups, nor any consumer, women's liberation, prolife, or other such public groups. However, generalizing about such residual extrarational categories of behavior as those that underlie environmental group politics, for example, is likely to be less coherent, less forceful. One can turn back to economic rationality arguments to say much about circumstances in which moral or miscalculated self-interest motivation may become more or less manifest in group political action. But it will be much harder to generalize about the distribution of moral sentiments on various issues, especially on potential issues. There need be no logical typology of issues that are susceptible to group action based on individual moral commitments, which may lead to group politics over both collective and private goods, both collective and private bads. The collective and private categories are subjective, and the morally committed can make my private concern their public issue. Nevertheless, one may expect to find some regularities in residual extrarational behavior.

First, it does not follow from the discussion above that one's extrarational response to a group good will be unrelated to one's valuation of the good. For example, as discussed in chapter 6, a contractarian should be more compelled to play fair when individual benefits from group action are high than when they are low. Of course, for a contractarian, the issue will not be whether one's benefit from one's own contribution will be more than the contribution costs, as in the logic of collective action, but whether one's group of like-minded activists benefits more from group actions than those actions cost. That is to say, one will be a calculating Kantian: one will do as one would have others do, so long as there are enough others who do likewise to produce net benefits to oneself, but one will not adamantly contribute to support a hopelessly lost cause or only to benefit others less responsible than oneself. For contractarians, therefore, what is of interest is not the size of the whole group that desires a group good, but rather the size of the k-subgroup that would be efficacious for itself on its own.

Note again a difference (discussed in chapter 5 under "Nonfungibility") between collective goods such as pollution control and goods such as wage increases. The distribution of benefits from a good like wage increases will probably be fairly uniform (or symmetric) among members of the relevant group. An academic analyst has little difficulty computing the ratio of benefits to contributions for individual members of the group. For goods like pollution control, however, the academic analyst is on uncharted terrain. A revealed-preference experiment might credibly suggest wide variations in individual valuations of increments of pollution reduction.[35] That is to say, there may be great asymmetry in valuations among a group of environmentalists, with some members willing to pay a very high tax to achieve the group's objectives and others willing to pay only a very limited tax. Consider two groups having identical average valuations of individual benefits from their group goods and similar in every other respect except that one group has no variation in individual valuations (as might approximate the case for many unions), while the other has great variation. The k-subgroups in the second group would include many far smaller subgroups than in the first group. Therefore, acting extrarationally, a far smaller number of contractarians in the second group could achieve successful group action than could that same number in the first group. It is not absurd to think that the politically motivated contributions of some of the current 180,000 members of the Sierra Club benefit *the contributors as a group*, in their estimation, more than the contributions cost. But if valuations of environmental programs were much more uniformly spread near the average level among the national population, the extent of such contributions should be markedly less than it is now. But given asymmetry of valuations, a modest number of contractarians may be carrying a large part of the society as free riders on some issues, including environmental issues.

A second regularity in extrarational behavior is that, even though individuals may contribute to collective actions for moral reasons, their contributions should still be subject to certain rational constraints. In particular, there should be predictable regularities in the ways they trade off such contributions against opportunities to acquire private goods and other collective goods. Most obviously, the more of everything else one has, the more one may be willing to trade against one's moral commitment to a marginal impact on the provision of a desired collective good.[36] Mackie Messer (or Mack the Knife) put it more forcefully: "Erst kommt das Fressen, dann kommt die Moral [First comes food and then morality]."[37] There are more pedestrian data that support Mackie Messer's view. For example, tax return data (not to be wholly trusted perhaps) reveal a strong correlation between income level and amount spent on charity—so strong as to suggest that people donate a larger percentage

[35] As suggested by poll data summarized by Dorfman, "Incidence of the Benefits and Costs."

[36] Recall Margolis's argument, discussed at the end of chapter 6, for a split psyche, half self-interested, half moral. (Howard Margolis, "A New Model of Rational Choice.")

[37] Mackie Messer's lament is in the finale of the second act of *Die Dreigroschenoper* [The threepenny opera], in Bertolt Brecht, *Stücke* [Plays] vol. 3, p. 99.

of their income as it rises.[38] Hence, other things being equal, one should expect that the upper middle class will contribute more readily than will the poor toward the provision of such group goods as environmental protection. To turn this rule around, those collective goods that the well-off want but that can only be collectively provided by extrarational actions are more likely to be provided than those collective goods that the poor want. The membership of the Sierra Club and other environmental groups is primarily upper middle class. Concomitantly, in an era of affluence, extrarational contributions to collective actions may be relatively easily generated.

Many other rational constraints will also apply. The institutionalization of organizations such as the Sierra Club makes collective political action much easier for environmentalists than it might otherwise be—not only are extrarational contributions more likely given such organizations, but the contributions are also likely to be more efficiently spent. Someone who would act out of morality or misunderstanding is more likely to contribute money, other things being equal, if the effort involved in making the contribution is made easy. The moral or misunderstanding environmentalist need not survey all possible ways to contribute, but need only satisfice[39] by sending in the membership amount requested in a mailing from the first environmental organization whose name he or she recognizes. In subsequent years members can satisfice even more easily—they need merely renew their memberships. Similarly, if one's motive is contractarian, to play fair, one can satisfice on one's definition of fairness by letting an organization set the level of contribution (its membership dues) that is fair, and one can take for granted that anyone of like mind facing this decision would do approximately the same.

A third regularity in extrarational behavior is that, despite the formal equivalence of their payoff structures, as mentioned in chapter 4 under "Collective Bads," extrarational cooperation may be more likely to oppose a loss or collective bad (such as pollution) than to support a gain. The goal in opposing a bad is likely to be more clearly focused than the goal in supporting a gain, since the bad may already exist or be specifically proposed (for instance, a new Westside Highway for New

[38] Gary S. Becker, *The Economic Approach to Human Behavior,* p. 274. Of course, the cost of giving a tax deductible dollar may fall as one's income rises, because marginal tax rates rise with income.

[39] The verb "satisfice" has been resurrected from obsolescence and given a new meaning by Herbert Simon. To satisfice means to seek a *satisfactory* solution to a problem. Satisficing is opposed to optimizing, which is seeking the *best* solution to the problem. For further discussion, see James G. March and Herbert Simon, *Organizations,* pp. 140–141, 169; and March, "Bounded Rationality, Ambiguity, and the Engineering of Choice."

York City, or an oil refinery for Durham, New Hampshire). Such clarity of focus may be especially important in very large groups, some of whose members are contractarians or are otherwise morally motivated to act, because there can be widespread agreement over what not to do even when there is little agreement over what to do. In small groups, contractarians may easily achieve constructive action, but agreement will become more difficult as the group grows larger (see further, chapter 6). Public response to the energy crisis is more diffuse than the response to building a new nuclear reactor in New Hampshire or the San Francisco Bay Area.

If the collective bad from which a group suffers comes from an external source, group members may suffer a sense of inequity to exacerbate the sense of loss and to motivate them to action. Perceived inequity commonly stimulates anger and action.[40] If the loss is internally generated by the group, people who would not cooperate in a collective action context might nevertheless be averse to harming others. Again, for example, many people have voluntarily stopped using fluorocarbon aerosols, although the large-number logic should apply to such a case with a vengeance. Those who have acted voluntarily for collective interests may then think it inequitable that others have not done so, and they may seek political change to coerce those others, just as they would if their loss were caused by an agent external to the group.

A fourth regularity in extrarational behavior is that when the action a group undertakes is political, the benefits may enormously outweigh the costs, even when the benefits are discounted by the probability of failure. If environmentalists had to bribe industrialists not to pollute, as suggested in Coase's analysis,[41] moral incentives would produce minuscule bribes and less effect. But they merely have to get Congress and an administrative agency to coerce industrialists into bearing the billions of dollars for cleaning up. All the money spent on electoral politics over the past decade is a tiny part of what will be spent on pollution control over the next decade. The small part of the population that contributes $2 million a year to Sierra Club political activity may well imagine that they seldom spend money so well. If the political system did not have a multiplier effect on group resources, many groups would be so inefficacious that only pristine Kantians and other peculiarly motivated individuals would still contribute. But political institutions have power that does not merely reflect the interests and power of all involved groups;

[40] George C. Homans, *Social Behavior: Its Elementary Forms*, p. 75; Morton Deutsch, *The Resolution of Conflict*, pp. 396–398.

[41] R. H. Coase, "The Problem of Social Cost." For further discussion, see chap. 4 under "Dimensions of Collective Action Problems."

and action by even a relatively weak group may be contagious or may otherwise broaden the scope of conflict to the eventual advantage of that group.[42]

In addition to rational constraints, there may be a moral constraint on moral and participatory motivations in purposeful collective actions. In coming to act from moral and participatory motivations, people may commonly put their actions under a contractarian constraint (as with the contractarian motivation to play fair, discussed in chapter 6). That is, one will put effort behind a moral commitment only if enough others do also, making the collective action possibly efficacious. Almost by definition, one would act from a desire to participate in one's history only if enough others were participating to make history (although obviously some must be early participants). This constraint need not apply to moral action in general, but only to purposeful collective action. Playing fair would usually not be involved, for example, in a situation such as helping someone in need. Its role is to govern actions when we are collectively helping ourselves.[43]

The extrarational considerations discussed here—especially moral motivation, but perhaps also ignorance and misunderstanding—may spur some people to contribute to public interest groups. On the evidence, they do not spur many people to contribute very much. But there is an interesting obverse of the fact that moral motives alone do not usually seem to be compelling enough to bring in large percentages of those interested in an organization's goals. Anyone who belongs to an organization only or primarily out of commitment to that group's goal of providing some collective good will quickly exit or try to change the organization if it seems not to serve its collective goal. Large groups, such as unions in union-shop states and those professional organizations that control certification, may undertake political effort as a by-product of their selective incentives, but in those groups there need be only a weak connection between members' collective interests or desires and organizational policy positions. If contributions to an organization are

---

[42] Schattschneider, *Semi-Sovereign People,* chap. 1; Deutsch, *Resolution of Conflict,* pp. 396–398.

[43] Hume notes that certain moral motivations ("the social virtues of humanity and benevolence") "have in view a single individual object, and pursue the safety or happiness alone of the person loved and esteemed. . . . And as the good, resulting from their benign influence, is in itself complete and entire, it also excites the moral sentiment of approbation, without any more enlarged views of the concurrence or imitation of the other members of society." Fair play is rather more like justice and fidelity, which are valued for "the whole scheme or system concurred in by the whole, or the greater part of the society." (David Hume, *An Enquiry Concerning the Principles of Morals,* app. 3, pp. 303–304.)

motivated by moral or political commitment to its goals, the organization's policy positions are far more likely to be consistent with positions of contributors.

The Sierra Club exemplifies both these cases. Some club members are in it for the activities and disagree with the politics; some are in it, in the sense that they contribute, exclusively to support the politics. If the club drastically changed its political focus or cut back its political activities, presumably the latter group would not stay with it long. Hence, more generally, organizations whose goals are supported by moral commitments, rather than merely by self-interest, are likely to be more assiduous in working toward their goals.

Just as selective incentives might induce one to contribute to a goal one does not support, so too the desire to participate in experiences of one's generation might lead one to participate in an action or movement whose purposes one does not support. The woman who would rather not be governed by ayatollahs might nevertheless have joined in marches and other actions whose intendment seemed to have been to install Khomeini in power. Civil rights and antiwar activities—such as an Indian summer march to Boston Common—might have attracted many whose commitment to these causes was not great. There might generally be a strong correlation between one's own desires for collective purposes and one's desire to participate for the sake of participation—a better correlation, indeed, than that between the goals of many organizations and their members' desires for collective purposes when the organizations' resources for "collective action" are a by-product of selective incentives for membership. But the latter correlation is one of the least-studied aspects of organized collective action, and the former correlation seems hardly to have been studied at all.

One might speculate that as a society becomes increasingly affluent, its politics may become less predictable, because individual desires vary more widely, sometimes wildly. Asymmetries of demand for various goods then may lead to numerous efficacious collective actions for diverse "public" purposes, and the scope of government may become increasingly broadened. As argued above, those collective goods that the well-off want are more likely to be provided, other things being equal, than those the poor want. The poor are more likely to want monetary collective goods—whose symmetry means that they suffer most severely from the logic of collective action. The skewness of this relationship is likely to increase as the class of collective goods being sought from government becomes increasingly dominated by nonfungible collective goods that are in part morally desired. To put old wisdom into new words, the well-off get better off. . . .

Less speculatively, a peculiar implication of the logic of collective action is that so little large-scale collective action *can be* narrowly rational that, indeed, very little *is* narrowly rational; thus, even perfunctory moral concern at the mass level may stimulate more collective action than self-interest does. Anyone trying to explain political activity may then be led to think that morality is relatively important as compared with self-interest. But as in the pluralist concern with decisions as opposed to nondecisions by political officials, this conclusion about the role of moral choice in the politics of the mass may be based on undue consideration of activity, when the more pervasive phenomenon may be explainable inactivity. It may be that only the wealthy can afford to act from narrow self-interest that coincidentally benefits the larger public (see further, chapter 8 under "Applications to Large Groups"). The rest of us all too often must act only morally, foolishly, or not at all.

8

DYNAMIC ANALYSIS
OF COLLECTIVE ACTION

Most of the preceding discussion has involved the static analysis of collective action, that is, analysis of one-time-only action. As Barry and Taylor have argued specifically for the Prisoner's Dilemma as a model of social life,[1] and as sociologists and anthropologists would argue more generally for social choice, such static analysis is fundamentally wrong-headed for many contexts of greatest interest to us. Most interesting group choices are probably made by groups that are ongoing; often those choices are even provoked by ongoing or repeated choice problems. One would wish to analyze the incentive structure in iterated, not one-shot, Prisoner's Dilemma to explain the choices of ongoing groups. This is done, sometimes only implicitly, in Olson's by-product theory and in the political entrepreneurship arguments of Wagner and of Frohlich, Oppenheimer, and Young, which were briefly discussed in chapter 2. It is done more explicitly and resolutely in Taylor's analysis of cooperation in anarchy.[2]

In chapters 9 through 14, I address the problem of collective action in ongoing groups facing variously iterated Prisoner's Dilemmas. Before turning to that, however, it is instructive to consider certain other dynamic analyses of collective action. Two recent analyses are especially interesting, although I will argue they are finally of quite limited applica-

[1] Brian Barry, *Political Argument,* pp. 253–255; Michael Taylor, *Anarchy and Cooperation,* p. 28.
[2] Ibid.

125

tion. The first of these is a generalization of the Cournot duopoly model[3] to voluntaristic provision of a collective good by *n* persons. The second is a more nearly contractarian analysis of "matching behavior" by members of a group in providing themselves a good. Neither of these assumes an iterated choice problem; rather, they model the one-shot resolution of a collective action problem. However, both require a dynamic interaction to achieve their resolutions. After treating these, I discuss how they might enhance our understanding of some actual groups' voluntaristic provision of their goods, while suggesting the limits of the Cournot and matching behavior arguments.

COURNOT ANALYSIS OF COLLECTIVE ACTION

John Chamberlin and Martin McGuire conclude from separate Cournot analyses that group size should not so clearly be a correlate of the likelihood of group failure.[4] In the usual Cournot analysis of duopoly, it is supposed that two firms are in competition in a given market. This is a small-group collective action problem, because if the two firms concert their pricing decisions they can expect jointly to obtain monopoly profits, which would substantially exceed competitive profits. Despite their joint interest, however, each firm has a private interest in undercutting the other in order to obtain a larger share of total sales and profits. If they cannot successfully collude to maintain a joint pricing strategy (perhaps because collusion is illegal), they may nevertheless be able to achieve a tacit equilibrium price from which it would not benefit either firm to change. Under the usual static assumptions of market economics, there will be an equilibrium. The Cournot model describes how firms acting under Cournot behavioral assumptions reach the equilibrium price if they are not already there. The Cournot assumptions are essentially the pre-game-theory assumptions that players in a market are relatively stupid: they are shortsighted; they assume that all other players are unstrategic while they are strategic; and they react to their environment, which includes the actions of others, while assuming that no other will take their actions into account.

---

[3] The Cournot model is named for the nineteenth-century French mathematician and philosopher Antoine-Augustin Cournot. A brief account of the Cournot duopoly model is given in Kalman Cohen and Richard Cyert, *Theory of the Firm: Resource Allocation in a Market Economy,* chap. 12.

[4] John Chamberlin, "Provision of Collective Goods as a Function of Group Size"; Martin C. McGuire, "Group Size, Group Homogeneity, and the Aggregate Provision of a Pure Public Good Under Cournot Behavior."

Suppose that a firm in a duopoly sees that it can increase its profit by changing its level of production, and so decreases or increases that level as necessary. As a result, price is likely to decrease or increase. Hence, the profits of the second firm will be affected, and it will react by changing its level of production, thereby again affecting the price of the common product. Now the profits of the first firm will be affected in turn, and it will react. For a duopoly under relevant conditions, this series of reactions will lead eventually to the equilibrium price.[5]

Chamberlin and McGuire extend this analysis by generalizing it from 2 to *n* participants and by applying it to any producers of any collective good. They then derive the level of production as a function of *n* to show that, under many logical conditions, the level rises as *n* increases.[6] This conclusion runs contrary to Olson's claim that for a very large group, "it is certain that a collective good will *not* be provided unless there is coercion or some outside inducements."[7] Chamberlin's and McGuire's contradiction of Olson on this point is not categorical, since it applies only under certain conditions. Although they discuss most of these conditions at some length, there is one whose importance may be clarified by the analysis of the cases presented in table 3-1 in chapter 3, and there is another of great importance that they do not discuss. The first of these conditions is that the collective good at issue is a pure public good, or very nearly so; the second is that, even if no one else was contributing to the provision of a group's collective good, some member or members would have a positive incentive to make some contribution independently. Each of these points merits further discussion.

For the first of these conditions, consider Chamberlin's discussion.[8] He notes that collective goods may be divided into "inclusive" and "exclusive," that is, pure and totally crowded, public goods. (Crowded goods, like highways, become less attractive as more people use them.) Olson's size argument applies to the latter, but not to the former. Goods with intermediate levels of crowding may approximate pure public goods and defy Olson's claim, or they may suffer sufficiently from crowding to fit his conclusion. Inclusive goods are represented by the comparison of rows 1 and 3 in table 3-1; exclusive goods, by the comparisons of rows 1 and 2 and rows 1 and 4. Hence, the Chamberlin and McGuire argument against Olson's general claim does not apply to collective actions whose

[5] This behavior fits the Cournot assumption because each firm in turn reacts to the current situation by changing to a level of production that would be optimal only if the other firm did not subsequently react, as it will do.

[6] McGuire, "Group Size," p. 112.

[7] Mancur Olson, Jr., *The Logic of Collective Action,* p. 44.

[8] Chamberlin, "Provision of Collective Goods," pp. 711–713.

costs rise substantially as n rises (row 4), or whose sums of individual enjoyments do not rise nearly linearly with n (row 2). Nevertheless, their conclusions do apply to some logically conceivable collective actions (which are similar in some respects to those represented in row 3), so that they are right to conclude that the logical analysis of collective action does not categorically square with Olson's claims.

One must conclude, in part, that whether larger groups are less likely to succeed than smaller ones is not entirely a logical matter, but rather that it is also in part an empirical question of what conditions correlate with size, and especially a question of whether the class of collective goods of interest includes many pure public goods. A clue to a possible answer is that most writers on public goods seem to agree that there are few credible cases of public goods that are not subject to crowding over any substantial range of group size n. The usual examples cited are nuclear deterrence and lighthouses, although the nighttime movies telecast by Hughes fit the analysis quite well over extremely large ranges of n (see chapter 3 at note 9). These examples, however, suggest the relevance of the second condition, which is not discussed by Chamberlin and McGuire, implicit in the Cournot analysis. It merits extended discussion.

"Cournot behavior" means that "each individual acting in isolation decides on a purchase of the public good on the assumption that everyone's purchase will not be influenced by his decision."[9] For the Cournot series of reactions to begin, some individual must decide to purchase *some* of the collective good. Given their cost functions, many public goods do not fit this assumption. For example, if cleaner air is a public good for residents in some metropolitan area, the Cournot analysis, if its other conditions are met, implies that adding more residents might lead to more expenditure on the public good—but *only if* we can assume that there was already some voluntary individualistic expenditure. One might reasonably assume no such thing and might expect voluntary expenditures to continue at their original level of nothing after new residents arrive.

McGuire assumes that the quantity of the collective good that an individual would buy even if no one else had bought any is a positive quantity, x_0.[10] One might suppose that Olson's argument is about whether size affects x_0. If $x_0 = 0$ for every member of the group, there will be no provision, even under the Cournot analysis. Hence, perhaps Olson is asserting that the larger the group, the greater the probability that $x_0 = 0$ for all members of the group. Indeed, he asserts this in the

[9] McGuire, "Group Size," p. 107.
[10] Chamberlin assumes the same, calling it x_i^0 for individual i.

second of his three arguments for why larger groups fail.[11] But, as argued earlier, this is basically an empirical issue, and a hard one at that. The more compelling point is that if group size is measured in terms of k rather than n, then by definition it follows that: if k is greater than 1 at all levels of supply (including very low levels), then $x_0 = 0$ for every member of the group. For the Cournot analysis to carry, *the group must be privileged at some level of supply.*

(The interpretation of Olson's logic in terms of k rather than absolute size might seem to be rejected by Chamberlin when he discusses Olson's vague equation of group size with per capita benefit. He says, "such an interpretation seems to be what Olson had in mind, for the 'fraction of the group gain' obtained by each individual plays a central role in his analysis. Such an interpretation seems to me to be fundamentally mistaken."[12] He then argues that in the case of a perfectly joint good, per capita share of benefits falls as group size increases, although, of course, absolute per capita benefits do not change. However, k is defined in terms of both costs and benefits, and it is not a function of actual group size—unless size affects costs or benefits—and k would be constant for a perfectly joint good.)

It is instructive to digress long enough to see why the Cournot analysis is compelling at all, even for a uniformly *privileged* group. The Cournot model of duopoly is concerned, as are the duopolists, only with money, with profits. The principal extension of that model to the provision of collective goods involves an extension from a money-only world to a two-good world in which the two goods trade off in each individual's utility function. *If* we were simplistically concerned merely with a good that each member of a group values more than its cost, the only issue at stake would be the (perhaps tacit) bargaining problem over who paid how much of the cost. In a more realistic case in which the collective good could be provided at various levels and consequently at a range of costs, the group might be privileged only up to a certain level of provision. This is the fundamental presumption of indifference curve utility theory: each succeeding increment of a good is valued less. The Chamberlin and McGuire analyses are based on this presumption.

Stated in terms of two desired goods, say x and y, in a two-good world, this fundamental presumption is that in order to compensate for losses of x, one will require increasingly larger additions of y for each successive increment of x that is lost. Hence, at the extreme limit in

---

[11] Olson, *The Logic,* p. 48. See above, chap. 3 under "Olson's Typologies of Groups."

[12] John Chamberlin, "A Collective Goods Model of Pluralist Political Systems," p. 104.

which one has a great lot of y and none of x, one should trade a lot of y for very little x. The rate at which one would trade y for x may also vary with one's income level, so that there will be a nested series of indifference curves—one for each income level. If x is beluga caviar and y is black bread, one will consume proportionately far more caviar on a luxurious income than on a subsistence income. If the abstract logic of the indifference curve theory is pushed to extreme limits for this example, the indifference curves for levels of consumption of x and y would be asymptotic to the axes representing levels of consumption of x and y. At some point one would be presumed to be willing, indeed glad, to trade many loaves of bread for a pinch of a beluga egg. Because economists are not commonly willing to admit to absurdity, they generally let their indifference curves tail off well before the region of bits of beluga egg and granules of bread is reached. They recognize as well as the rest of us that one whose income was measured in kopecks might sensibly spend all on black bread and none on caviar.

Given the usual form of indifference curves representing rates at which the collective good is traded for the private good in Chamberlin's and McGuire's analyses, it follows that a privileged group at a low level of supply for the collective good might voluntarily generate contributions to purchase further increments of the collective good *beyond* the level that only one member acting alone would have provided, that is to say, beyond the level at which the group ceased to be privileged in Olson's static terms. This is the essence of Chamberlin's and McGuire's conclusion. It does not apply to groups that are privileged at *no* level of supply of their collective goods. Among the groups to which it does not apply, then, is virtually every large-scale political group that seeks a costly good whose value to each member of the group is a small fraction of its cost.

(Chamberlin's "collective goods model of pluralist political systems" is, on this account, less than a full model, because it generally considers only perfectly joint goods. For these he analyzes "the behavior of two types of groups, unorganized [that is, groups that are characterized by Cournot behavior] and perfectly organized groups, those which provide an optimal amount of the collective good. All other groups fall somewhere between these two polar cases."[13] For both types he assumes that, for some level of actual provision, they are privileged groups. Again, this assumption makes good sense for numerous important groups, such as the major oil companies, automakers, chemical firms, and so forth. Even without organization, each of these groups can,

---

[13] Ibid., p. 98.

under Cournot behavioral assumptions, commonly act to provide high levels of, for instance, lobbying in the interest of the entire group. Numerous other important groups, including most larger public interest groups, are likely to be unorganized and, under Cournot assumptions, cannot be expected to provide any collective benefits. These groups are excluded from Chamberlin's model, although some of the details of the model can be applied to such groups. In a model which, like Chamberlin's, is based on the assumption of narrow self-interest, certain large groups, contrary to his conclusion, *are* certain to be losers.)

To summarize, the Cournot analysis makes sense for highly valued goods that can be supplied virtually at a continuum of levels, that are valued at decreasing marginal rates at higher levels of provision, and that are sought by groups privileged with respect to their goods at some level of provision. For example, oligopoly pricing (and hence oligopoly profits) should fit the Cournot analysis. For another example, under the Cournot assumptions, we would expect a substantial level of oil company lobbying for various benefits even if there were no organized efforts by the seven sisters to cooperate in such lobbying. But many of the goods that interest groups seek cannot well be fitted to the Cournot assumptions.

One cannot disagree with Chamberlin's and McGuire's claim that Olson's size thesis is not logically determined. Still, one can sensibly conclude that there are logical reasons for expecting the thesis to hold for groups and goods of political interest. In particular, goods commonly of interest to political groups are unlikely to be the pure public goods to which the Cournot analysis most clearly applies. When they are approximately pure public goods (that is, when they do not suffer significant cost increase or individual benefit decrease) over a relevant substantial range of group size, they are likely to have very high costs, so that few, if any, group members could rationally contribute even if others did not. In the latter case, as in any other case as well, there may be some group members whose valuation of the good is so high that they would contribute (in which case the group is privileged), but this is unlikely to be true of very many people, so that the Cournot analysis will apply only to the very small group composed of the wealthy members of the larger group.

MATCHING BEHAVIOR

Despite their limited relevance, a clear merit of the Chamberlin and McGuire analyses is that they introduce a dynamic element into the problem which is absent from Olson's essentially static analysis of benefits minus costs. As is discussed at length in chapter 9, although narrow self-interest recommends not cooperating in a one-shot, 2-person Prisoner's Dilemma, it may recommend cooperating in an iterated Prisoner's Dilemma. This is because I can make my choice of cooperation or defection in future plays of an iterated game contingent on your choice in the present play. If I can communicate this strategy, even by tacit means such as by playing tit for tat, then you may be convinced that mutual cooperation is possible and desirable. In a one-shot play, there is no way to employ a contingent strategy.

Often this distinction seems odd in real contexts, even though it is compelling in game experiments. For example, although it seems like a one-shot problem, Hume's meadow will take time to drain, and the two neighbors will either both participate or both not participate (unless they constitute a privileged group), so that the Prisoner's Dilemma interaction will be ongoing for a while, not strictly one-shot. There will be no serious likelihood of achieving the Prisoner's Dilemma outcomes in which one player is taken for a sucker. Such outcomes are possible in game experiments, but they are often not possible, or at least not likely, in real-world, 2-person Prisoner's Dilemmas. Although for real-world, *n*-person Prisoner's Dilemmas it is possible and indeed likely that some will not cooperate even while others do, it may still be possible to elicit contingent contributions and to achieve a high level of cooperation, whether in one-shot or ongoing collective actions.

In an analysis related to those of Chamberlin and McGuire, Joel Guttman similarly concludes that very large groups can achieve substantial, even Pareto-optimal degrees of cooperative behavior.[14] He imagines that members of a group enter a two-stage game. In the first stage, they propose their various matching rates for each other's contributions. In the second stage, each puts forward a "flat rate," which will then determine all others' matching contributions under the previously proposed matching rates. Total contributions will be the sum of all flat rates plus the consequent matching contributions.

To spell this out: suppose I propose to match all others' contributions at some rate, perhaps 5 percent, and all others likewise propose their matching rates. Knowing all the matching rates, I now decide on a flat rate, say, $10. All others contribute their flat rates, which sum, say, to $200. I now contribute my promised matching rate, 5 percent of $200, or $10, and all others contribute their matching rates. The final group contribution is the sum of all flat and matching rates. (If we were a group of twenty-one members each proposing the same flat and matching rates, we would have a final contribution of $420.)

[14] Joel M. Guttman, "Understanding Collective Action: Matching Behavior."

Guttman concludes that with n identical actors, the contributions will be Pareto-optimal, which is to say that the group will behave as though it were a single rational individual.[15] But with more than two nonidentical actors, Guttman's model is not entirely determinate, and suboptimal levels of contribution are possible. Note that this is the reverse of the conclusion argued above (and further below), that it is only in highly asymmetric large groups that the Cournot analysis suggests substantial levels of contribution.

Guttman's model is intended to explain voluntary provision of a collective good itself. His characterization of the model as a game inadvertently suggests its greatest weakness: that it is subject to gaming, or strategic behavior. No one is finally obligated to follow through with matching contributions consonant with the matching rates proposed in the first stage of the game. That is precisely why there is a problem of collective action—it is often in no one's interest voluntarily to contribute anything toward providing a particular collective good. In groups that are relatively small in the ordinary sense of the word, however, the matching analysis may seem pertinent if individuals can make their own contributions contingent on others' living up to their bargains, as often they can. As group size increases, however, the efficacy of contingent behavior or threats is likely to decline. Among the implications of the iterated Prisoner's Dilemma and Guttman analyses is that Olson's category of "intermediate groups" may be considerably larger than he seems to imply, even if we define size in terms of k rather than n, because in a dynamic situation contingent contributions are possible. This is true whether the dynamic aspect of the situation is due to something like matching behavior in a one-shot collective action like Hume's meadow project, or to an ongoing collective action as in an iterated Prisoner's Dilemma.

APPLICATIONS TO LARGE GROUPS

If, even on these dynamic analyses, collective action must rationally break down for very large groups, how are we to comprehend the many very large groups that seem to have followed in the wake of Olson's book? There is perhaps no collective good of significant national political interest that costs so little per unit of supply that a typical citizen of the United States could rationally contribute some amount, say, twenty dollars, to its provision if by "rationally" is understood "out of narrow self-interest." Nevertheless, the foregoing analysis can contribute to the

[15] *Ibid.*, p. 254.

understanding of even extraordinarily costly large-group collective actions. For example, consider again a collective good that evidently interests tens of millions of contemporary Americans: creating laws to eliminate much air and water pollution, which can probably be achieved only through large-scale political activity at the national, or perhaps at the California-state, level. The vast majority of us seem voluntarily to spend as little on that collective good as on beluga caviar: nothing at all. If the group of those interested in antipollution legislation were very symmetric (homogeneous) with all members' valuations near the modal actual valuation, we should expect no supply at all.

But as certain industries know all too well, there has been a substantial supply of antipollution legislation over the past decade or so. No doubt at least part of the reason is that not everyone is always narrowly self-interested. Another part presumably is that politicians are entrepreneurs who follow mass sentiment in order to enhance their own careers, as discussed in chapter 2. Another important part of the reason, however, is that the group of antipolluters is far from symmetric, so that its "tens of millions" size is deceptive. How deceptive? Consider the Sierra Club. In comparison with the group of all antipolluters, the Sierra Club is extremely small (178,000 members in 1978). Furthermore, the number of its members who actually contribute to the club's political activities is still smaller, since dues, fees for services, and sales receipts do not appear to cover significantly more than the cost of nonpolitical club activities.[16] Mitchell reports that 4,200 members of the club each donated $50 or more beyond dues in 1977.[17] Even this is a large number of people, and it seems unlikely that many of them could sensibly be seen as narrowly rational contributors on any analysis. At least many of them must be acting extrarationally. Keep in mind for a moment, however, the small

[16] For the four fiscal years 1975–78, the Sierra Club spent a total of about $7.5 million "studying and influencing public policy." "Contributions" to the club (i.e., revenues other than dues, fees for outings, earnings from publications, and a very small amount of miscellaneous revenues and investment income) totaled $6.9 million, the bulk of which were clearly designated by donors as political contributions. (*Sierra Club Bulletin*, April 1976, February 1977; *Sierra*, May 1978, March/April 1979.) As noted in chapter 7, a substantial fraction of members claim to join solely in support of the club's political goals, and the bulk of their annual dues essentially constitutes political contributions. (Don Coombs, "The Club Looks At Itself.") Hence it seems likely that none of the political activity of the club can be seen as a by-product of private good functions of the club—except in the important sense that, if the club had no private good functions, it might not be available for political functions.

[17] Robert Cameron Mitchell, "National Environmental Lobbies and the Apparent Illogic of Collective Action," p. 109. This figure represents 2.4 percent of the membership of the club.

number of people who contribute substantial sums, while considering the rational calculation that might occur to *them.*

Clearly, the Sierra Club's political contributions, reaching $2 million a year from 1975 to 1978, constitute an effective level of contribution only because environmentalists achieve their purposes not directly by providing themselves their good, but indirectly by getting governments to enforce provision of the good in various ways. If it were up to the Sierra Club to contract with a polluter, the ratio, $r,$ of group benefit to cost of such a contract would likely be bathetically far less than 1, so that the contract would not be entered. But since pollution control can be accomplished indirectly by law, the club faces only the costs of getting the enforcement adjudicated. The cost of these activities is conspicuously low compared with the cost of environmental control—on the order of a few thousand times lower. The total environmentalist political budget may be about $10 million per year; politically mandated pollution abatement at the national level cost about $23 billion in 1978.[18] Hence, a dollar's worth of politics may buy over $2,000 in pollution abatement. If benefits from abatement and conservation were uniformly spread over the population, Sierra Club members *as a group* would be getting back only about $3 of abatement per dollar of contributions to politicking.[19] Presumably, however, the value placed on abatement would exceed its cost, and, as argued in chapter 5, the members of the Sierra Club would value it far higher than the average American. Hence, it is barely possible that r for the Sierra Club political actions is very high, on the order, say, of 1,000 or even higher depending on the value placed on government-mandated conservation programs whose "cost" is largely uncounted, but whose value may be very high. For such a high rate of return on the effort, it is conceivable that it is an attractive investment, even considered only in narrow self-interest

[18] The $10-million figure is a rough estimate from data in ibid. The Sierra Club puts up $2 million of this (see n. 16 above). The $23-billion figure is from Council on Environmental Quality, *Environmental Quality 1978,* p. 424. It represents the direct expenditures, and not such expenses as the profits and wages forgone, which several industries cite in their public pronouncements. It also omits the costs of conservation of land and natural resources. Politically mandated expenditures for 1978 were only about half the total pollution abatement expenditures, since much would have been spent even without environmental legislation. Hence the larger figure for total abatement expenditures in 1977 cited in chap. 7, n. 22.

[19] If $2,000 in benefits per dollar of expenditure were spread equally over the population of the United States, each person would receive 1/100,000 of a dollar. Sierra Club members and their dependents number at least 300,000, so that the *group* receives benefits of $3 per dollar of political expenditure (300,000 × 1/100,000).

terms, to a select few of the wealthy class of Laurence Rockefeller, for instance, who is thought to be a principal benefactor of the environmental movement.

Recall now the very small number of people who might contribute substantial sums to the Sierra Club. Their contributions might, with some qualifications, fit Chamberlin's and McGuire's Cournot model of voluntary collective action, whereas $20- to $50-contributions surely cannot be seen as Cournot behavior. For a very large group, the extent of group asymmetry will be an important determinant of the likelihood of group success. A very homogeneous group can generate no contributions in the simplest static analysis, and also none on a Cournot analysis, because no one in the group can be so wealthy as to be privileged with respect to provision of the group's good. A very asymmetric group might also generate little or no contributions from strictly rational motives on the static analysis, but once it is represented by an ongoing organization, an asymmetric group might generate a significant level of contribution from its intense members (where intensity is likely to be a positive function both of level of income or wealth and of desire for the group's good). Because there is a Sierra Club with a considerable political fund built up from past contributions, someone like Rockefeller could sensibly see it as worth his or her while to add to the fund. In turn, those who give small sums (for extrarational reasons) may be encouraged to do so in part because they see that the Sierra Club is increasingly active politically, and often seems to be effective. Hence, there is a dynamic interaction between the small number of what might be rational, large contributors and the large number of extrarational, small contributors—each group is encouraged to donate to the Sierra Club because the other group does.

The number of major contributors needed to make the Sierra Club go might be wealthy enough to make the Cournot analysis go. In this case, as in many others of contemporary group politics, however, the process gets started not strictly as a Cournot-like calculus of contributions. Rather, it almost surely gets started by extrarational efforts of some to establish an organization or to piggyback a political movement onto an extant organization, efforts that could be seen as narrowly rational only if they were an act of political entrepreneurship, or if they were initiated by someone of extensive wealth whose behavior might fit a Cournot model. Again, however, even after a relevant national organization (such as the Sierra Club, National Association for the Advancement of Colored People, or other) exists and has a political fund available, it is difficult to suppose that its small-scale contributors (for example, those giving $20 or $50) are motivated by narrowly rational choice. Only very large contributors can convincingly be seen as Cournot-like oligopolists. Furthermore, not even a Rockefeller could be seen as rational if the Sierra Club required total contributions even vaguely approaching the scale of the cost of the political policies it seeks.

Indeed, a large donor's behavior may seem analogous to the actions of a corporation that enters and supports an industrywide trade association because of asymmetries among firms, as discussed in chapter 5. The corporation may not defy Olson's analysis even if it seems on general grounds to be logically a latent member of its group, because it may receive clear, specialized benefits from its group's political or other program. As Stigler notes, "With trivial exception, every industry produces a wide variety of goods or services."[20] The mix will vary significantly from firm to firm. Hence, any firms not represented in their industry associations may lose as a result. "The proposed tariff may neglect *their* products; the research program may neglect *their* processes; the labor negotiation may ignore *their* special labor mix."[21] The impact of a major contributor on the Sierra Club's ability to undertake political actions might be so great that the club would bend its program to the contributor's wishes to some (perhaps great) degree. Hence, a major donor might have a far greater effect on public policy than small-scale contributors, not merely to the extent that the large donor's contribution is, say, 10,000 times greater, but more so because the contribution buys the specific policy initiatives that interest the donor. Indeed, the contribution may even cause the redirection to the donor's initiatives of a large percentage of the small-scale contributions. From the large donor's perspective, such influential impact increases the attractiveness of contributing to the "collective" effort.

[20] George J. Stigler, "Free Riders and Collective Action: An Appendix to Theories of Economic Regulation," p. 362.
[21] Ibid.

9

RATIONALITY IN THE PRISONER'S DILEMMA

In the literature of rational choice, there are several apparent paradoxes that lose their paradoxical air upon investigation. Two of these, the Voter's Paradox and the Prisoner's Dilemma (and its generalization in collective action, *n*-person Prisoner's Dilemma), are particularly important in social theory. (The Voter's Paradox is the problem of cyclical majorities. Majorities of voters may prefer A to B, B to C, and C to A, so that no candidate can defeat every other.) They result from the aggregation of individually rational choices into social choices. Their paradox is this: that by the canons of rationality applied to individual choices, the social choices are irrational. Individual rationality requires that preference orderings be transitive, and that more-preferred alternatives be chosen over less-preferred. The social or group equivalent of the latter requirement is commonly taken to be that collective choice be Pareto-optimal (that is, that no one can be made better off without making someone else worse off). But in the Prisoner's Dilemma, the collective result of individually rational choices is not Pareto-optimal, and in the Voter's Paradox it is not transitive.

These two paradoxes have very different qualities. Neither is a paradox in the strong sense of Willard Quine's "antinomy."[1] Rather,

This chapter is a revised version of an article by the author, "Mutually Expected Rationality: A Critique," in *The Papers of the Peace Science Society (International)* vol. 28 (1978) pp. 37–48.

[1] Willard V. Quine, *The Ways of Paradox and Other Essays,* pp. 3–20.

the Voter's Paradox is a "veridical paradox"—that is, its conclusion (that majority choice is cyclic) is true. A veridical paradox "packs a surprise, but the surprise quickly dissipates itself as we ponder the proof."[2] There are also falsidical paradoxes. The male barber who shaves all and only those men in his village who do not shave themselves is a figment of the logician's imagination. There can be no such barber, as is clear from the reductio ad absurdum that follows our assuming there can be.

The Prisoner's Dilemma, however, is neither veridical nor falsidical. The sense of paradox that it conveys comes from two mingled misapprehensions. One of these is similar to that informing the initial sense of paradox in the Voter's Paradox. The other misapprehension grows out of the problem of strategic interaction and the presumption of mutually expected rationality, and is similar to the misapprehension that informs the initial sense of paradox in Daniel Bernoulli's St. Petersburg Paradox, discussed later in this chapter.

MUTUALLY EXPECTED RATIONALITY

An antinomy is a statement that is true only if it is false. The sense of paradox in the Voter's Paradox is obviously weaker than this. There is nothing a priori illogical in the fact that the properties of an aggregation are not the properties of its constituents. Indeed, it does not require a sophisticated intellect to recognize that the state of affairs in a Voter's Paradox is logical, possible, and perhaps even somewhat likely. After a while, one has difficulty imagining that anyone is surprised at the Voter's Paradox, so that one may think that calling it a paradox is an exercise in persuasive definition. That there can be cyclical majorities is structurally too obvious for consternation.

The problem of Prisoner's Dilemma is less obvious, because it is less merely a result of the structure of preferences. It requires a much more deceptive bit of persuasive definition to take us in. The players in Prisoner's Dilemma are said to be not only rational but *strategically* rational—that is, they take each other's rationality into account: they play with mutually expected rationality. And yet their strategic rationality leads them to a joint outcome considerably worse than what irrational players might achieve. The persuasive definition here is deceptive for two reasons: (1) the most compelling analysis of the game involves no *strategic* calculations and should not be expected to produce col-

[2] Ibid., p. 11.

lectively rational results; (2) the most telling critique of this analysis invokes strategic calculations, but these carry no behavioral weight.

At the first level, without strategic calculations, Prisoner's Dilemma is merely a veridical paradox. One might at first think that individuals acting rationally to maximize their well-being should collectively make themselves so well off that they would not miss any potential gains. This is a compelling assumption in market activity: if bargaining and communication are costless, trading for mutual benefit will lead to a Pareto-optimal state of affairs in which no further gains are possible. When, however, collective goods are added to private consumption goods, market behavior may no longer be collectively rational and may result in Pareto-suboptimal outcomes. If enforceable contracts are possible and costless, 2-person collective goods and those n-person collective goods that would not yield net benefits to $n - 1$ persons may be provided, but goods that are more interesting and more beneficial may not. Individual behavior in welfare economics is not very strategic.

The source of paradox in the Voter's Paradox is structural: it follows clearly from the preferences of the individuals. The source of the first sense of paradox in Prisoner's Dilemma is similarly structural: it depends only on the individuals' preferences over their own outcomes, and takes no account of their strategic interactions with their adversary-partners. It follows from the fact, discussed in chapter 2, that each player has a clear preference for the outcomes from one strategy over those from the other strategy. This can be seen in matrix 1a in figure 9-1, which displays the semigame played by the Row player in the Prisoner's Dilemma game of matrix 1 in the same figure. (These matrices basically duplicate those in figure 2-1, and are included here for ease of reference.) Row's strategy II dominates Row's strategy I in the very strong sense that Row is not only always at least as well off, but is always better off with the strategy II payoffs for a given strategy choice by Column. So long as behavior is said to be rational when we are so unstrategic as to consider only our own payoffs in such cases, then no surprise inheres in the result that the collective outcome is Pareto-suboptimal. If this were the prin-

Figure 9-1. Prisoner's Dilemma.

Matrix 1 Row's and Column's payoffs				Matrix 1a Semigame: Row's payoffs		
Row	*Column*			*Row*		
	I	II				
I	1,1	−2,2		I	1	−2
II	2, −2	−1, −1		II	2	−1

cipal problem with the Prisoner's Dilemma, the dilemma would merely
be a veridical paradox.

However, at the second level of analysis, in which strategic calculations
are assumed, Prisoner's Dilemma sounds suspiciously like an antinomy.
If I am strategically rational, "I am rational in my interactions with you
only if I take into account that you may also be rational."[3] The condition in quotes clearly involves self-reference, because the clause "you
may also be rational" requires for its explication the entire sentence of *Hofstadter*
which it is a part. Self-reference is known on occasion to lead to paradox
in Quine's strong sense of antinomy, as in Russell's paradox of the set,
S, of all sets that do not contain themselves. *S* contains itself if and
only if it does not contain itself. But self-reference need not lead to
paradox, and, indeed, the definition of rationality that includes taking
others' rationality into account is eminently sensible in the context in
which it first arose in game theory, as well as in some other contexts.
The definition underlies two very different game solutions, which are
both compelling in their realms: von Neumann's maximin solution of
2-person, zero-sum games, and Schelling's "prominence" solution of
many coordination games.[4] Consider these for a moment.

In a 2-person, zero-sum game, if you choose an equilibrium strategy
(that is, a strategy from which you have no incentive to change unilaterally), I cannot do better, and may do worse, if I choose any but
one of my own equilibrium strategies. (In a 2-person, zero-sum game,
an equilibrium strategy is a maximin strategy: it is a strategy in which
the worst payoff is as good as or better than the worst payoff in any
other strategy—hence, it is the best of the worsts, or maximin.) This
does not guarantee that everyone always chooses equilibrium strategies
in such games. But it does virtually guarantee that sophisticated players
in such games will choose equilibrium strategies if they are convinced
that their adversaries are also sophisticated. If one had to make one's
own strategy choice known before one's adversary chose, one would
have no choice but an equilibrium strategy. The logic is so compelling
that rational choice under the condition of mutually expected rationality
yields determinate payoffs. John Harsanyi notes that the von Neumann–
Morgenstern rationality postulates do not generally produce determinate
solutions, but that they do for 2-person, zero-sum games; he implies
("it is no accident") that this is why the von Neumann maximin solution
of the latter games "has been so particularly fruitful in all sorts of appli-

---

[3] For such a definition of game-theoretic rationality, see John von Neumann and
Oskar Morgenstern, *The Theory of Games and Economic Behavior,* pp. 11–12;
and R. Duncan Luce and Howard Raiffa, *Games and Decisions,* p. 6.

[4] Thomas C. Schelling, *The Strategy of Conflict,* pp. 54–58.

cations."[5] In a sense he is right, but his implication has no point. The maximin solution in this context is fruitful because it is logically unimpeachable. To look for determinate solutions to more general games, as Harsanyi does, is partly misguided. One should rather look for logically unimpeachable solutions based on compelling assumptions. The von Neumann–Morgenstern assumptions are attractive not because they produce a determinate outcome in some context, but because they compel us to adhere to them in our choices. And when we adhere to them under Harsanyi's postulate of mutually expected rationality, we reach determinate payoffs in 2-person, zero-sum games.

Similarly compelling is Schelling's notion of prominence, which leads to solutions in certain games of coordination played with restrictions on communication. It is, of course, very different from mathematical game theory solution concepts in that it involves not simply the payoffs associated with outcomes, but also various apparently irrelevant characteristics of the outcomes, characteristics that make the outcomes psychologically "prominent." Harsanyi rightly excludes such characteristics from consideration under his rationality postulates for generalized mathematical games.[6] In Schelling's ostensibly real-world situations, however, they are clearly relevant, although one would be hard pressed to give general rules for assessing the prominence of outcomes. The notion is not logical in the manner of von Neumann's maximin solution theory, but it is not hard to imagine circumstances in which one could be extremely confident of the rightness of one's selection of the prominent outcome.

What is the content of the sense of paradox at this second level with its supposed strategic calculations in Prisoner's Dilemma? Although the self-reference in the definition of strategic rationality has implications in the case of 2-person, zero-sum games and in some mixed-motive games with limited communication, it often has none in the general class of games. In particular, I will argue, it has no implications in Prisoner's Dilemma. We are persuaded by the following assertion—that *even* strategically rational players defect in Prisoner's Dilemma—to suppose that more is being claimed than that players take their own payoffs into account. Alas, there is no logical basis for the supposition. One who insists it is necessary to take others into account has not taken them into account merely with that assertion. Players in single plays of Prisoner's Dilemma cannot intentionally with logical certainty take more than their own payoffs into account unless there is a social or other overlay that alters the apparent payoffs in the game.

[5] John C. Harsanyi, "Rationality Postulates for Bargaining Solutions in Cooperative and in Noncooperative Games," p. 141.

[6] Ibid., pp. 150–151.

To show that an assumption and its implications are compelling, one can best present them, and let one's readers be compelled. To show, contrariwise, that an assumption has no compelling implications in a given context, it will not do simply to present some conclusions that would compel no serious reader. A common device in mathematical and logical demonstrations is the reductio ad absurdum, but I have none for the present argument that mutually expected rationality has no content in various contexts, including that of Prisoner's Dilemma. In lieu of better devices, I will argue, in part, by example from other supposed paradoxes.

There is a class of apparent paradoxes which, like the falsidical paradoxes, depends on a combination of analytic and factual claims. Unlike the falsidical paradoxes, however, they are resolved not by concluding by reductio ad absurdum that their facts are false (there is no such barber), but by showing that they do not, upon investigation, sustain their supposed conclusions. That is to say, they are paradoxical only in the subjective sense that too casual attention to their statement may lead to misapprehended conclusions. The solution of one of these, as Wittgenstein says, is seen in the disappearance of the problem.

One of the oldest of such paradoxes is also perhaps the oldest of the rational choice paradoxes: the St. Petersburg Paradox. At the risk of entering upon an infinite regress, I will present what I think is the only compelling resolution of this paradox, show that this resolution is related to what I think is the most compelling resolution of the peculiar paradox of iterated-play Prisoner's Dilemma by showing how the latter is related to the resolution of the Hanged-Man Paradox, and finally, by this indirection, argue that the notion of mutually expected rationality is factually hollow in the context of single-play Prisoner's Dilemma. Standing alone, the final argument in this chain is one whose force might not instantly compel the reader. However, I think it likely to compel after mulling, in lieu of which I hope to prepare the ground sufficiently that the argument will seem natural, if not obvious.

THE ST. PETERSBURG PARADOX

In the St. Petersburg Paradox it is supposed that one is offered an interesting gamble. A fair coin will be tossed repeatedly until it turns up heads. If the first heads occurs on the nth toss, one will be paid $\$2^n$. Hence, if the first heads is at the first toss, the payoff is \$2; if it is at the twentieth toss, the payoff is slightly more than \$1 million. The expected value of the gamble is:

$$\tfrac{1}{2}\ (\$2) + \tfrac{1}{4}\ (\$4) + \tfrac{1}{8}\ (\$8) + \ldots = \$1 + \$1 + \$1 + \ldots$$

There is no limit to this sum. Hence, by the expected utility hypothesis, one should be willing to pay any amount whatsoever, say, $10,000, for the gamble. But clearly one would do no such thing. This is the paradox. One might resolve it as a falsidical paradox by concluding that the expected utility hypothesis is absurd. The eighteenth-century Swiss scientist Daniel Bernoulli and others resolve the paradox by assuming that utility is not linear with money, although this resolution merely invites restatement of the gamble with payoffs in utility rather than in money. Ultimately, as Menger argues, the paradox can be resolved in this fashion only by assuming that one's utility has an upper bound.[7] This assumption is compelling in its own right, but to invoke it as the resolution of the St. Petersburg Paradox is to grant that the paradox is not an antinomy. Whether utility is bounded is more a factual than a logical issue.

If we are to resort to factual issues, we need not debate the limits or forms of our utility, since the slightest bit of realism is sufficient to do in the St. Petersburg Paradox. Consider a real gambling house that offers the Bernoulli gamble. It must have limited resources; hence it cannot make payoff beyond some finite level; hence it cannot credibly offer a Bernoulli gamble that is not truncated at some point for which the payoff is less than or equal to the house's assets. For a truncated Bernoulli gamble to have an expected value of a mere $40 would require that the house be prepared to meet a possible (but exceedingly unlikely) payoff of slightly more than $1 trillion. The requirement is absurd (at least at this writing in 1981). An expected value of $20 would require that the house have assets of slightly over $1 million. Bernoulli concludes that, paradoxically, no one would pay an unlimited sum for the full Bernoulli gamble. However, there are no doubt many people who would pay $20 for a Bernoulli gamble truncated at twenty tosses and guaranteed by a reliable house (or state).

The French mathematician Bertrand and, alas, the Chicago economist Stigler seem to think such realism yields no resolution of the paradox. Stigler says of the limited-house-assets argument (already proposed in 1837 by Poisson) that "even its spurious plausibility depends on the particular formulation of the problem."[8] He adds, "Bertrand was surely right in this respect: 'If one plays with centimes instead of francs, with grains of sand instead of centimes, with molecules of hydrogen instead of grains of sand, the fear of insolvency [on the part of the house] may be reduced without limit.' "[9] Nothing may be reduced without limit, and Stigler's and Bertrand's point is wrong. Suppose the house pays in mills

[7] Karl Menger, "The Role of Uncertainty in Economics."

[8] George J. Stigler, *Essays in the History of Economics,* p. 113.

[9] Ibid., n. 128.

rather than in dollars, so that heads on the first toss pays two-tenths of a cent instead of $2. Now it will take ten additional (for a total of thirty) tosses with the first heads on the thirtieth toss for the payoff to reach $1 million. The commonsense response to this is to value the gamble far less. Indeed, if the original gamble with payoffs in dollars and a maximum run of twenty tosses was worth $20, the new gamble with payoffs in mills and a maximum run of thirty tosses is worth only 30 mills, or 3 cents, although both gambles afford a maximum potential payoff of a little more than $1 million. The success of contemporary state lotteries suggests that large numbers of people would spend 3 cents for such an outside chance at a million dollars.

Why is there no paradox? Because even in a thought experiment it is not possible to conceive of a Bernoulli gamble that would not be truncated long before one's expected utility from the gamble became large. Further, how could one use $1 trillion without radically altering any contemporary economy beyond understanding of one's resultant benefits? The assumptions in the logic of the full Bernoulli gamble simply cannot be fulfilled. Hence, the expected utility hypothesis, though one may wish to question it on other grounds, is not undermined by Bernoulli's supposed paradox, because the hypothesis depends for its meaning on the valuation a person could place on real occurrences. The supposed paradox does not even test very severely the reasonableness of asserting that utility is linear with money.

ITERATED PRISONER'S DILEMMA AND THE HANGED-MAN PARADOX

Consider now the peculiar paradox of the iterated Prisoner's Dilemma game. Iterated play is different from single-play in mixed-motive games without communication (such as Prisoner's Dilemma) in that it yields opportunity for tacit communication, so that one may sense that the other player's future choices are contingent on one's own immediate choice. (In some games, including all 2-person, zero-sum games, this may make no difference, since communication may not affect the outcome.) Hence, it is generally agreed that players may rationally cooperate in iterated Prisoner's Dilemma. When there is even tacit opportunity for making one's choices contingent on those of one's adversary-partner, that is, of threatening the partner with defection in return for defection, rationality can become strategic. As in Schelling's notion of prominence, there is no guarantee of this, since one player may not recognize the other's threats for what the other intends them to be. However, there is voluminous evidence that many relatively unsophisticated players do comprehend such threats in the long run.[10] Among sophisticated players, cooperation in iterated Prisoner's Dilemma may be the norm.

Luce and Raiffa, Harsanyi, and presumably most other sophisticated players would defect in single-play Prisoner's Dilemma,[11] but many, including Luce and Raiffa, would cooperate in iterated play.[12] One must append "sometimes" to the latter claim, however. In a perverse twist, Luce and Raiffa note that if the game is played exactly twice, then the second play should be played as though it were a single-play game. Hence, one should defect in the second play. Of course, one's adversary should do the same, so that against a sophisticated player, one should assume that the outcome of the second play is determinate and therefore not contingent on the first play. In that case, the first play should likewise be treated as a single-play game, so that one should likewise defect in it. Alas, the brutality of that logic leads as well to defection in a series of exactly 100 plays, beginning with the last play and working back to the first. Not knowing when the experimenter will terminate the game, one should cooperate 100 times in succession (unless, of course, one's partner misses the point). But knowing that there will be exactly 100 plays, one should defect 100 times. A little knowledge is not merely dangerous, it is perverse.

That this paradox is not to be taken seriously can be intuited quickly enough if we imagine being placed before *exactly 1 million* or, alternatively, before *about 1 million* plays of Prisoner's Dilemma. Would any sophisticated human being really behave so differently in these two situations as always to defect in the first and always (or almost always) to cooperate in the second? Luce and Raiffa grant that they would not defect repeatedly in a long, fixed series. Why does the logic of their double-play analysis not compel them when stretched over 100 plays? They do not finally have an argument much stronger than that they "do not think it 'reasonable' to single out" continuous defection when the game is iterated many times. "It is not 'reasonable' in the sense that we predict that most intelligent people would not play accordingly."[13] (Alas, they "know some individuals who, although brilliant in other ways, insist they would. . . .") I think their "sense" is right and that it has compelling grounds. This can be exemplified more clearly with a digression into the Hanged-Man Paradox.

[10] In Anatol Rapoport and Albert M. Chammah, *Prisoner's Dilemma.*
[11] Luce and Raiffa, *Games and Decisions,* p. 96; Harsanyi, "Rationality Postulates."
[12] Luce and Raiffa, *Games and Decisions,* pp. 100, 102.
[13] Ibid., pp. 100–101.

In the Hanged-Man Paradox, a man, K, is sentenced on Sunday to be hanged, but the judge, who is evidently French or enamored of the French wit for surprising those sentenced to the guillotine in their last moments, orders that the hanging take place on one of the next five days at noon. Smiling wistfully, he says to K, "You will not know *which* day until they come to take you to the gallows." K, who has evidently been condemned for logical perversions, cannot prevent his mind from nevertheless trying to figure out in advance which day will be his last. He quickly realizes it cannot be Friday, because if he has not been hanged by Thursday noon, he will know nearly a full day before they come to get him that he will be hanged on Friday. He is simultaneously pleased at his cleverness and depressed that he has pushed his date with the gallows closer to Sunday. Soon enough, he realizes that if Friday is logically excluded, then so is Thursday, because if he has not been hanged by noon Wednesday, he will know that, Friday being excluded, his date must be Thursday. In like manner, he can exclude Wednesday, Tuesday, and Monday. As a logician, he smugly concludes that the judge's decree is false. On Thursday noon he is hanged. The paradox is that he is surprised when they come to take him to the gallows. (One can easily think up less macabre relatives of the Hanged-Man Paradox, such as the Surprise Quiz, a device with which we are all familiar and by which no doubt many of us have illogically been surprised.[14])

Is the Hanged-Man Paradox not an antinomy? Initially it may seem that it is. But its terms are in part very different from those of Russell's paradox and other classical antinomies. Russell's paradox involves no facts, but only formal definitions and logical relationships. The Hanged-Man Paradox requires contingent facts. One cannot construe as analytic the truth of a statement that is not analytic. Hence, one cannot know, for example, that one will be hanged in the next five days in the same way one knows that A is either B or not B. Though our judge might have had great authority, he could not guarantee the certainty of a hanging within five days. Wittgenstein asks, "But when is something objectively certain? When a mistake is not possible. But what kind of possibility is that? Mustn't mistake be *logically* excluded?"[15] In his backward deduction from Friday, K neglected the important possibility that he might not be hanged, and therefore he suffered his terrible surprise, compounded by the second-order surprise that he was being surprised that the judge's decree was being fulfilled. Quine remarks, "It is notable that K acquiesces in the conclusion (wrong, according to the fable of the Thursday hanging) that the decree will not be fulfilled.

[14] For other relatives and references, see David Kaplan and Richard Montague, "A Paradox Regained."

[15] Ludwig Wittgenstein, *On Certainty,* p. 27.

If this is a conclusion he is prepared to accept (though wrongly) in the end as a certainty, it is an alternative which he should have been prepared to take into consideration from the beginning as a possibility."[16] Had he done so, he would have rejected his reductio ad absurdum conclusion that the judge's decree was wrong. Though he might then have put his hopes in uncertain possibilities, his Thursday surprise would have been mitigated. His problem was that facing a hangman focused his mind a little too admirably.

Similarly, the player who deduces backward from the presumed final play in a presumed series of exactly 100 plays of Prisoner's Dilemma has let logic be polluted with uncertain terms. Perhaps if Jehovah himself guaranteed that there would be exactly 100 plays. . . . But even then, how could one trust one's senses that *this* was Jehovah? There is yet a second uncertainty: over what one's adversary-partner will do in the course of 100 plays. The paradox is hence doubly resolved. One cannot logically deduce backward from the last play. On this account there may be some subjective difference between a 2-play and a 100-play iteration in that the degree of both uncertainties may increase with the number of specified iterations. Moreover, one may think the prospects of contingent choosing are less in a very short than in a long string of plays (as seems to be evidenced by the relatively unsophisticated players in the long, iterated games of Rapoport and Chammah[17]). Hence, one might choose to defect on both plays of a 2-play game, but expect to cooperate (if one's adversary seemed to respond to tacit communication) on most plays of a 100-play game. Let us make this general conclusion stronger.

Suppose you claim that one should not play iterated Prisoner's Dilemma with contingent choosing if the number of plays is specified in advance. You presumably are not claiming that defection is the best strategy in such a game against every other player, but only that it is best against a sophisticated player. Hence, to reject your claim, it is insufficient for me to assert that in playing against me you could do better than always defecting because I would play tit for tat for at least the first ninety or so plays. You can answer that assertion by derogating my level of sophistication. To reject your sophisticate's claim, I should better hope to show it specious on its own terms. It is specious because it derives a supposedly logically certain conclusion from various assumptions, some of which are incapable of certainty.

In particular, your claim requires three assumptions: (1) that one know the game will be terminated exactly on the *x*th play, (2) that one know the other player's sophistication has led the other to the same

---

[16] Quine, *Ways of Paradox*, p. 22.
[17] Rapoport and Chammah, *Prisoner's Dilemma*.

logical conclusion (that is, that one should always defect), and (3) that the other will be sufficiently bound by this logic as to make only defecting choices. The second of these assumptions is very strong, because for some Prisoner's Dilemma payoff structures (for example, that in matrix 1 of figure 9-1), the long-term gain from a successful effort at coordinated cooperation heavily outweighs the short-term risk of taking the sucker's payoff for a few plays. In any case, the sophisticate must grant this: that the instant the other player chooses to cooperate for a play of the game, the sophisticate must reject (2) or (3) and with it the whole strategic conclusion that continued defection is still necessarily rational.

Knowing this, even if you, the sophisticate, were quite sure of assumption 1, you should yourself prefer to enter a cooperative choice early in the game to rule out the possibility that I act under your presumption that defection is rational against a sophisticated player. That way, you give us a chance to succeed in contingent choosing for your own benefit. Indeed, only if you expect me to be too stupid tacitly to coordinate contingent choosing should you then expect to defect on almost all plays of the game. Still, you should not *plan* to defect on every play unless you are firmly convinced that you face a partner (such as a simplistically programmed computer) whose choices will not be contingent on your own. These last two statements apply generally to any iterated Prisoner's Dilemma, whether or not it is known in advance when the game will terminate. If one is quite sure that this is the last play, one can sensibly defect. Or, if one is quite sure there are exactly two plays left, one can sensibly defect on both, on the ground that it will be hard to establish contingent choosing over these two plays. The conclusion for two plays is less compelling than that for one play, however, since it is at least conceivable that the other player is using a contingent strategy, in which case cooperation on the first of the two plays is more rewarding than defection on both plays. That is, in a two-play Prisoner's Dilemma, there is no strategy that dominates all other strategies against all of an adversary's possible contingent and noncontingent strategies. In general, unless the whole fixed-number iteration is extremely pristine, one cannot get the deduction going from the nth play back to the first.

Before going on to the discussion of single-play Prisoner's Dilemma, it might be noted here that Rapoport provides a matrix of eight possible contingent and noncontingent strategies in twice-played, 2-person Prisoner's Dilemma [18] (the strategies are given in chapter 10, section on "Ambiguities in the Notion of Convention"). In two-play Prisoner's Dilemma, a complete strategy says what one will choose in each of the plays, or gives a rule from which each choice can be determined. Tit for tat says one will cooperate on the first play, and then do on the second

---

[18] Anatol Rapoport, *Two-Person Game Theory*, p. 134.

play whatever the other player did on the first play. The strategy of always defecting is noncontingent (one defects no matter what the other player has done). Clearly, the strategy of always defecting (defect-defect) is not the best choice against a player playing tit for tat—for example, cooperate-defect would yield a higher payoff. Hence, defect-defect does not dominate all other strategies against tit for tat. But it is also the case that tit for tat does not dominate all other strategies against defect-defect—for example, defect-defect yields one a higher payoff against the other player's defect-defect. Indeed, in general in two-play Prisoner's Dilemma, there is no dominant strategy, that is, no strategy that is always better than or at least as good as any other strategy against every possible strategy of the other player.

Although there is no dominant strategy for 2- or n-play Prisoner's Dilemma, Michael Taylor suggests that players might view the joint tit-for-tat strategy as a Pareto equilibrium for early plays in the sequence of iterations.[19] The notion of an "equilibrium" over part of an iterated game is somewhat peculiar, since an equilibrium is normally defined in terms of joint strategies over a whole game, not over a part of it. Nevertheless, players might grasp that if there are n iterations altogether (or if at any stage there are n plays remaining), unilateral defection from tit for tat to continuous defection may not pay. In Rapoport's and Chammah's terminology, let Row's payoffs be R (*R*eward for jointly cooperating), T (*T*emptation to defect while Column cooperates), S (*S*ucker's payoff for cooperating while Column defects), and P (*P*unishment for jointly defecting).[20] Unilateral defection from tit for tat to continuous defection will not pay if $nR \geq T + (n-1)P$ for an individual playing Row with payoffs as shown in figure 9-2 for *C*ooperation and *D*efection (payoffs for Column are not shown):

Figure 9-2. Row's payoffs.

	C	D
C	R	S
D	T	P

There will be some payoff matrices for Prisoner's Dilemma that will satisfy this inequality for n as small as 2. However, there can be "coordination equilibria" (in the sense defined in chapter 10 below) in iterated Prisoner's Dilemma if play is open-ended, but not if play is for a fixed number of iterations (see below, chapter 10 at note 20).

[19] Michael Taylor, University of Essex, personal communication, 1980.
[20] Rapoport and Chammah, *Prisoner's Dilemma*, pp. 33–35.

SINGLE-PLAY PRISONER'S DILEMMA

Note how this account of various paradoxes informs our understanding of such notions as Schelling's prominent solutions in some games and the tacit communication that allows for contingent choosing in iterated Prisoner's Dilemma. These notions are not logically derived (as the equilibrium outcomes of a 2-person, zero-sum game are). They are merely intuitively sensed. Their appeal lies in the likelihood that others would also intuitively sense them. Their "proof" lies not in logical deduction, but in the statistical distribution of their appeal. Among sophisticated players, the appeal of contingent choosing, and hence of generally cooperating in iterated Prisoner's Dilemma, is presumably distributed widely. Anyone who has tested seminar or party groups for the spontaneous choice of prominent solutions to various coordination problems can probably attest to the frequency with which some solutions have nearly universal appeal among given groups. What is the status of single-play Prisoner's Dilemma? In the context of this game, there is self-evidently no notion of *mutually expected rationality* that has wide appeal among the sophisticated; however, the *unstrategically self-interested strategy* of choosing a totally dominating strategy has very wide appeal.

The most compelling argument for cooperation in Prisoner's Dilemma is probably the argument from symmetry, which supposedly takes one's adversary into account. The argument is that if I choose a strategy as rationally best, my adversary, if similarly rational, must choose the same strategy. Hence, the outcome can be only the upper-left or the lower-right cells of matrix 1 of figure 9-1, for payoffs of $(1,1)$ or $(-1,-1)$. Clearly we both prefer $(1,1)$ to $(-1,-1)$. Hence, I must cooperate by choosing strategy I. Unfortunately, the only sense in which this argument is compelling is in a psychological sense, like that of Schelling's prominence. But prominence leads to cooperation in some coordination games because both players value successful cooperation far more than they value any alternative. In Prisoner's Dilemma, each player would prefer to defect while the other foolishly cooperates. One may deduce from symmetry that similar thought processes will lead to symmetric payoffs, but this deduction is binding on one's actual choices in the game only if one is playing, and knows it, oneself. If a computer was playing the game and was programmed to carry out such deductions, and if by oversight it was instructed to act on its deductions, then it might cooperate. But this is because it would be acting as though it "knew" what it could not know—that its adversary would also act as though bound by the deduction from symmetry. A sophisticated player knows one can know no such thing about one's unknown adversary, not least because one would probably not put absolute trust in anyone, but surely not in an unknown and presumably self-interested adversary.

In what sense is one bound by relevant intuitions and deductions from the assumption of mutually expected rationality in Schelling's coordination games or in 2-person, zero-sum games? If one fails to have a common intuition as to the prominent solution of a coordination game with restricted communication, then one may have lost, compared with what one could have done by changing *one's own behavior only*. Similarly, in iterated Prisoner's Dilemma, if one fails by way of tacit communication to achieve cooperation enforced by contingent choosing, then one may have lost, compared with outcomes that could have been achieved by changing *one's own behavior only* toward more cooperation. In single-play Prisoner's Dilemma, it will *never* be true that one could have done better by changing one's own behavior only toward more cooperation. If I think my adversary in a zero-sum game is sophisticated, there is a clear inducement for me to choose an equilibrium strategy. I am bound by self-interest. Whether I think my adversary in single-play Prisoner's Dilemma is sophisticated or not, there is an inducement for me to defect.

In sum, mutually expected rationality has no implications for behavior in Prisoner's Dilemma. Like Quine's K awaiting the hangman,[21] one can suspend judgment and hope for the best and choose to cooperate for reasons of the appeal that symmetry gives to mutual cooperation, but one has strong reasons not to. Of course, one might also cooperate for reasons other than self-interest, but one would still have strong reasons for thinking that one's self-interest for the short run of the single play of the game lay in defection. The aura of paradox about Prisoner's Dilemma comes from the misapprehension that strategic rationality has implications for players' knowledge in the game. Even in Quine's sense that "a paradox is just any conclusion that at first sounds absurd but that has an argument to sustain it,"[22] there is no paradox in the Prisoner's Dilemma. When the nature of the game is properly stated—that is, without the persuasive definition of the "mutually expected rationality" of the players—there is neither surprise nor paradox in the conclusion that narrowly self-interested actions by individuals may produce collectively bad outcomes. If there is a seemingly paradoxical result of narrowly self-interested behavior, it is the opposite kind of result: that in some contexts such behavior can produce collectively good outcomes, as in Mandeville's *Fable of the Bees* or Smith's argument for *The Wealth*

---

[21] Quine, *Ways of Paradox,* p. 23.
[22] Ibid., p. 3.

of Nations. The latter result is possibly a veridical paradox—at first it seems odd, but it may nevertheless be true.

Note the irony that anyone who maintains that 100 consecutive defections is the rational strategy in a 100-play iterated Prisoner's Dilemma should contrariwise concede the rationality of cooperating in single-play Prisoner's Dilemma. The always-defect strategy in the iterated game depends for its deduction on the assumption of sure knowledge of how the other player will behave. If one could have such knowledge, one could as well know that the other has comprehended the deduction from symmetry that the payoffs will be symmetric, and hence that both must cooperate or both must defect with deterministic surety in the single-play game.

If one still senses a residue of paradox in single-play Prisoner's Dilemma, the sense may come from the extreme difficulty of imagining oneself into a purely anomic, one-shot situation. The only way to do that which is compelling may be in an experimental setting. If one thinks one would defect in the anomic experimental setting, one should not think there is any paradox. But this result is often projected into social situations that are less certainly one-shot and anomic. Hence, one may think that in real life one would cooperate. That is because the situation is not certainly or anomically Prisoner's Dilemma.

Indeed, in real life, one is likely to be anomically involved only in very large group interactions and rarely if ever in 2-person interactions (see further, chapter 12). In the case of n-person games, strategic rationality seldom has implications for behavior. In n-person, zero-sum games there is no compelling "best" strategy. And in iterated n-person Prisoner's Dilemma, or collective action, strategically rational behavior may be very hard or virtually impossible to engineer, because a group of cooperators may be able to punish any defectors only by suffering losses themselves (in 2-person Prisoner's Dilemma this is not true). Thus the device of tacit communication to induce cooperation by contingent choosing is undercut.

The sort of coordinated contingent strategies that Taylor[23] argues should lead to success in collective actions in anarchic situations, that is, when there is no state or other authority to regulate cooperation, will be very difficult in a larger-number Prisoner's Dilemma. His argument depends on having the relevant number of the n members of a group coordinate on identically the same strategy of cooperating only if at least $m - 1$ others cooperate. Hence, success would be ruined if one too few cooperated. The "one too few" result presumably would produce strategic bargaining to induce another member to cooperate. In such bar-

[23] Michael Taylor, *Anarchy and Cooperation.*

gaining one would agree to become the additional cooperator only if one were relatively sure of two things: that no one else would if one did not, and that those who had already agreed on the contingency of an additional agreer would really withdraw for want of one additional cooperator. The second conviction could be confidently held only if one knew very much about those already cooperating, or was confident that the number of those already agreeing to cooperate was just exactly one short of being enough to yield them net benefits from their cooperation. In the latter case, the issue would be trivial, since the value to oneself of joining them would most likely be marginal. The first conviction could be confidently held only if one knew very much about those not already cooperating, or if there were nearly certainly no other potential cooperators because there were no other potential beneficiaries of the collective action. In general, in a large-number Prisoner's Dilemma that is iterated but is otherwise isolated from external sanctions, whether one should be the *m*th cooperator in Taylor's scheme is ill-determined. How one might forcefully be induced to cooperate will be the subject of the next three chapters, especially of chapters 11 and 12. Much of the interest there will be in incentives present in games that are not isolated from other social interactions.

10

CONTRACT BY CONVENTION

The notion of *contract* commonly carries with it the implication of explicit agreement. While the literature on social contract may not provide convincing arguments for any specific social contract, it nevertheless seems compelling in its common assumption that people can obligate themselves by implicit agreement. As Lewis argues, "Many social contracts will be sustained by the moral obligation of tacit consent or fair play, as recognized by the agents involved."[1] Such contracts may arise by *convention,* in a technical sense to be defined below, which involves calculations of self-interest. The self-interest may be somewhat muddled by norms or moral codes which themselves are sustained in part by other conventions, perhaps held by a larger or partially different population. Few would agree that there is any overarching social contract of the stature of Locke's or Rousseau's that carries with it obligations to contemporary or otherwise-designated "nations." Nevertheless, one could reasonably explain a large part of the group-oriented collective action in advanced, diffuse nations as contract by convention.

Such an explanation is important, not least because it makes comprehensible much activity that might seem to defy the narrow rationality of self-interest. However, it may do so in part by fitting modest, even surprisingly modest, degrees of extrarational behavior into a larger and largely rational social context. The extrarational behavior may do no

[1] David K. Lewis, *Convention,* p. 94.

155

more than serve as the catalyst to initiate and perhaps establish a contract by convention, which can then be sustained without further extra-rational support.

I will argue that for groups in ongoing Prisoner's Dilemma or collective action situations, or in games, it is often possible to achieve cooperative contract by convention directly from a straightforward coordination of self-interested behavior without any extragame incentives. The possibility is hedged about substantially by various factors, including, most notably, the likely debilitating effects of very large group size and such difficulties in the nature of a group's collective good as would balk explicit contractual agreement (as discussed in chapter 6), even if this could be enforced by some sanctioning authority. In addition, contract by convention may be achieved less directly with the support of extragame incentives. In the latter case, successful group action has obvious affinities with Olson's collective action as a by-product of selective individual incentives.[2]

In chapter 9, I argued that ordinary single-play Prisoner's Dilemma is distinguished from Schelling's coordination games and from iterated Prisoner's Dilemma by the fact that self-interest may prescribe cooperation in both of the latter, but not in the former. Yet the prescription is not strictly a logical derivation. I wish here to exploit an ambiguity in Lewis's analysis of convention to show that cooperation in iterated Prisoner's Dilemma can be achieved by convention. Lewis himself sanctions this exploitation, albeit perhaps unwittingly, because it leads to some difficulty in the notion. The ambiguity is itself inherent not merely in Lewis's definition, but in the problems themselves that one would wish to analyze. Lewis's analysis is best explained in terms of Schelling's coordination games.[3]

COORDINATION PROBLEMS

Consider the strategic differences in two classes of games: Prisoner's Dilemma and Schelling's coordination games.

1. It is widely agreed that in an anomic situation, that is, when players are not bound by social contexts of friendship or other extra-game incentives, defection is the individually rational choice in single-play, 2-person Prisoner's Dilemma, as represented in the payoff matrix

[2] See chap. 2 above, and Mancur Olson, Jr., *The Logic of Collective Action*, pp. 132–167.

[3] Thomas C. Schelling, *The Strategy of Conflict*, pp. 83–118.

of game 1 in figure 10-1. Defection implies choosing strategy D in game 1; if both players choose their strategy D, the resultant payoff to each is worse than what each could get if both cooperated by choosing strategy C. But, alas, if one cooperates, the other is better off defecting, and the cooperator suffers the greatest possible loss. Hence, there is strong incentive for mutual defection if there are no extragame incentives.

Figure 10-1.

Game 1
Prisoner's Dilemma

Row	Column	
	C	D
C	1,1	−2,2
D	2, −2	−1, −1

Game 2
Pure coordination (with
two coordination equilibria)

Row	Column	
	I	II
I	2,2	1,1
II	1,1	2,2

Game 3
Pure coordination (with one coordination equilibrium)

Row	Column	
	I	II
I	2,2	1,1
II	1,1	0,0

2. In a coordination game like game 2 in figure 10-1, both players are best off if their joint strategy puts them in the upper-left cell, an outcome which Schelling calls the "prominent solution."[4] Choices in such a game may not be wholly logically determined if it is played under conditions of limited communication and without benefit of a visible matrix of payoffs, so that some sophistication or intuition may be required to "coordinate" choices.

If one fails under point 2 above to have a common intuition as to the prominent solution of a coordination game with restricted communication, then one may have lost, compared with what one could have done by changing one's own behavior only. In the case of 1 above, on the contrary, it will *never* be true that one could have done better by changing one's own behavior toward more cooperation. In game 2 there is a *coordination equilibrium*, that is, a combination of strategies producing an outcome "in which no one would have been better off had

[4] Ibid., pp. 57–58.

any one agent alone acted otherwise, either himself or someone else."[5]
Indeed, in game 2 there are two coordination equilibria: the upper-left
and the lower-right cells. In game 1 there is only one equilibrium, the
lower-right cell, in the usual game-theoretic sense. If both players
have chosen strategy D, neither can improve his or her own lot by
unilaterally changing strategy. However, this equilibrium is not a coordination equilibrium. If Row unilaterally switched from strategy D to
strategy C, Row would not benefit; however, Column would benefit
from Row's switching strategies.

CONVENTION

The distinction between the two games discussed in the preceding
section underlies Lewis's definition of convention, which follows. If
the players of the iterated coordination game successfully achieve tacit
communication to cooperate, they are adhering to a convention. We
may generalize from the 2-person game to *n*-person games to obtain
Lewis's final definition (presented here in his words to ensure against
distortion) :

> A regularity *R* in the behavior of members of a population *P*
> when they are agents in a recurrent situation *S* is a *convention* if
> and only if it is true that, and it is common knowledge in *P* that,
> in almost any instance of *S* among members of *P*,
> 1. almost everyone conforms to *R;*
> 2. almost everyone expects almost everyone else to conform to *R;*
> 3. almost everyone has approximately the same preferences
>   regarding all combinations of actions;
> 4. almost everyone prefers that any one more [person] conform
>   to *R,* on condition that almost everyone conform to *R;*
> 5. almost everyone would prefer that any one more [person]
>   conform to *R',* on condition that almost everyone conform
>   to *R',*
> where *R'* is some possible regularity in the behavior of members of
> *P* in *S,* such that almost no one in almost any instance of *S* among
> members of *P* could conform both to *R'* and to *R*.[6]

The "common knowledge" requirement is much stronger than what he
could realistically claim of some of his examples of conventions. In part
at least, this is because he means, with Hayek,[7] to include under knowl-

---

[5] Lewis, *Convention,* p. 14.

[6] Ibid., p. 78.

[7] Friedrich A. Hayek, *Law, Legislation, and Liberty* vol. 1 *Rules and Order.*

edge a great deal that is inarticulate and unconscious, that could never fill out a sentence beginning "I know. . . ." The behaviorist's stimulus–response learning evidently produces what would qualify as "knowledge" in this definition.

For Lewis it is important that there be alternative possible conventions in a game for us to speak of convention. Hence, if players repeatedly achieved the outcome of the upper-left cell of game 3 in figure 10-1, their behavior would not be a convention, because strict self-interest *without* tacit coordination is sufficient to reach that outcome. Strategy I is dominating, that is, it is individually rational in the sense that each player in the game is better off playing strategy I no matter what the other does. More generally, for there to be a conventional play of a game, there must be at least two coordination equilibrium outcomes, two outcomes from which one cannot unilaterally move with profit to oneself—or to others.[8] In an iterated version of game 2, players could probably manage, even without communication, to coordinate their strategies so as always to achieve thereafter the outcome of the upper-left cell—or so as to achieve the outcome of the lower-right cell. There is no logical reason for a priori preferring one of these two outcomes to the other. Therefore the final choice is partly conventional in the ordinary sense of the word, just as the way that Americans dress for various functions is largely a matter of convention rather than of a priori rightness. Conforming to the convention, in the ordinary sense, of a dress code generally becomes a convention in Lewis's sense, because violation of the code provokes censure, which is commonly not in one's self-interest if one prefers approbation to disapprobation from the relevant community.

Lewis's own interest in and analysis of convention was sparked by the philosophical debate over whether language arises by convention, and by Quine's short answer to the problem. In Lewis's words, Quine's answer is that "conventions are agreements, [but] the conventions of language could not possibly have originated by agreement, since some of them would have been needed to provide the rudimentary language in which the first agreement was made."[9] For the present discussion, however, the more interesting conventions involve collective behavior of other types. The following examples of possible social choice conventions might clarify the notion.

1. It is well known that the Voter's Paradox, with its cyclic majority preferences, is an occasional barrier to successful prediction of policy

[8] Lewis, *Convention*, p. 70.
[9] Ibid., p. 2.

outcomes. Yet for all the analytical interest in such problems, they do not seem to bother the members of legislative bodies that supposedly are afflicted by them. Why? For the simple reason, as Haefele argues with different words,[10] that legislative bodies commonly adopt conventions that substantially ensure finality in a finite, indeed small, number of votes. Though a body might not agree as to which of three cyclic majority preferences should be made into policy or law, it might readily adopt procedures that prevent stasis in the face of such preferences. If legislators understood these problems better, and if they understood the full implications of their rules in relevant moments, their convention might break down. Until that happens, we may rely on the ignorance and even stupidity of legislators to keep them infallibly voting significant measures up or down in ways that prevent cycles. This example incidentally suggests what sort of knowledge might be involved in Lewis's definition above.

2. Why do we care about truth in relating events of interest when a bit of untruth might add even more to the interest? In part, our regard for truth in relating events is perhaps an instance of Gilbert Ryle's scrupulousness.[11] But consider how, once it has arisen, a convention of truth in relating events would govern behavior in a community. Other conventions are possible: for example, silence and interest value of one's tall tales. Since entertainment is part of the reason for relating events, interest value may be in competition with truth, and Dr. Seuss does not sully his tales with mere truth. But another value is sharing knowledge that is desired, which is to say that learning the truth of some events is of interest to us. Others cannot, as a rule, figure out as adeptly as I which parts of various truths are of interest to me and which can be embellished for entertainment's sake without harm to my interests; therefore, I am likely to prefer to hear an event related by someone who I have reason to believe will be fairly truthful, rather than interesting at the expense of truth. Dual conventions may arise, one for tall tales, another for relating events, and those unable to parcel their telling into appropriate categories may find their telling holds little of anyone's interest. Hence, once the convention of truth in relating events has arisen, almost everyone may find it in his or her interest to conform, to a considerable degree, even though there may still be some self-interested or merely interest-value embellishment—no doubt far more cars are totaled in the telling than in the wrecking even in the most truthful of modern societies. Note that a convention of truth in relating events might arise entirely from and be applied entirely in very small-

10 Edwin T. Haefele, "A Utility Theory of Representative Government."
11 Gilbert Ryle, "Conscience and Moral Convictions."

scale, even dyadic interactions. This is not a necessary feature of conventions, but in particular cases it may enhance both the recognizability of what constitutes conforming behavior and the immediacy of the application of incentives to conform.

3. If there is some strongly held notion of fairness—it need not be uniformly strongly held, but need only be more or less randomly distributed among a fraction of the population—and if some kinds of violation of that notion may often be observed, and if those who hold the notion react very badly to those who violate it if violations are infrequent and much less badly if violations are commonplace, then avoidance of the often-observable kinds of violation of that fairness notion may be a convention. Almost everyone might then observe the convention, which is to say that we all might act as though we held to the norm of fairness. But some would observe the convention strictly from self-interest, on the expectation that to violate it would yield greater expected cost than gain (the expected cost being vaguely a product of the harshness of adverse reaction by the probability that the violation might be observed by one of the fraction who actually hold the fairness norm). If one were choosing, under conditions of limited knowledge, how to act, one might choose to act as though one held to the fairness norm in almost all situations, because the burden of thinking out the balance of expected costs and benefits might itself seem to outweigh the sometime benefit of unfair action. Just as an ethical utilitarian might follow rules of thumb rather than be a foolishly determined act-utilitarian who weighs the costs and benefits of every action without including the costs of the weighing itself, so also might a perfect egoist behave like an (almost) perfectly fair-minded person, all because of convention. The egoist might agree with the Greek sophists that "convention is merely a contract into which the weak enter in the hope of depriving the strong of their natural rights"[12] but might nevertheless feel constrained to submit out of self-interest. The convention itself, however, might depend not only on self-interest and success in coordinating strategies, but also on some normatively motivated sanctioning behavior, if only a small bit of it.

AMBIGUITIES IN THE NOTION OF CONVENTION

Lewis notes that his use of Schelling's coordination games is scaffolding—he can restate his analysis of convention without it.[13] In fact,

[12] J. E. Raven, *Plato's Thought in the Making*, p. 8.
[13] Lewis, *Convention*, p. 3.

the scaffolding is not perfectly fitted to the final structure. There are ambiguities in the terms of the scaffolding and in the terms of the final structure (the definition above, of convention). Lewis acknowledges ambiguity in the notion of R in his definition (see section on "Convention" above). But there are also ambiguities in the notions of strategy and equilibrium in his game-theoretic analysis, and there is a related ambiguity in the way in which coordination, and hence convention, is achieved. Consider first the ambiguity in the notion of R—the notion of "a regularity R in the behavior of members of a population P."

Lewis says, "One thing we do *not* tolerate is a convention to which most people want there to be exceptions, however few the exceptions they want."[14] It is only a slight distortion of his context to read in this a reference to his later discussion ruling out mixed-strategy equilibria, which he says are equilibria "only in an extended sense and still not" coordination equilibria.[15] The latter claim seems to derive its meaning from the fact that he is speaking of mixed strategies over a part of a larger matrix, a part which is zero-sum (unlike the larger matrix). But consider the optimal-mix situations of Schelling, which are part of a more general class of games involving binary choice in a variably large population.[16] (Schelling uses L for left and R for right, but to avoid confusion with Lewis's R, I will use L for left and Q for right.) Some of these games are like binary-choice Prisoner's Dilemma in that each player prefers to choose L while all others choose Q, although as a group all are better off if all choose Q than if all choose L. The beauty of Schelling's graphic L-Q representation is that if one has a relevant binary-choice issue to test, one can easily enough contrive a pair of binary-choice curves to represent the issue. Suppose, for example, that the "regularity R in the behavior of members of a population P" is to choose Q 98 percent of the time and L 2 percent of the time. We can easily construct a Schelling L-Q graph in which L and Q choosers are equally rewarded at the overall *and* individual optimal mix of 98% Q-2% L. Consider the graph in figure 10-2. Should 98% Q-2% L count as a coordination equilibrium? If it does count, there are two coordination equilibria in the game (the other being 0% Q-100% L), so that either coordination equilibrium outcome could be a convention. From the verbal definition of coordination equilibrium, surely both of these outcomes qualify. Lewis's caveat against mixed strategies is not logically derived from his analysis, but rather is tacked onto it. But he has reason

14 Ibid., p. 77.
15 Ibid., p. 96.
16 Thomas C. Schelling, "Hockey Helmets, Concealed Weapons, and Daylight Savings"; and Schelling, *Micromotives and Macrobehavior*, pp. 213-243.

Figure 10-2.

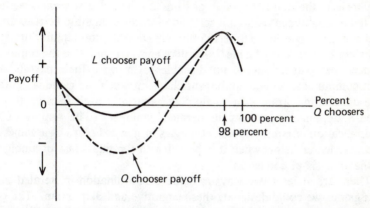

for the tacking, because permitting mixed strategies makes the notion of a regularity in behavior somewhat murky. Is everyone doing the *same* thing when 98 percent choose Q and 2 percent choose L? Suppose each person decides randomly whether to choose L or Q by drawing a chit marked L or Q from a hat filled with the relevant mix of chits. It should not be surprising that the notion of such regularity is hard to define, since the notion seems similar to the likewise ill-defined notions of synonymy and similarity.

This ambiguity, although it will play some role later, is not centrally important for the present discussion. Consider again the payoff matrix of game 2, a pure coordination game, in figure 10-1. There are two conspicuous coordination equilibria in the single-play game. However, for coordination to occur without communication and for the players to feel confident that they were thence coordinated might require several plays. In a lengthy iterated version of game 2, there would be many coordination equilibria, each resulting from each player's choosing the same strategy. For example, each might choose the peculiar strategy 10111001010110100 . . . , where the first entry is for the first play, the second for the second, and so forth, and 1 in an entry represents a choice of row or column I in that play, and 0 represents a choice of row or column II. The most likely coordination equilibrium for real players is presumably 000 . . . , or 111 . . . , but a pair of lovers of iambic poetry might coordinate on 0101010 . . . , and younger lovers of the new math might coordinate on the binary representation of the square root of 2. Lewis discusses games like game 2 as though they had only a pair of coordination equilibria (the pair that obtains in the single-play version of the game). However, if life were not limited, neither would be the set of coordination equilibria we could discover for stubbornly iterated plays of game 2. Although the explosion of coordination equilibria in the iterated version of game 2 might at first seem unsettling for the notion of convention, it seems on further thought to be reassuring, in that game 3 continues to have only one coordination equilibrium even in its iterated version. Game 3 is unlike games 1 and 2 in the important respect that players should not be able to improve their payoffs with tacit communication and contingent choosing when the game is iterated. The dominating strategy in single-play game 3 is itself iterated to produce a dominating strategy in iterated game 3. (The import of the multiplication of equilibria and strategies in iterated plays of a game will become clearer below when it is joined with the final class of ambiguity in the analysis of convention.)

There are at least two ways *to achieve* coordination in iterated plays of a game: we could designate these cognitive and Skinnerian. The cognitive way is to share, for whatever reasons, a common intuition. For example, if Byron and Shelley knew they were in the iterated version of game 2 with each other, both might begin to smile and to muse, "te-tum, te-tum, te-tum . . . ," and then go on to play by the strategy 010101 . . . , and thereby assure themselves the maximum payoffs. The Skinnerian way involves rewards and punishments, such as hitting the other player until that player learns to coordinate. One punishes or rewards the other player by making one's own future choices contingent on the other player's present choice. This can best be illustrated with a non-coordination game, the Prisoner's Dilemma of game 1.

Recall from the payoff matrix for Prisoner's Dilemma that the clear incentive is to defect in a single-play game under anomic conditions. For a convention to arise, play must be iterated. But as discussed in chapter 9, in iterated Prisoner's Dilemma the incentives change. One can make one's future choices contingent on the present choice of the other player. Hence, it is possible to create "extraplay" incentives to influence choices in the current play of the game. Of course, the possibility is not a logical necessity because, for example, the Row player may not perceive that the Column player is choosing contingently. For the extraplay incentives from contingent choosing to affect choices before hardened positions are established may require some sophistication in understanding the strategic implications of the game, as well as a successful bit of tacit communication between the two players.

For the iterated Prisoner's Dilemma, representation of possible strategies is painfully complex. As has been mentioned, Rapoport presents eight strategies (shown below) for the play of a twice-played, 2-person Prisoner's Dilemma.[17] In these strategies, let a noncontingent choice of

[17] Anatol Rapoport, *Two-Person Game Theory*, pp. 132–134.

Cooperation or Defection be represented simply as C or D. And let a contingent choice be represented by a sidewise tree, $<$, with as many arms as there are contingencies on which to base a choice, followed by shorthand entries, such as, "C if C on first play," which means "Choose C on this play if the other player chose C on the first play." Rapoport's eight strategies for twice-played Prisoner's Dilemma are as follows:

1. CC

2. C $<$ C if C on first play
       D otherwise

3. C $<$ D if C on first play
       C otherwise

4. CD

5. DC

6. D $<$ C if C on first play
       D otherwise

7. D $<$ D if C on first play
       C otherwise

8. DD

For single-play Prisoner's Dilemma, of course, there are only two strategies, C and D. Listing strategies analogous to Rapoport's for an open-ended Prisoner's Dilemma would be impossible, but the task could be undertaken by finite methods over infinite time. Most of the strategies (for example, cooperate the first two plays, defect the next thirty-seven, cooperate the next eleven, and so on) would seem uninteresting, if not ridiculous. (Incidentally, one should perhaps be leery of judging too quickly that a particular strategy is uninteresting. The great mathematician G. H. Hardy tells of visiting Srinivasa Ramanujan, lying ill with tuberculosis of which he soon died. Having difficulty with what to say, Hardy noted that he "had ridden in taxi-cab No. 1729, and remarked that the number seemed to me rather a dull one, and that I hoped it was not an unfavorable omen. 'No,' he replied, 'it is a very interesting number; it is the smallest number expressible as a sum of two cubes in two different ways.' "[18])

Since there was no coordination equilibrium in single-play Prisoner's Dilemma, one might expect to find none in the iterated game. If all strategies were noncontingent, clearly there would be no coordination equilibrium. For example, if both of us chose the strategy CCC . . . , you could improve your own net payoff by switching to a strategy of

[18] James R. Newman, ed., *The World of Mathematics* vol. 1, p. 375.

defection on one or more plays. If we both chose DDD . . . , one could make the other better off by switching to cooperation on some plays. One or the other of these conclusions will apply to every noncontingent strategy.

Contingent strategies are considerably more interesting. Consider the strategy, C < C if C < C if C < . . . , where "C if C" is very shorthand for "Choose C if the other player chose C on the previous move, and choose D otherwise." If both players have chosen this strategy, neither can be made better off by having one of the players switch to another strategy.[19] Indeed, for most alternative strategies one is likely to devise, both would suffer net losses. Hence, iterated Prisoner's Dilemma has a coordination equilibrium. Given one, it takes little ingenuity to devise another: D < C if D < C if DC < C if DCC < . . . , where "C if DC" means "Choose C if the sequence DC was chosen on the previous two plays, and choose D otherwise." These and numerous other contingent strategies (or "regularities in behavior") produce coordination equilibria in iterated Prisoner's Dilemma. (Unlike game 3 in figure 10-1, therefore, Prisoner's Dilemma has a dominating strategy in single play, but not in iterated play. This last claim is true even if the iterated-play game is not open-ended, but of fixed duration. But if the game is of fixed duration, there can be no coordination equilibrium.[20] Hence, there is no conventional outcome for a fixed-duration, iterated-play Prisoner's Dilemma.) Hence, there are conventional outcomes in iterated Prisoner's Dilemma, so that cooperation in the iterated game has strong rational motivations. I can say that I prefer to defect while the other player

[19] When Prisoner's Dilemma is iterated, it generally makes sense to add a further restriction to its definition. Let the payoffs to Row in a 2-person Prisoner's Dilemma be $R, S, T,$ and P as defined in text above at figure 9-2. The ordinal definition of 2-person Prisoner's Dilemma is $T > R > P > S$. (Anatol Rapoport and Albert M. Chammah, *Prisoner's Dilemma,* pp. 33–35.) If you and I are able to coordinate to maximize our payoffs, however, we need coordinate on always cooperating only if $R > \frac{1}{2}(T + S)$. If $R < \frac{1}{2}(T + S)$, we can do better if we alternate between my cooperating while you defect and your cooperating while I defect. There will still be coordination equilibria, but they will occur for joint strategies that are opposites in the sense that whenever you play C, I play D, and so forth, with your strategy and mine fully contingent on each other's actual plays. Rather than deal with such complications in the text we can simply assume that 2-person Prisoner's Dilemma requires that $R > \frac{1}{2}(T + S)$.

[20] Suppose there were. It would follow from having both players choose a given strategy S. That joint strategy must yield a choice of C for both players or D for both players (or some probabilistic mix of these) on the final play of the game. If one of the players now switched to the strategy identical to S except that it changed the final C or D (or the ratio of the mix), then either that player would benefit or the other would benefit, according as the joint strategy SS had produced a terminal play CC or DD (and analogously for the mixed strategy).

cooperates, but I cannot reasonably say that I prefer not to conform while the other player conforms to the convention of cooperating, because the convention is to cooperate if and only if the other does.

THE STAG HUNT

The discussion so far has been given over to setting up the central argument by clarifying its terms in the context of 2-person games rather than in the context of central interest—namely, the context of groups, even of very large groups. Rousseau's powerful, almost visual parable of the stag hunt is commonly taken as a metaphorical statement of this central interest in group cooperative action. A comparison of two different interpretations of the stag hunt parable should clarify the final analysis of contract by convention.

Midway through the *Discourse on the Origin and Foundations of Inequality Among Men* (the so-called *Second Discourse*), Rousseau is discussing how, in an anomic, nascent society of shortsighted men who command at least a rudimentary language,

> men could imperceptibly acquire some crude idea of mutual engage-ments and of the advantages of fulfilling them, but only insofar as present and perceptible interest could require. . . . Was it a matter of catching a deer, everyone clearly felt that for this pur-pose he ought faithfully to keep his post; but if a hare happened to pass within reach of one of them, there can be no doubt that he pursued it without scruple, and that having obtained his prey, he cared very little about having caused his companions to miss theirs.[21]

As is common in the writings of Rousseau, this passage is too summary to be entirely clear. It lends itself readily to two elaborations, such as those by Lewis and by Kenneth Waltz, with their different implications for group cooperation.[22]

Lewis fills in some of the detail omitted by Rousseau:

> Suppose we are in a wilderness without food. Separately we can catch rabbits and eat badly. Together we can catch stags and eat well. But if even one of us deserts the stag hunt to catch a rabbit, the stag will get away; so the other stag hunters will not eat unless they desert too.[23]

[21] Jean-Jacques Rousseau, *The First and Second Discourses*, p. 145.
[22] Lewis, *Convention*, pp. 7, 47; Kenneth N. Waltz, *Man, the State, and War*, pp. 167–169.
[23] Lewis, *Convention*, p. 7.

As Lewis points out,

> Each . . . will eat better by staying and taking his share of the stag
> when it is caught. But . . . [each] prefers to catch rabbits if even
> one of the others does.[24]

Note that this is not strictly a Prisoner's Dilemma. If everyone else
chases the stag, I too prefer to chase it, because I'll eat better that way
than I would if I went off alone to catch a rabbit. (That the situation is
not Prisoner's Dilemma also follows from the fact that a captured stag
is not a collective good in the sense of being available to all members of
the group whether or not they contribute to its capture. Exclusion is
not difficult, as any shirker who came along later to ask for a shank
or rib would no doubt learn soon enough.) Hence the hunt is a
coordination problem, because in any given play of the game, each
prefers to do what all others are doing, whether they are all chasing
a stag or all chasing rabbits. If the hunt is iterated daily, the outcome
may be a convention.

As was true of game 2 in figure 10-1, the conventions that may arise
from the nascent society of Rousseau's stag-hunting group in Lewis's
presentation are as numerous as one can imagine. The group may come
together every Monday for a stag hunt, and live off the carcass the
whole week. Or it may scatter daily into individual hare hunts. Or it
may alternate—a stag hunt this week, seven days of hare hunting
next week. Somewhere there is a twelve-year-old logician who would
have the patience to extend the list considerably. In this respect, as with
game 2, the two coordination equilibria of the single-play game multiply
into numerous coordination equilibria in the iterated game. Indeed,
since the stag hunt has meaning in life rather than merely in a matrix of
payoffs, one might expect an eventual quest for variety to lead even the
most individualistic or the most cooperative group into an occasional
stag or hare hunt. Hence, one would not expect the conventional outcome of the game to be simply an iteration of one of the coordination
equilibria in the original single-play game, but a mixture of the two.

In Lewis's version of the stag hunt, the problem of social cooperation
does not seem intractable. Any time a group of adequate size can stick
together long enough for the successful capture of a stag, its members
can expect others to want to join them for the next hunt. Even in its
single-play version, the stag hunt is a coordination game, not a Prisoner's
Dilemma, because it has two coordination equilibria, and it has no
dominating strategy. This is surely not the elemental problem of social
order that motivates social contract theory. The elemental problem is

24 Lewis, *Convention*, p. 47; see also ibid., n. at p. 95.

how to get someone to be orderly—when it is in his or her self-interest not to be. This is the problem of Prisoner's Dilemma and collective action.

As the reader may have noticed, there is an omission in the quotation above from Rousseau. The words left out are these: "for foresight meant nothing to them, and far from being concerned about a distant future, they did not even think of the next day." Waltz relies on this aspect of Rousseau's argument to interpret the stag hunt in such a way that it seems to be a Prisoner's Dilemma.[25] If one has a sufficiently limited time horizon, one might value an anticipated share of a stag less than an immediately available hare. In that case, one would see no point in the silly pun "hare today, gone tomorrow," and would prefer to defect whenever the opportunity arose to catch a hare. To pass up an opportunity to defect and grab a hare might be costly, because another in the group might defect, leaving the others unable to catch a stag and perhaps unable to find hares for themselves (at best, their gratifications would be delayed and therefore presently discounted). Hence, in a single play of Waltz's version of the stag hunt, there is not a coordination equilibrium, but rather a dominating strategy to defect at the first opportunity.

Does the *n*-person stag hunt or, more generally, the *n*-person Prisoner's Dilemma have coordination equilibria in its iterated version? As with 2-person Prisoner's Dilemma, the answer is that there are coordination equilibria if the game is open-ended. Consider the strategy:

$$C < C \text{ if all others chose } C < C \text{ if all others chose } C < \ldots$$

If all players have chosen this strategy, there can be no benefit to anyone from having one or more players switch strategies.[26] There are other strategies, on analogy with such strategies for iterated 2-person Prisoner's Dilemma, which produce other coordination equilibria in the game. (Again, as with 2-person Prisoner's Dilemma, there is neither a coordination equilibrium nor a dominating strategy in an iterated *n*-person Prisoner's Dilemma of fixed duration.)

[25] Waltz, *Man, the State, and War*, pp. 167–168.

[26] As discussed in n. 19 above, this joint strategy will yield a coordination equilibrium in 2-person Prisoner's Dilemma only if $R > \frac{1}{2}(T + S)$. We may generalize this condition from 2- to *n*-person Prisoner's Dilemma. The claim in the text would apply to any *n*-person Prisoner's Dilemma in which the best joint payoffs result when all choose C. If the best joint payoff results when some choose C while others choose D (as in games such as those represented in figure 10-1), to achieve coordination equilibria will require that players not all have the same strategy. While this qualification on the discussion in the text is messy, it does not undercut the argument for a contract-by-convention resolution of *n*-person Prisoner's Dilemma.

INCENTIVES IN PRISONER'S DILEMMA CONVENTIONS

We have now produced multiple coordination equilibria and, hence, the possibility of conventional outcomes in open-ended iterated Prisoner's Dilemma. Even for long interactions of fixed duration, we have some reason to expect conventional, largely cooperative outcomes during most of the interaction if the players are sophisticated. As discussed in chapter 9, only near the end of the fixed duration might we expect, from arguments of self-interest, that there will be defection. Prisoner's Dilemma differs from games of pure coordination in this last respect, because a convention in a game of pure coordination should be sustained down through a previously denoted terminal play. This difference is related to yet another ambiguity in Lewis's final definition of convention.

Condition 4 in the definition of convention (see above, section on "Convention") is: "almost everyone prefers that any one more conform to R, on condition that almost everyone conform to R." Suppose we are in an n-person Prisoner's Dilemma, and almost everyone is conforming by playing cooperatively. But I am *not* conforming; I am taking a free ride. Now "almost everyone prefers that any one more [for example, I] conform." Indeed, only I would not prefer that I conform. In a pure coordination game, of course, I would prefer to conform if almost everyone is doing so. Hence, Lewis's conditions seem to encourage conforming behavior when the best coordination equilibrium is almost being attained in a game that is a pure coordination game in its single-play version—but not in a game that is Prisoner's Dilemma in its single-play version. Nevertheless, it is possible in iterated Prisoner's Dilemma to achieve optimal joint payoffs for all players through implicit contract by convention. To show why, and to show that the resolution of a Prisoner's Dilemma by convention is not a contrivance, it is useful to compare the present argument from convention with Taylor's argument for substantial degrees of cooperation in iterated Prisoner's Dilemma.[27]

The direct conventional resolution of an isolated instance of iterated Prisoner's Dilemma is essentially the same as Taylor's in that it is achieved by staunch adherence to a strategy of making choices in each play or time period of the game contingent on the previous choices of others. Such contingent choosing by some might not seem compelling to others, either because they are too dense or because they hope the threat of following through on the contingent strategy will not be realized

[27] Michael Taylor, *Anarchy and Cooperation.*

(just as one might devastate one's enemy with nuclear weapons in the hope that the enemy after the fact will view counterdevastation as pointless, even though it was the enemy's avowed deterrent policy before the fact). The latter hope is not entirely unreasonable in some contexts, and it generally becomes more reasonable the larger the relevant group. There is a significant explanatory difference, however, between Lewis's focus on coordination equilibria and Taylor's focus on standard game-theoretic equilibria. All coordination equilibria are equilibria, but not all equilibria are coordination equilibria. In particular, in an iterated Prisoner's Dilemma, the outcome resulting from all players' always defecting is an equilibrium, but not a coordination equilibrium. Nor is any outcome in which there is a net of defecting over cooperating choices a coordination equilibrium. Outcomes of overwhelming defection can be achieved only by failure of convention.

Achievement of a standard equilibrium is often taken to be the characteristic outcome of rational choice. But certain equilibria can be achieved in a sense anomically, that is, by taking no one else's behavior into account. The peculiar fellow who at 4:30 P.M. on a Friday workday ventures out for a pleasure drive on a main urban thoroughfare will soon find himself in the unpleasurable equilibrium of a traffic jam. By taking others into account and coordinating his behavior with theirs, he could have given himself far greater pleasure. Similarly, players who are not oblivious of each other's interests in an iterated Prisoner's Dilemma might methodically ignore those interests and secure themselves an equilibrium outcome of continuous defection when they could have done much better. A coordination equilibrium, however, has great appeal over the Prisoner's Dilemma equilibrium of total defection. The appeal is that the coordination equilibrium can result from convention, in which event it is supported by a double incentive to each player. Each player has an interest in his or her own conforming and an interest in others' conforming. It is not in my interest for you always to defect in iterated Prisoner's Dilemma, and therefore total defection is not a coordination equilibrium. My interest in your conforming means that, if there is a way to do so at little or no net cost to me, I will want to give you further incentive to conform.

Smith argues that when a man "injures or insults us," or, we may add, takes a free ride on our backs,

> the glaring impropriety of this conduct, the gross insolence and injustice which it seems to involve in it, often shock and exasperate us more than all the mischief which we have suffered. To bring him back to a more just sense of what is due to other people, to

make him sensible of what he owes us, and of the wrong that he has done to us, is frequently the principal end proposed in our revenge, which is always imperfect when it cannot accomplish this.[28]

In small-scale, especially two-person, interactions our sanctions of failure to conform may be repaid well enough by subsequent conformance. In larger-scale interactions, however, my sanction of you may not return enough to me to allay the burden on me of endeavoring to effect the sanction. Hence, it would seem that more—such as the instinctual anger that Smith also discusses—is required to override the costs, because even if my "revenge" is *not* "imperfect," still I may gain only a minuscule part of the larger group's benefit from your being brought back "to a more just sense of what is due to other people. . . ." The problem of collective action is merely put off onto the group need for sanctioning nonconformers. But this need not be so difficult a problem as the original collective action itself.

Most obviously, perhaps, the problem of sanctioning nonconformers may be resolved by ethical motivations, as for example by a demand for fair play. But there is a more interesting resolution, which is related to the way in which the defining conditions for convention are likely to be met in actual collective action situations. Apart from (1) the incentive to cooperate (which is automatic in pure coordination games), these conditions are (2) knowledge of one another's preferences and comprehension of the situation, and (3) the sequential repetition of the same situation. It might seem that the latter two conditions are no more likely to be met than is the condition requiring the sanctioning of noncooperators. But, as discussed in the following chapter, all of these stringent conditions may be met through the overlapping nature of one's group-related activities, which may turn a sequence of one-time-only, apparently unrelated activities into the rough equivalent of an iterated Prisoner's Dilemma in which generally cooperative behavior may become rational.

[28] Adam Smith, *The Theory of Moral Sentiments*, pt. 2, sec. 3, chap. 1, p. 96.

11

ENFORCEMENT OF CONVENTIONS

A conspicuous difference between contract by convention in a Prisoner's Dilemma and a coordination game convention is that the former requires a larger cognitive element. Mere behavioral learning may lead away from the likelihood of successful contract in Prisoner's Dilemma situations, whereas it may be sufficient to induce the wayward to conform with newly arising coordination game conventions. Once established, either type of convention may be reinforced and sustained by behavioral motors in the absence of clear understanding of why the conventions are supported. But the motor that drives coordination games to conventional outcomes is absent from Prisoner's Dilemma, except to the extent that the expected value to me of the effect of my contribution on the behavior of others is greater than zero.

Olson argues that a group will fail strictly from the fact that no individual stands to benefit from the individual's own contribution alone. This conclusion is forceful for a one-shot effort, but not for an ongoing effort in which contingent choosing may be effective. Even in one-shot efforts, Olson's conclusion may not apply if the group itself is ongoing, since it may assimilate the present one-shot effort to a series of group-related efforts. Nevertheless, Olson's strong claim that larger groups are more likely to fail than smaller groups (smaller groups measured not in terms of absolute size, but in terms of k—which, it will be recalled is the size of the smallest efficacious subgroup) continues to have force even for ongoing efforts, because the effect of my contribution on the behavior of others is bound to be less in very large than in smaller groups.

The assimilation of one-shot efforts to the ongoing life and cooperative activities of a particular group can be generalized across efforts of
overlapping groups. The overlapping nature of various activities and
groups allows cooperative conventions to arise and, more importantly,
to be enforced. Below, I discuss the ways in which the overlapping
nature of varied activities in turn (1) provides opportunities for low-cost
sanctions, (2) creates the knowledge requisite for conventional behavior, and (3) establishes the rough equivalent of an iterated Prisoner's
Dilemma. In contexts in which the sanction, knowledge, and iteration
conditions are even approximately met, we can expect some degree of
success in enforcing Prisoner's Dilemma conventions. We can also
expect some degree of failure, for reasons discussed in chapter 12.

OVERLAPPING ACTIVITIES: SANCTIONS

As Hayek argues more generally of social institutions,[1] one cannot
simply look at the present set of apparent incentives deriving directly
from a particular group's structure and goals to obtain an adequate
accounting of why the members of the group behave as they do. Consider
how incentives in a large-group interaction can be built up out of
incentives in small-group interactions. For example, the backpacker's
norm of not littering might build from small-scale into large-scale
interactions. On the smallest scale, dyadic interaction, the disapprobation of one backpacker for another who litters may not be provoked by
what one would conceive of as a positive moral code. Rather, it would
have much in common with the momentary dislike or annoyance one
might feel toward a stranger who has gratuitously insulted oneself or
one's child. That is to say, its motives have more in common with
motives of self-interest than with commitment to a moral code or
norm: it might even approach the perfect revenge to which Smith
suggests we aspire; it might lead to correction of the disapproved
behavior to the advantage of the disapprover. If one sets up a
camera for a scenic shot, focuses, and discovers refuse in the view, one
has suffered a loss because one has a genuine self-interest in the beauty
of that bit of wilderness at that time. Though there may be no conventional way to obtain restitution from the litterers if they are identified
later on the trail, there still may be conventional ways to let them know
of one's disapproval.

Many conventions may be of such character that whether one conforms to them partly determines whether one can associate pleasurably

[1] Friedrich A. Hayek, *Law, Legislation, and Liberty* vol. 1 *Rules and Order*.

with a relevant group. For example, if one litters a wilderness area, the quality of one's relations with other backpackers may be affected. The same may not be true of littering at a crowded public park or beach where interactions may approach an anomic state (see further the discussion of the third interpretation of the stag hunt in chapter 12, section on "Failure to Arise"). Furthermore, self-interest may be much more intensely felt with regard to one's relations with the few other backpackers on the isolated trail than with the crowd on the beach. In Schelling's titular terms, micromotives produce macrobehavior,[2] but the results may be opposites in the littering examples, indeed almost perversely so: beach users might litter a beach to which they expect to return week after week, while backpackers might refrain from littering an area they may never expect to see again.

In these two examples there seem to be substantial size effects. But it is not only group size per se that makes the difference. Many clubs of backpackers with their separate conventions of not littering the wilderness might have a grand meeting on a beach, and they might there readily follow their conventions. In part, this would no doubt be because ongoing relationships among subgroups would make this large crowd less anomic than the usual beach crowd, but it would also be because this crowd would have a convention already available to it. And there is more.

Is the behavior of backpackers on the beach somehow necessarily moral, while their behavior on the trail was perhaps rational? No. This is the essential meaning of Lewis's convention: a convention is honored because, once it exists, it is in our interest to conform to it. Because we have a convention, we have expectations about each other's behavior; and because we have expectations, we suffer costs if we do not live up to them. The unfavorable responses evoked by my failure to conform are an additional cost of my not conforming. Conventions are like social institutions that have power over individual decisions because there are expectations built on the institutions, implying costs to those who challenge the institutions. For the backpackers, the cost of delivering a sanction is even lower at the beach gathering than it would be out on the trail, because on the beach the sanctioner will be backed up by the larger society of other backpackers—indeed, one might sooner expect sanctioners to feel rewarded than burdened by their own sanctioning of miscreants. The costs of being sanctioned, on the contrary, will be escalated on the beach.

Lon Fuller remarks that the "central problem of 'interpretation' in customary law is that of knowing when to read into an act or a pattern

2 Thomas C. Schelling, *Micromotives and Macrobehavior.*

of repetitive acts an obligatory sense such as that which may attach to a promise explicitly spelled out in words." He offers the following resolution:

> Where by his actions toward B, A has (whatever his actual intentions may have been) given B reasonably to understand that he (A) will in the future in similar situations act in a similar manner, and B has, in some substantial way, prudently adjusted his affairs to the expectation that A will in the future act in accordance with this expectation, then A is bound to follow the pattern set by his past pattern of actions toward B. This creates an obligation by A to B. If the pattern of interaction followed by A and B then spreads through the relevant community, a rule of general customary law will have been created.[3]

Long before courts would support them in such interpretations, individuals may presume that when such a pattern spreads through a relevant community, others have established obligations, and they may sanction those others for failure to fulfill the obligations. If this argument seems implausible, that is perhaps because it is stated so generally. Consider an easy example. Suppose I yell "Fire!" in a crowded theater. I would be a fool to claim lack of responsibility for the ensuing havoc on the ground that I was misunderstood because when I yell "Fire!" I mean "Atchoo." No doubt the mangled crowd would seek me out for sanctions. When courts stand behind such sanctions, the pattern of interaction has become a legally binding contract by convention.

All of this may sound circular. But the circularity is only apparent and is more a matter of fact than of reasoning.[4] The creation of Fuller's obligations requires induction from the past existence of the relevant customary behavior, so that his argument is not simply that one is obligated because one is obligated. It is commonplace that social concepts, such as "money" and "institutionalization," are founded on such

[3] Lon L. Fuller, "Law and Human Interaction," pp. 66–67.

[4] Hume concludes that justice is an artificial rather than a natural virtue, because there would otherwise be circularity in our understanding of justice. He first argues that "we have naturally no real or universal motive for observing the laws of equity, but the very equity and merit of that observance; and as no action can be equitable or meritorious, where it cannot arise from some separate motive, there is here an evident sophistry and reasoning in a circle. Unless, therefore, we will allow, that nature has establish'd a sophistry, and render'd it necessary and unavoidable, we must allow, that the sense of justice and injustice is not deriv'd from nature, but arises artificially, tho' necessarily from education, and human conventions" (David Hume, *A Treatise of Human Nature*, bk. 3, pt. 2, sec. 1, p. 483).

apparent circularity, as Weber and others point out, because the concepts imply (one might say "mean") the processes through which they come to apply. Without citing Weber, H. L. A. Hart notes that "it is true, as we have already emphasized in discussing the need for and the possibility of sanctions, that if a system of rules is to be imposed by force on any, there must be a sufficient number who accept it voluntarily. Without their voluntary cooperation, thus creating *authority,* the coercive power of law and government cannot be established."[5] On Reinhard Bendix's account, Weber is even more explicit:

> Like the other types of authority, legal domination rests upon the belief in its legitimacy, and every such belief is in a sense question-begging. For example, charismatic authority depends upon a belief in the sanctity or exemplary character of an individual person, but this person loses his authority as soon as those subject to it no longer believe in his extraordinary powers. Charismatic authority exists only as long as it "proves" itself, and such "proof" is either believed by the followers or rejected. The belief in the legitimacy of a legal order has a similarly circular quality. . . . [L]aws are legitimate if they have been enacted; and the enactment is legitimate if it has occurred in conformity with the laws prescribing the procedures to be followed. This circularity is intentional.[6]

Similarly, to establish a convention in a particular group is to give the members of the group power to sanction each other's violations of the convention.

In support of Weber's argument on charismatic authority, we may note that history is rife with examples of the sudden loss of charismatic legitimacy. Sabbatai Sevi, the seventeenth-century "mystical messiah," might today have a religious following in the millions, had he let himself be executed rather than convert to Islam. But he let his charisma die that he might live.[7] In a very different manner, the King of Kings, Shahanshah Mohammad Reza Pahlavi, another victim of Islam, lost his authority in part from the rapid creation of charisma about an alternative convention that was built up out of ever larger bits of evidence that the alternative was possible.

[5] H. L. A. Hart, *The Concept of Law,* p. 196; see also, ibid., p. 193; and Lon L. Fuller, *The Morality of Law,* pp. 200–224.

[6] Reinhard Bendix, *Max Weber: An Intellectual Portrait,* pp. 418–419. See also, Bendix, *Nation-Building and Citizenship,* pp. 21–27; and Karl Marx, *The Eighteenth Brumaire of Louis Bonaparte,* p. 87.

[7] Gershom Scholem, *Sabbatai Sevi: The Mystical Messiah.*

Apparent circularity may not only lie beneath social institutions, but also beneath personal values. Swann discovered the features of his beloved Odette in a Sistine fresco by Botticelli, and

> albeit his admiration for the Florentine masterpiece was probably based upon his discovery that it had been reproduced in her, the similarity enhanced her beauty also, and rendered her more precious in his sight. Swann reproached himself with his failure, hitherto, to estimate at her true worth a creature whom the great Sandro would have adored, and counted himself fortunate that his pleasure in the contemplation of Odette found a justification in his own system of aesthetic. He told himself that, in choosing the thought of Odette as the inspiration of his dreams of ideal happiness, he was not, as he had until then supposed, falling back, merely, upon an expedient of doubtful and certainly inadequate value, since she contained in herself what satisfied the utmost refinement of his taste in art.[8]

Of course, Swann is so obsessive as to be able to turn anything in upon anything else in his head, and social institutions such as money and the role of charismatic leaders may seem nearly unique in the scheme of daily life. But circular reinforcement is merely clearer in the cases of Swann, earlier-day money, and charisma, than in numerous other pervasive instances.[9] The circular creation of obligations in conventions may be among the more commonplace of these. And once others think I am obligated to them in some way, they may feel justified in sanctioning me, if need be, to force me to live up to my obligation.

In what forms are sanctions delivered to those members who violate a group's convention? Not least in effectiveness can often be mere disapprobation. But there are also other devices more nearly in the nature of economic exchanges. Groups may create, by their cooperation, not only collective goods from whose enjoyment exclusion is not possible, but also other goods from whose enjoyment exclusion *is* possible. Such auxiliary goods may be used as incentives to reward or punish con-

[8] Alas, this is Proust, and Swann's dreams of ideal happiness are not to be: "He failed to observe that this quality would not naturally avail to bring Odette into the category of women whom he found desirable, simply because his desires had always run counter to his aesthetic taste." Marcel Proust, *Remembrance of Things Past* vol. 1, pp. 171–172.

[9] For some less elegant instances of circular reinforcement, see Russell Hardin, "Rationality, Irrationality, and Functionalist Explanation." Fuller notes of the circular interaction which makes law work that a "complete failure in this interaction is so remote from ordinary experience that the significance of the interaction itself tends to be lost from our intellectual perspective" (Fuller, *Morality of Law*, p. 219).

formance or nonconformance to the more difficult Prisoner's Dilemma convention. The use of such sanctions need not require conscious intent. One may simply not trust those who do not conform to a convention that evidently serves them well if those same individuals benefit additionally from their nonconformance. Hence, in forming groups to benefit from other conventions, one may have a natural proclivity to exclude those who have not conformed in the past. Furthermore, one may exercise the sanction of exclusion not only with respect to the larger group affected by a Prisoner's Dilemma convention, but also with respect to subgroups or even substantially different groups.

Before leaving the discussion of sanctions, note how they can be turned to perverse uses. If conventions are to be supported in part by sanctions, the conventions may stray from serving our interests. Consider how strong and commonplace the claim of obligation may become. John Rawls argues that "when a number of persons engage in a mutually advantageous cooperative venture according to rules, and thus restrict their liberty in ways necessary to yield advantages for all, those who have submitted to these restrictions *have a right* to similar acquiescence on the part of those who have benefitted from their submission [emphasis added]."[10] Whereas Fuller based laws on conventional expectations, Rawls more boldly deduces rights from them. He makes an even stronger claim than did Gompers, in his argument for the union shop, that "persons who are desirous of becoming beneficiaries of an agreement should become parties to that agreement, and that they should bear the equal responsibility which such an agreement involves."[11] Whatever philosophers or social scientists might think of these views, people in their daily lives may instinctively hold some variant of them and may act accordingly.[12]

---

[10] John Rawls, *A Theory of Justice,* p. 112. Hart, to whom Rawls is indebted for this view, gives a fuller account. (H. L. A. Hart, "Are There Any Natural Rights?" pp. 185–186).

[11] Samuel Gompers, "Discussion at Rochester, N.Y., on the Open Shop—'The Union Shop is Right'—It Naturally Follows Organization," p. 221.

[12] Heidler lectures Marya, the woman at the hollow center of Jean Rhys's *Quartet,* on an excessive convention:

"My darling child," said Heidler with calmness, "your whole point of view and your whole attitude to life is impossible and wrong and you've got to change it for everybody's sake."

He went on to explain that one had to keep up appearances. That everybody had to. Everybody had for everybody's sake to keep up appearances. It was everybody's duty, it was in fact what they were there for.

"You've got to play the game." (Jean Rhys, *Quartet,* p. 113.)

Robert Nozick strongly objects to the Rawls view:

> One cannot, whatever one's purposes, just act so as to give people
> benefits and then demand (or seize) payment. . . . So the fact
> that we partially are "social products" in that we benefit from
> current patterns and forms created by the multitudinous actions
> of a long string of long-forgotten people, forms which include
> institutions, ways of doing things, and language . . . , does not
> create in us a general floating debt which the current society can
> collect and use as it will.[13]

Less vociferously, one can note that sanctions for nonconformance to
some convention may be applied to someone whose interests are actually
harmed by general conformance to that convention (the power of the
law, for example, may be directed against malefactors *or* against
victimized groups).[14] This being so, it is in the interest of some to
protest (even contrary to fact) that their nonconformance should *not*
be sanctioned because they do not benefit from general conformance and
should not have their losses compounded by their conforming or being
sanctioned. Hence, a sophisticated egoist might successfully take a free
ride on a convention for dealing with an iterated Prisoner's Dilemma,
which would make no sense in a convention for dealing with a pure
coordination game. It is also true, however, that in conventions of
interest to us in the collective resolution of Prisoner's Dilemma situations,
we will often, perhaps commonly, have good reason to judge whether
another's protestations are honest, and the other will know that we do,
so that we often should not expect wholesale deception. Revelation of
preferences per se will generally not be the central problem in establishing or maintaining cooperative Prisoner's Dilemma conventions.

OVERLAPPING ACTIVITIES: KNOWLEDGE

From the following statement of Lewis regarding the knowledge conditions for conventional behavior, preference-revelation problems might
seem to be a very serious obstacle to the generalization of convention to
cooperation in iterated Prisoner's Dilemma situations. He says, "The
common knowledge requirement involves universal quantifications over
[the relevant population] *P*. . . . We need not allow any exception to
these [quantifications]; anyone who might be called an exception might
better be excluded from *P*."[15] This seems to be a devastating exclusion

[13] Robert Nozick, *Anarchy, State, and Utopia*, p. 95.
[14] Again see Hart, *Concept of Law*, pp. 196–197.
[15] David K. Lewis, *Convention*, pp. 76–77.

for the class of conventions—conventions of language—which most interest Lewis. But the exclusion is not as sweeping as one might infer.

In Lewis's account, convention is often much too conscious and articulated a process, perhaps because of its paternity in Schelling's coordination games, which, like game theory more generally, approach the ultimate in conscious rationality. But the apparently imposing "universal quantifications" involved in Lewis's knowledge requirement are in fact not very forceful, because the knowledge may be a very weak version of knowledge. It may be merely potential, irremediably non-verbal (for example, dancers' knowledge of how to coordinate their movements), and liberally generalized from many particular instances.[16] Thus it may bear little resemblance to the knowledge of a player of some of Schelling's coordination games. It may be more nearly like the "meanings" inherent in common law, since the common law, in Lord Mansfield's elegant formula, "does not consist of particular cases, but of general principles, which are illustrated and explained by those cases."[17]

That many of these principles may be nowhere written down or articulated need not reduce their force in governing our expectations of one another's behavior in relevant contexts. Fuller recalls the old-fashioned legal term "intendment" which, significantly in the present context, is a term commonly applied to meaning as established in common law. "Our institutions and our formalized interactions with one another are accompanied by certain interlocking expectations that may be called intendments, even though there is seldom occasion to bring these underlying expectations across the threshold of consciousness."[18] For example, when one votes, one presumably expects that the vote will be properly counted. We may say that the institution of elections carries an intendment that the votes be faithfully counted. Such an intendment may so be taken for granted that it need not be specified by statute. A striking example may be found in the institution of (large) gift-giving, which seems, on Fuller's very brief account, to carry with it the intendment of some degree of reciprocity. Fuller notes that

> our courts do not openly avow the principle of Roman and Con-
> tinental law that ingratitude by a donee gives the donor the power
> to revoke a gift. And yet, if we look to what our courts do, rather
> than what they say, it is arguable that the principle receives con-
> siderable recognition in this country. Frequently where the donee

16 Ibid., pp. 63–68.
17 Hayek, *Rules and Order*, p. 86.
18 Fuller, *Morality of Law*, pp. 217–219.

proves himself ungrateful, our courts are able to find that the gift was made on the condition of a certain line of conduct by the donee, or was induced by fraud.[19]

What, then, is the nature of our common knowledge that it may enable us to achieve a convention? No one of us need know who all of us are. There need merely be overlapping networks of knowledge, possibly even disjoint networks. Thus, I may not know whether A's interests are well served by our convention, but B will know. Further, others' knowledge of my preferences, of my comprehension of a relevant collective action situation, and of my knowledge, in turn, of their preferences and comprehension may be influenced not only by the present circumstances, but also, and perhaps more importantly, by the evidence of previous interactions largely unrelated to our present Prisoner's Dilemma. Hence, for me to free ride without serious expectation of sanctions may require that I have already established a pattern of iconoclastic free riding. Whether it would be rational to establish such a pattern may be a question beyond answering. However, one could generalize that it would be more likely rational if one's collective action interactions were more commonly with large than with small groups, and that it would be the more likely rational the more others established such a pattern. That there are many perhaps rationally determined cantankerous people is evident from experience. That it could be easy to establish a pattern of obstinate free riding while escaping some conceivable sanctions is suggested by commonplace arguments that one can establish a reputation for almost anything, including self-serving irrationality.

Clearly, however, the degree of cooperation may depend on the quality of knowledge generally available. The fund of common knowledge is likely to be far more narrowly defined for very large than for small groups. Hence, a large group is less likely to be able to focus on a mutually cooperative behavior that involves precise or complex understanding of alternative ends or means to group ends. For example, if a large group is to coordinate by a rule of fairness, the rule will have to be relatively unobjectionable in the sense that attractive alternative rules not be available to compete with it.

All of the conclusions in chapter 10 about the force of contingent strategies in iterated Prisoner's Dilemma would follow readily if, as with the uncontrollable Doomsday Machine to deter nuclear war, every player could make all others believe without doubt that he or she would resolutely follow through on the contingent threats. But believing such

19 Lon L. Fuller, *Legal Fictions*, n. at p. 80.

things without doubt is not always possible—indeed, belief without doubt may be an empty category for many of us. Suppose that ninety-nine players in an iterated Prisoner's Dilemma chose the strategy "C if ninety-nine others chose C on the previous play," while the one remaining member of the group chose the noncontingent D strategy, and that all received a substantial net benefit even when only ninety-nine members cooperated. It might seem foolish of the ninety-nine cooperators to defect just because they had planned or threatened to. Indeed, after trying, at substantial loss, to punish the loner for stubborn defection, the ninety-nine might all begin to suspect that they would gain more over the long run by tolerating a free rider than by further attempting to get the loner to cooperate. Hence, what one's strategy ought to be may be learned after playing for a while, because what is the best strategy depends on the behavior of other players.

It may seem that this observation pushes us back to Olson's logic of collective action, in particular to the conclusion that large groups will fail to cooperate—because if one player can defect profitably in this game, then probably so can two, and so forth, until the returns for cooperation no longer justify cooperation by the dwindling number. Sometimes this dismal conclusion will be valid, but not always. One may not only follow through on one's contingent threat not to cooperate if others do not, but one may even feel rationally compelled to do so— because whether one follows through in the present game may affect one's credibility in other games. Suppose I am the hundredth player, the lone defector in the game above, and you are one of the contingent cooperators. I may have come to believe from your past record that your contingent threat to defect if I continue to defect is, say, roughly 50 percent credible. My defection, then, would yield an expected loss to the group of my own contribution plus 50 percent of yours, plus relevant percentages of others' contributions. (The functional relationship would presumably be more complex and more severe than simply additive.) It may therefore be irrational for me to continue to defect, given my beliefs about others' credibility.[20]

Since a major factor in making rational choices in Prisoner's Dilemma games is one's knowledge of others—of their threat credibility as well as their sophistication and their actual interests—group size will be important for reasons other than that argued by Olson. In iterated Prisoner's Dilemma involving a very large group (where large means large k), I cannot judge well enough from most others' past behavior whether my contingent threats will affect their present behavior or

[20] This is a central issue in Norman Frohlich, Joe A. Oppenheimer, and Oran R. Young, *Political Leadership and Collective Goods*.

whether their contingent threats are credible.[21]   Therefore, only if this large group is overlaid by a network of much smaller subgroups, each concerned with its own conventional behaviors with respect to specific subgroup goals, can my choices in the large-group Prisoner's Dilemma seem to have compelling strategic value in influencing others (as, for example, by affecting the assessment made by members of my subgroup about my credibility in carrying out contingent threats or contingent promises). It is hard to imagine that conventional behavior or strategies of contingent cooperation could resolve Prisoner's Dilemmas if these occurred exclusively in very large groups. Large-group Prisoner's Dilemmas might be resolved as a by-product of smaller subgroup interactions. But this could be a strictly spontaneous voluntaristic by-product —not the organized by-product of Olson's analysis as discussed in chapter 2.

The argument for large-scale contract by convention as a product of overlapping small-group interactions recalls Peter Laslett's "The Face to Face Society." Laslett argues that "it seems to be the case that any given sample of individuals capable of acting collectively has only one procedure open to it. It must discover from within itself, or have discovered for it, a group of a critical size which can act, and act continuously, as a face to face society."[22] He seems to be concerned with decision making under crisis, not with acting more generally. Crisis decision making requires "total intercourse between the personalities, conscious and unconscious, and it may well be that the solution of the crisis takes place as much as a result of what is neither formulated nor expressed as of . . . ratiocination."[23] This is possible because in a face-to-face society "everyone in it *knows* everyone else in it . . . [and]

[21] Taylor thinks mistaken the view that promises and threats in noncooperative games will not be credible merely because "the player in question is not bound to carry them out . . . and it may not be in his best interest to do so" (Michael Taylor, *Anarchy and Cooperation,* p. 32). The view is not wholly mistaken, as one can observe from parenting, one of the most difficult tricks of which is actually to carry out threats that have failed to deter. The parent who says "No movie if . . ." may find that indeed "This hurts me worse than it does you." It is not easy to adopt a threat strategy and then stick to it if alternatives are more attractive when threats fail. But Taylor's unexplicated belief is at least partially explicated by Thomas C. Schelling, *The Strategy of Conflict,* esp. chap. 1. Among other possibilities, one can establish a reputation for carrying out one's threats (such as actually following through after saying "No movie if . . ."). This is the striking difference between anomic single-play Prisoner's Dilemma and iterated Prisoner's Dilemma: one can establish a reputation in iterated play. Clearly, one can do so as well in a diverse set of Prisoner's Dilemma interactions.

[22] Peter Laslett, "The Face to Face Society," p. 160.

[23] Ibid., p. 158.

is never called upon to co-operate in any other way than by being present at what is going on."[24] These are conditions that commonly enhance the prospects for tacit coordination of mutually beneficial action, whether in crisis or otherwise.

To summarize, in general, contract by convention depends on knowledge conditions—the more people whose behavior one must know well enough to consider it predictable, the less one will be able to know about each of them on average. Hence, the prospects for successful contract by convention decline as group size increases. Moreover, the credibility of a strategy of contingent choosing must commonly fall off as the size of the population being "threatened" with contingent defection increases. (This will, of course, not be true if cooperation by virtually all group members is required to produce net benefits.) One's credibility is perhaps most likely to be judged from one's behavior in similar circumstances in the past. (Unfortunately, lack of the sophistication needed to understand conventional behavior could be confused with opportunistic free riding. Hence, one might follow through with contingent defection not because others have attempted a free ride, but because they have been too dense to comprehend one's threat.) Overlapping activities are therefore perhaps most important for their relation to reputation, or rather for the dependence of one's reputation on one's behavior in a cluster of activities.[25]

Finally, note that knowledge and sanctioning may interact constructively. The incidence of the actual use of sanctions may not be very high, because the possibility of invoking sanctions may make coordination far easier.[26] Two parties to a potential contract can enter into it because there is a law of contracts backed up by the sanctioning power of the state. Without such law, they would be more constrained. In particular, they could not so confidently enter into one-shot contracts, and hence might never or only far more slowly come to establish ongoing exchange relations. This is perhaps the least misanthropic interpretation of Hobbes's arguments about the state of nature. He argues that "though the wicked were fewer than the righteous, yet because we cannot distinguish them, there is a necessity of heeding, anticipating, subjugating, self-defending, ever incident to the most honest and fairest conditioned."[27] For Hobbes, coercion is necessary to prevent the few who may be ill-intentioned from harming the many

[24] Ibid., pp. 157–158.
[25] See n. 21 above.
[26] See further, Fuller, "Law and Human Interaction," p. 73, on the coordination function of most branches of law.
[27] Thomas Hobbes, *De Cive*, p. 100.

who are well-intentioned. Even more important in the present context, the possibility of sanction is valuable for letting the well-intentioned, who do not require sanctions, risk being cooperative on the secure knowledge that those with whom they come to interact are similarly well-intentioned.

OVERLAPPING ACTIVITIES: ITERATION

In addition to the possibility that conformance with one convention may be enforced by sanctions derived from other conventions, a specific game need not be iterated for a specific group in order for a convention to develop. Rather, various members of a large class of related or similar games may be faced more or less sequentially by substantially over-lapping groups. In this manner, a convention covering the behavior of a very large class of people, none of whom interacts personally with more than a fraction of the class, can be built up out of smaller sub-group interactions in a large class of situations.

Barry argues that "it would require trust, but hardly altruism, for all concerned to settle on some scheme from which all would benefit compared with the alternatives of deadlock or anarchy."[28] The difference between altruism and trust, he suggests, is illustrated in the difference between single-play and infinitely iterated Prisoner's Dilemma. In essence, one can trust another if one knows there will be opportunity to sanction the other if one's trust proves to have been misplaced. This may seem to distort the meaning we often have in speaking of "trust," since some of us may trust selected others under more difficult circumstances, such as when the only sanctions against them for abusing our trust would be from their own consciences. But it captures much of the behavioral source of trust, perhaps even all of it for such people as Ruskin, who wrote, "I cannot trust other people without perpetual looking after them."[29] It also suggests that our expectations about one another's behavior in, say, a particular Prisoner's Dilemma situation may be based on more general evidence than merely past behavior in the same situation. The confidence we place in our trust of someone may be built up out of varied experiences. And if we are so doubting as to require "perpetual looking after them," we can often count on varied future interactions to offer us opportunity for retribution against any abusers. Hence, it is not necessary that we be locked into a sequence of plays of the same particular Prisoner's Dilemma for us to be able to

---

[28] Brian Barry, *Political Argument*, p. 253.
[29] Cited in *Oxford English Dictionary* under the word "trust."

react to each other as though we were.[30] Hence, we can command cooperation among ourselves through our devices for achieving narrowly, behaviorally defined trust.

The simplest generalization from an actual instance of iterated Prisoner's Dilemma would be to a set of diverse Prisoner's Dilemma interactions. If these were entered sequentially by a given set of people, and if the sequence were not contrived to yield substantially decreasing returns for cooperation as the sequence progressed, the resulting "game" would be strategically equivalent to an iterated Prisoner's Dilemma. The most complex generalization would be to the sort of social context in which we commonly find ourselves. Not only the games in the sequence, but also the group membership varies. As Hayek says of his "spontaneous orders," "The significance of the abstract character of such orders rests on the fact that they persist while all the particular elements they comprise, and even the number of such elements, change."[31] This is also the significance of an institution in Philip Selznick's analysis.[32]

The sociologist's traditional notion that a weave of mutual expectations holds society together is not an extrarational notion. Indeed, it is not even necessarily cut through, as is often supposed, by the demands of egoistic self-interest in Prisoner's Dilemma situations, which are now seen to be pervasive.

[30] Runciman and Sen wrongly dismiss consideration of the cooperative aspects of iterated Prisoner's Dilemma on the ground that "pure repetitions are normally not possible in social games. . . . In fact, in the case of the 'prisoner's dilemma' itself, pure repetitions will be difficult and many repetitions unlikely" (W. G. Runciman and Amartya K. Sen, "Games, Justice and the General Will," n. at p. 555).

[31] Hayek, *Rules and Order*, p. 39.

[32] Philip Selznick, *Leadership in Administration*.

12

LIMITS TO CONTRACT
BY CONVENTION

The last chapter closed with the sociologist's dream of ideal happiness, which seems all too often not to be. If the analysis of contract by convention is apt, there are conspicuous issues to investigate in the hope of finding structured explanations as to why such contracts often do *not* regulate behavior in ongoing Prisoner's Dilemmas. Against contract theories of the *formation* of the state, Comte argued that "to attribute to [the principle of cooperation] the formation of the social state, as it was the fashion of the last century to do, is a capital error; but when the association has once begun, there is nothing like this principle of cooperation for giving consistency and character to the combination."[1]

The issue in chapter 11 was largely how to maintain a contract by convention. But before one can be maintained, it must first arise. This chapter deals with issues related to the beginnings and endings of conventions: the first section discusses obstacles to creating conventions; the second section, ways in which they are created; and the final section on termination considers ways in which nascent and even long-enduring contracts by convention may fail. Here, two of the best-studied contracts by convention—oligopolistic cooperation (as in cartels) and arms control—give ample insight into the circumstances that put cooperation under stress.

[1] Auguste Comte, *Auguste Comte and Positivism*, p. 272.

FAILURE TO ARISE

Under what circumstances will conventions fail to develop? In a large-number group or a society in which single-play Prisoner's Dilemma is encountered repeatedly and anomically so that one cannot identify one's adversary-partner in any play, and cannot expect others honestly to reveal how they choose in plays of the games, and does not meet the same adversary in sequential encounters—under these conditions there can be no conventional outcomes, and narrowly self-interested members of the group would never play cooperatively. This is a third possible interpretation of Rousseau's stag hunt parable. Perhaps the coming together of a particular group of, say, five potential stag hunters is anomic and noniterative in the sense that the five will scatter after their one-time group effort, whether successful or unsuccessful. Each might, the next day or next week, join a new group of five, but there might be slight chance that any group would re-form for a second hunt. Moreover, it might be unlikely that any one hunter would remember enough about the behavior of specific others to enable the larger population to develop a conventional behavior of its own as an alternative to costly individualism. Contingent choosing and sanctioning would be impossible.

Recall Marx's vivid characterization of the nineteenth-century French peasantry, who

> live in similar conditions but without entering into manifold relations with one another. . . . Each individual peasant family is almost self-sufficient; it itself produces the major part of its consumption and thus acquires its means of life more through exchange with nature than in intercourse with society. . . . [Without ongoing relationships among themselves,] the great mass of the French nation is formed by simple addition of homologous magnitudes, much as potatoes in a sack form a sack of potatoes. . . . [The peasants] are consequently incapable of enforcing their class interest in their own name. . . .[2]

In a more mundane context, the so-called "market for lemons" is a problem of anomie. An individual who owns a defective car, a lemon, can expect to be able to sell it for about the going market rate for that kind (quality, age, *apparent* condition, and mileage) of car so long as there is no reasonable way for prospective buyers to know it is a lemon. Hence, owners of such cars have extra incentive to sell privately, and presumably do so more often than owners of very good cars in order to

[2] Karl Marx, *The Eighteenth Brumaire of Louis Bonaparte*, pp. 123–124.

be rid of their lemons before the next rounds of repairs have to be made. Hence, the market price, reflecting the disproportionate frequency of sales of lemons, will be lower for a given kind of car than the average value of that kind of car. But as a result, owners of nonlemons have incentive not to sell their cars (or incentive to sell them to trusting friends), being generally unable to prove their cars are better than the average for the market, and thus able to sell only at prices substantially below values.[3] There is, therefore, a Gresham's law for used cars. A seller involved in ongoing relationships with a prospective buyer would have incentive to state the actual value of the car even if it was a lemon, and the buyer would have reason to trust a claim that it was not a lemon. But sales through classified ads in the newspapers seldom involve seller–buyer pairs with ongoing relationships. Hence, the general quality of anomie implies that the possibilities for beneficial exchange are depressed. The best recourse for buyers may be to go to large dealers who depend on maintaining a good reputation and who may therefore stand behind the—higher-priced—cars they sell. Individual sellers have no comparable recourse.

The anomie of the third interpretation of the stag hunt is perhaps the most obvious barrier to conventional resolution of a Prisoner's Dilemma, because it reduces the interaction to unrelated single-play occurrences. But conventions may fail to arise in more favorable contexts as well. Indeed, that one convention has arisen means that numerous others have not. Hence, it may be that of a set of possible conventions—all preferable to no convention, but some of them preferable to others—a less beneficial one will arise, blocking a more beneficial one.[4]

In the static analysis of choice, one simply checks the costs and benefits of alternative actions and then determines which action is best. In the dynamic analysis, the fundamental problem often is to explain how the costs and benefits have come to be what they are. For this reason, to see that a convention "works" and to understand how it is maintained may be easy. To explain how it arose may be beyond our capacity, because it may have arisen out of a series of accidental choices,

---

[3] George A. Akerlof, "The Market for 'Lemons': Quality Uncertainty and the Market Mechanism." See also Geoffrey Heal, "Do Bad Products Drive Out Good?" and Thomas C. Schelling, *Micromotives and Macrobehavior,* pp. 99–100. This argument has affinities with the exit part of Albert O. Hirschman's *Exit, Voice, and Loyalty.* See further, chap. 5 above, under "Inequality," where it is argued that those who want more or better than they get from group effort may withdraw from the group and seek market substitutes. In the market for lemons, those who want more for their cars and those who want more for their money withdraw.

[4] See further, Russell Hardin, "Rationality, Irrationality, and Functionalist Explanation."

insights, and interactions too numerous for anyone to know, and mostly unpredictable even though each seems explicable in hindsight. A strong claim of rational explanations is that they yield clear predictions on relatively little data. This is often considerably less true than it would seem. A careful microanalysis of a particular case may require far more knowledge than is assumed in the common claim, and yet the case may nevertheless be powerfully explained by the assumption of rationality. But there may be a post hoc one-sidedness to what we explain. We may often have confidence in our understanding of the rise of a particular convention without having similar confidence in our understanding of why some other convention did not arise in its place.

THE RISE OF CONTRACTS BY CONVENTION

How do conventions arise? Clearly, some pure coordination game conventions arise spontaneously, and some come into being through the agency of a central coordinator. A local convention by which one should not arrive at a party until half an hour or more after the appointed time is presumably an instance of spontaneous generation. The coordination of American clocks and watches onto standard time was accomplished by central coordinators. Until 1883, clocks were set more or less by local sun time; hence, at noon in Washington, it was 12:24 P.M. in Boston and 11:43 A.M. in Savannah. The multiplicity of times became problematic as the railways developed; they established Standard Railway Time and cut down the number of railroad times from at least fifty-six to four. Seventy of the hundred principal cities in the United States adopted the system immediately, and another ten followed within five months.[5] Progress was set back by the introduction of daylight saving time after the First World War, and in the sixties it was possible to take a 35-mile bus trip from Steubenville, Ohio, to Moundsville, West Virginia, that required seven time changes, and to enter a government office building in Minneapolis–St. Paul where the time differed from floor to floor for part of the daylight saving period. In 1966 Congress took over as a somewhat more coercive central coordinator, but left enough discretion to the states that in 1979 the nation was still only 97 percent standardized.[6]

Prisoner's Dilemma conventions likewise may arise spontaneously or through the agency of a central coordinator. The convention of back-

---

[5] Ian R. Bartky and Elizabeth Harrison, "Standard and Daylight Saving Time," p. 46.

[6] Ibid., pp. 49, 53.

packers not to litter on a beach, discussed again below, is presumably a spontaneous convention. Ronald Manzer argues that the rise of Canadian provincial teachers' unions depended in part on the leadership of zealots—central coordinators—who could not convincingly be called narrowly self-interested.[7] Nathan Smith Davis of the movement to establish the American Medical Association also seems to have been a zealot.[8] In the wake of such zealots, selective incentives may play a great role in further building and maintaining an organization, but contract by convention may often be more important. For example, the American Medical Association is one of the most powerful interest organizations ever formed, and yet today one would probably agree that its most important incentive to membership is voluntarily exercised by individual members rather than by the organization: member doctors selectively refer patients to other member doctors. Hence, doctors in private practice have strong reason to be in the association, but this is a function of conventional rather than of organizational sanctions.[9]

Spontaneous coordination to mutual benefit in an iterated Prisoner's Dilemma may come about in much the same ways as in a pure coordination game. As Schelling notes, "The fundamental psychic and intellectual process is that of participating in the creation of *traditions;* and the ingredients out of which traditions can be created, or the materials in which potential traditions can be perceived and jointly recognized, are not at all coincident with the mathematical contents of the game," that is, with the strict assessment of the interests of the parties to the interaction.[10]

Concerning the convention of justice, particularly the rules of property, Hume notes that

> no questions in philosophy are more difficult, than when a number
> of causes present themselves for the same phaenomenon, to deter-
> mine which is the principal and predominant. There seldom is any

[7] Ronald Manzer, "Selective Inducements and the Development of Pressure Groups: The Case of Canadian Teachers' Associations," p. 110.

[8] Jeffrey L. Berlant, *Profession and Monopoly,* pp. 225–234. See also chap. 2 above, under "The By-Product Theory" and "Political Entrepreneurship."

[9] As Joe Oppenheimer suggests, referrals may be to other members mainly because the association publishes directories of its members, which ease the task of selecting relevant doctors. (Joe Oppenheimer, University of Maryland, College Park, Md., personal communication, 1980.) If so, then if another institution published more complete directories and distributed them to all doctors, the distribution of referrals should change.

[10] Thomas C. Schelling, *The Strategy of Conflict,* pp. 106–107. See further, Brian Barry, *Political Argument,* pp. 253–256.

very precise argument to fix our choice, and men must be con-
tented to be guided by a kind of taste or fancy, arising from
analogy, and a comparison of similar instances. Thus, in the
present case, there are, no doubt, motives of public interest for
most of the rules, which determine property; but still I suspect,
that these rules are principally fix'd by the imagination, or the
more frivolous properties of our thought and conception.[11]

How coordination is reached the first time a pure coordination game
is played does not always depend on the prospect of iteration as it does
for Prisoner's Dilemma games. Nevertheless, what is at stake in reaching
a coordinated rule of choice may be the same in both classes of games.
In order best to show how a contract by convention may arise in a
Prisoner's Dilemma, it is perhaps well to consider first the strongest
arguments against cooperation in n-person Prisoner's Dilemma, even in
iterated play. This involves a regression almost to the cruder assumptions of earlier chapters on the static analysis of collective action.

Size Effects

In chapter 3 it was shown that if the smallest efficacious subgroup
(k) has at least two members, then the group is latent in this strong
sense: that narrowly self-interested players will not cooperate if there is
no incentive external to the payoffs in the collective action game to induce
cooperation in the game. Hence, the only size effect logically inherent
in the payoff structure of a collective action game is that which distinguishes games with k equal to 1 from all other games. In chapter 9,
I argued that in a 2-person, binary-choice Prisoner's Dilemma that is
iterated in an open-ended sequence, cooperation is rational. This conclusion may be generalized. If $k = n$, cooperation is rational for all
players, although if n is large, the benefits of cooperation may be sufficiently small that cooperation may hardly be worth the effort, especially
if some players in the game are too slow-witted to understand it. (For
2-person Prisoner's Dilemma, $k = 2$.)

The interesting size effects for iterated games are for group sizes
between 2-person groups and very large groups in collective actions for
which k is less than n. Consider a collective action in which n is greater
than 2, and the minimal k is 2. Unless there is only one k-subgroup, it
might be narrowly rational of any two members who comprise a k-sub-
group not to cooperate, if they believed they could expect others to
cooperate instead. Their situation is similar to that of each of two or
more privileged members of a privileged group: each would be bene-

---

[11] David Hume, *A Treatise of Human Nature*, bk. 3, pt. 2, sec. 3, n. at p. 504.

fited by supplying the group good alone, but each would rather have another privileged member supply it. Iteration makes cooperation rational in a 2-person Prisoner's Dilemma. How would it affect these two collective actions?

Recall that iteration makes cooperation by both players in our binary-choice Prisoner's Dilemma rational because if you defect, I benefit by also defecting, and while my defection benefits me, it punishes you. Hence, punishing you is not merely cheap, it is rewarding to me. For groups of larger n (or for multiply privileged groups) this conclusion does not follow. Consider a symmetrical, binary-choice, n-person Prisoner's Dilemma with k less than n. A cooperating k-subgroup cannot punish other players who are defecting without hurting themselves at least in the short run. Only to the extent they can convince the others that they are willing to suffer a loss in the long run can they induce the others to cooperate out of self-interest. If all the defectors fully understand the situation, the cooperators cannot successfully argue, as is possible in a 2-person Prisoner's Dilemma, that they would themselves benefit immediately from every act of punishing the defectors. But they can successfully argue that the benefit they (the k-subgroup) receive for cooperating while the others defect is too slight to be of great interest, while the gain they might get from inducing the others also to cooperate is substantially greater. Hence, only by suffering a short-term loss or by using strategies that are outside the payoff structure of the game could the cooperators induce the defectors to join in cooperating. The relevant external strategies are such devices as bluffing, external commitments, external incentives, and so forth. For example, we may make compelling our claim that we will defect, even at a loss to ourselves in the present game, by making a large enough bet with an outside party that we will not be taken for a free ride. One of the most important external strategies in social contexts is to have one's reputation be at stake.

If it is not binary choice, even 2-person Prisoner's Dilemma need not have a uniquely determined rational outcome when played in open-ended iteration. For example, in a continuous-contribution, 2-person Prisoner's Dilemma, I might propose to match your contributions. But you might counter with a proposal that I match your contributions two for one, because, say, you think I am secretly wealthy, or merely because you are willing to lose all rather than contribute more than half of what I do. External strategic considerations cannot be precluded. Only a binary-choice Prisoner's Dilemma in which the smallest k-subgroup includes all members is proof against such external strategies by any member.[12] If we restrict attention to only those groups whose benefits from their collective goods are substantially greater than the costs of the goods, we may conclude that only for very small number, binary-choice Prisoner's Dilemmas is cooperation rationally mandated in iterated play. In certain other small-number Prisoner's Dilemmas with wider ranges of possible contributions but with some level of contribution somehow prominently selected, we may also conclude that cooperation is rational. In either case, "small" means very small, not much more than two. If, for example, $k = 10$ for a particular 10-person Prisoner's Dilemma, the game is unlikely to yield benefits significantly greater than costs, although it might, as in a cartel to raise prices.

Amalgamation

This game-theoretic strategy discussion must seem foreign to most actual experience. People do not behave that way or even think that way, at least not most of the time. Indeed, that way of thinking seems most reminiscent of international politics and of childhood. Most of us can probably recall a familiar childhood scene in which having an adequate number to play some game was important, so that the threat, "If you don't play fair and let me have a turn, I'm going home," was a powerful one. The rationality assumed in game theory is one of what James March calls "models of calculated rationality." He distinguishes such rationality from "a quite different kind of intelligence, systemic rather than calculated. Suppose we imagine that knowledge, in the form of precepts of behavior, evolves over time within a system and accumulates across time, people, and organizations without comprehension of its full justification."[13] Those who behave as though they were rationally conforming to a convention might often meaningfully be said to do so even though they understand their behavior in no such terms. Despite this strong objection to the realism of imputing careful micromotives to people in ordinary life, it is instructive to build up to a more realistic view by beginning from the crudest game-theoretic analysis, as just presented. The more systemic understanding of rationality in actual contexts

[12] It is possible that only some members have external strategies available. For example, if one or more members do not belong while all others do belong to the only k-subgroup, the k-subgroup is proof against external strategies by the subgroup's members irrespective of whether the other one or more members of the larger group cooperate.

[13] James G. March, "Bounded Rationality, Ambiguity, and the Engineering of Choice," pp. 591–592.

will be seen as a pervasive form of bounded rationality, which characterizes relatively deliberate choice by individuals and organizations.[14]

If the incentive in an ongoing, small-number Prisoner's Dilemma is to cooperate while the incentive in a large-number Prisoner's Dilemma is the opposite, how may cooperation in the latter rationally be achieved? Just as many large-number conventions are. Many conventions that cover substantial groups or populations are built up out of dyadic or very small number interactions. For example, the convention of truth telling is generally practiced in face-to-face encounters. Only with the rise of the modern national executive and the electronic media has lying to millions become routinely feasible. But the convention has no force except through the fact that it is widely observed. A party to the convention follows it in a dyadic interaction because the other party, whoever it is, can also be expected to follow it. An outsider entering a community of truth tellers would not be able to profit long from violating the convention of truthfulness, because the outsider would soon be trapped in a damaging reputation. An outsider may soon become party to the convention merely by following it. If too many dyadic interactions begin to involve "outsiders," growing anomie can as well destroy the convention of truth telling as original anomie would have prevented its rise (as in the third interpretation of the stag hunt above). Most of the conventions Hume and Lewis discuss—for example, language, Lewis's most important convention, and Hume's justice—are built out of dyadic and small-number interactions.

One should expect similar results for Prisoner's Dilemma conventions whenever a k-subgroup comes into interaction. This is generally improbable except for collective actions with relatively small k-subgroups. But ongoing games in the absence of other relationships are not plausible in many social circumstances. The firms in an oligopoly may be run by managers who do not enjoy, as Marx puts it, "manifold relations with one another," but the members of many common interest groups do. If we are members of a large group facing an ongoing Prisoner's Dilemma, we are likely to have dyadic and small-number relationships on other issues. My failure to conform to the implicit contractual obligations of our large-number convention may call into doubt my reliability in our small-number convention. My violation need have no perceptible impact on you—it is merely the generalization of such behavior to our other interactions that would affect you. In this respect, my violation would be analogous to my violation of a quite different

---

[14] For the most developed account, see Oliver E. Williamson, *Markets and Hierarchies*.

convention: if, while in your presence, I lie to a third party in order to serve my interests, you may sensibly wonder whether I would lie to you as well.

Obversely, your failure to sanction me for a violation of a convention that covers a very large group to which we belong may seem to involve costs to you. Even though you will not perceptibly benefit from my conformance to our large-group convention, your failure to sanction might reduce the credibility of your sanctioning me in much smaller-group conventions under which you would perceptibly benefit from my conformance. One cannot easily separate sanctions under one convention from those under another. Hence, the interweaving of dyadic and small-number conventions with large-number conventions may make it possible to enforce the latter, as argued in chapter 11.

Finally, note that the construction of a large-number contract by convention out of dyadic or small-number interactions does not necessarily depend on the value of the small-number exchange interactions, because it may be the convention and general conformity to it that give value to the small interactions. Hume characterizes justice as different from benevolence in an important respect. He argues that, "as the good resulting from [an act of benevolence] is in itself complete and entire, it also excites the moral sentiment of approbation without any reflection on farther consequences, and without any more enlarged views of the concurrence or imitation of the other members of society." The good resulting from acts of justice is distinctively different; it is not, he says, "the consequence of every individual single act, but arises from the whole scheme concurred in by the whole or the greater part of the society." Justice is a convention. If we all often enough conform to it, it prevails. If too many of us too often violate it, it collapses. And it is the convention, not the acts themselves under it, that defines whether acts under it are just and that gives them their virtue. Indeed, as Hume notes, justice in its individual applications may not be pleasing, as, for example, when a poor man who steals food from the wealthy is punished.[15]

---

[15] David Hume, *An Enquiry Concerning the Principles of Morals* (App. 3: "Some Farther Considerations with Regard to Justice"), pp. 304–305. For further discussion, see Russell Hardin, "The Emergence of Norms." Kafka has a similarly but more systematically rude view of the particular instances of the institution, which he honors, of marriage. "I do not envy the particular married couple, I only envy all couples—even if I envy a particular couple, I really envy the whole of marital bliss in its manifold variety, I would probably doubt the bliss of a particular marriage even in the most favorable case" (Franz Kafka, *Tagebücher* [Diaries], p. 391 [entry dated 17 Oktober 1921], my translation).

Generalization

Whether we are likely to initiate a contract by convention in a very large number Prisoner's Dilemma depends in part on whether there is a relatively obvious, natural, or prominent generalization from extant small-number Prisoner's Dilemma conventions to the large-number case. A convention of truth telling can expand to cover a large population and to accommodate numerous new entrants if interactions do not become too predominantly anomic. Recall the backpackers who carry their convention of not littering with them when they congregate en masse on a beach, as discussed in chapter 11 under "Overlapping Activities: Sanctions." It is because they have a convention from which they can generalize that they can easily reach coordination on not littering the beach. In many complicated problems, how to generalize from extant conventions would not be so obvious—there might be competing conventions from which to generalize, or there might be none that is a compelling analogue. It is important in the example of the backpackers on the beach that they not only have a prominent coordination outcome available—prominent because of its "rightness," uniqueness, optimality, or whatever—but that they also have an ongoing convention for dealing with such problems. To invoke mere rightness, uniqueness, or optimality either to serve as a sanction or to justify a sanction is not as powerful as to invoke obligation, in this case the obligation of an implied contract. It is more powerful and, moreover, it is easier, to invoke the obligation than, say, rightness, simply because there is a history that makes the obligation a universal principle in the group, and there may not be the same history for rightness, however defined. When the obligation of an implied contract is invoked, the invoker knows there can hardly be any misunderstanding or disagreement over the issue.

When such a generalization is not possible—and it is not possible if a sufficiently large fraction of the relevant group does not honor it—creating an effective convention may be very difficult, especially if the relevant population is very large. There may be no small-number Prisoner's Dilemma that is prominently analogous to a given large-number Prisoner's Dilemma. For example, it appears that there is no small-number Prisoner's Dilemma common in ordinary social life that is analogous to the larger Prisoner's Dilemma involved in automotive pollution. Hence, even in a very homogeneous community in which small-number Prisoner's Dilemma conventions were common and were often generalized to larger-number Prisoner's Dilemmas, a convention of voluntarily spending extra to make private cars nonpolluting might be hard to establish, although perhaps not impossible. In a community that is asymmetric in the sense used in chapter 5, with some members having a more intense demand for some commonly desired collective good, provision by convention may be still harder, even if a relevant generalization from some small-number convention is obvious. For example, those who can afford only relatively old used cars would have to bear a proportionately larger share of the costs of a convention against polluting. Certain conventions of fairness might weigh against such an outcome, and yet there might be no feasible conventional way for the well-off to offset part of the larger burden of the less well-off. Hence, asymmetries, which as argued in chapter 5 may enhance the prospects of organized collective action to enforce the provision of a collective good, may impair the prospects of direct provision by convention.

The possibility of generalization depends on elements of commonality of information, experience, and understanding, and also on the lack of conflicting principles from which to generalize. But the way in which generalization occurs is often not likely to be articulated. An organized group may achieve quite articulate prescriptions for policy. But the members of a group creating and conforming to a convention may be much less conscious of what they are doing. Being more conscious makes little sense for all the usual bounded rationality reasons: there are costs involved in becoming theoretically astute, in assessing alternative choices, in building consensus, and so forth. In addition, too precise an understanding of what principle of convention is being generalized is likely to involve relevant differences in the small- and the large-number Prisoner's Dilemmas to be resolved. What the members of a group can choose to do almost instinctively without too much reflection is likely to be a better—both more coherent and more efficient—guide to action than is any carefully analyzed program.

Consider further the import of the tacit character of contract by convention. Recall the passage from Fuller (at note 3 in chapter 11) describing how a rule of general customary law may be created. Fuller goes on to discuss the "familiar phenomenon of the spread of customary law *from one social context to another* [emphasis added]." He says,

> Where customary law does in fact spread, we must not be misled as to the process by which this extension takes place. It has sometimes been thought of as if it involved a kind of inarticulate expression of group will; the members of Group B perceive that the rules governing Group A would furnish an apt law for them; they therefore take over those rules by an act of tacit collective adoption. This kind of explanation abstracts from the interactional processes underlying customary law and ignores their ever-present communicative aspect. Take, for example, [the practice] of offering a twenty-one gun salute to visiting heads of state. . . . It is apparent that once the pattern of twenty-one became familiar any departure

from it could generate misapprehension; spectators would spend their time, not in enjoying the grandeur of cannon roar, but in counting booms, attributing all sorts of meanings—intended and unintended—to any departure from the last allocation. Generally we may say that where A and B have become familiar with a practice obtaining between C and D, A is likely to adopt this pattern in his actions toward B, not simply or necessarily because it has any special aptness for their situation, but because he knows B will understand the meaning of his behavior and will know how to react to it.[16]

Similarly, the accidental fact that a relevantly generalizable convention already obtains among ourselves or among others with whom we are familiar may make it easy for us to reach a spontaneous resolution of our collective action problem. If we are suddenly put into a situation in which we do not perceive that there is a relevant convention, however, we may not be able to cooperate successfully even though we all wish to do so.[17]

TERMINATION OF CONTRACTS BY CONVENTION

Almost every Prisoner's Dilemma is potentially competitive in the sense that each player would rather others pay all the costs of providing the mutually beneficial outcome. Only when contributions are binary (for example, to vote or not to vote), so that no one can bear another's share of the costs, or when successful collective action requires cooperation by all, is the competitive edge sometimes dulled (see further, chapter 6). But there is a class of Prisoner's Dilemma games that are more fundamentally competitive—those that seem like iterated Prisoner's Dilemma in their ongoing payoff structure, but with this difference: that they involve as the best outcome for one player the elimination of one or more other players.[18] For any particular interaction there may be a prospect of elimination not in general, but only under certain circumstances. But the possibility that such circumstances may arise sooner or later puts ongoing cooperation at risk.

The most commonplace iterated Prisoner's Dilemma with a substantial gain possibly to be made from elimination of other players is perhaps

---

[16] Lon L. Fuller, "Law and Human Interaction," pp. 68–69.

[17] Shibutani notes that "specialists in disaster relief complain that the major problem they face is not mass panic but lack of coordination" (Tamotsu Shibutani, "On Sentiments and Social Control," p. 160).

[18] The argument that follows was stimulated in part by discussions with my colleagues Adam Przeworski and Phillippe Schmitter.

the conflict of oligopolists in a given market. Unless one entrepreneur can be fairly confident of bankrupting another, both may be best served over the long run by oligopolistic cooperation. Unless there are other ties that lead them to be contractarian with each other, however, there is likely to be tension in their mutual cooperation, because each must commonly suffer a strong sense of risk. Among the ties that may reduce the sense of risk are beneficial cooperation against unions and government.

With perfect collusion, oligopolists who face no other competitors in a given market can achieve monopoly profits (assuming there are no further returns to scale from combining the production facilities into a smaller number). This is, of course, a long-run incentive. In the short run, cheating by cutting prices to increase market share and total profits might be beneficial. If competitors are quick to undercut a cheater's price cuts, however, any short-run gains from cheating may be wiped out in the ensuing price war. Hence, there may be a strong incentive in the long run to cooperate in the oligopolists' iterated Prisoner's Dilemma.

One of the best-studied oligopolistic collusions is the series of cartels on the Chicago–East Coast railways in the three decades before such cartels were outlawed by the Supreme Court in decisions in 1897 and 1898.[19] Paul MacAvoy models these cartels with what is essentially a Cournot duopoly model like that discussed in chapter 8. One of the duopolists is the price-cutting firm, the "cheater." The other duopolist is the set of all other firms in the cartel, which act in unison to maximize their profits in competition with the cheater. MacAvoy shows that a threat merely to match any cheater's price cuts will not be a deterrent to cheating. To deter cheating requires a threat of deeper cuts than the cheater's own, although even a credible threat to make deep cuts will be effective only under certain market conditions. In the face of such a threat, "there can be 'reasons' of profit for remaining loyal to the agreement." [20]

Since the value of collusion is generally in the long run, the incentive for collusion will be considerably weaker during periods when long-run prospects are poor in any case. For example, during the Great Depression of the thirties, numerous collusive agreements in diverse industries were short-lived.[21] James Scott argues of the peasants of Southeast Asia

[19] Paul W. MacAvoy, *The Economic Effects of Regulation*, pp. 187–188.

[20] Ibid., p. 19; related discussion in ibid., chap. 2 and app.

[21] John R. Bowman, "New Deal, Old Game: Competition and Collective Action Among American Capitalists 1925–1934"; Simon Whitney, *Trade Associations and Industrial Control.*

that when their survival is often likely to be threatened in the short run, they are not concerned to maximize production in the long run.[22] They do not appear to be peculiar in that respect. They are risk-averse in their game with nature just as oliogopolists, especially in a period of economic duress that threatens survival, may be risk-averse in their game against each other. In both cases, the purpose is to avoid elimination.

Consider a long-enduring and extensive contract by convention that was broken in the face of the great Calcutta credit crisis of 1829–34. In the first half of the nineteenth century, two of the biggest English agents in Canton for trade—mostly in opium—with India were Dent and Jardine. Ostensibly in competition with each other in the Canton market, they also cooperated extensively—in part perhaps as a means of risk spreading. They had combined in 1805 in forming a highly profitable insurance company in Canton. The company expired and was renewed every five years, with its management alternating between Dent and Jardine. Furthermore, since communications were by sea mail, and since the terms and fortunes of business fluctuated suddenly, it was in the interest of all firms to carry mail for one another in order that all might be quick to respond to changes in market conditions.[23]

Dent was closely associated with the House of Palmer, one of the great English trading houses in Calcutta. Palmer failed in 1830 as a result of the sudden collapse of the London market in indigo, and with its failure Dent suffered badly. Dent reputedly suspected that its suffering was made worse by Jardine's "withholding of the correspondence brought from Calcutta in a Jardine clipper which bore the news of the failure of Palmers." [24] One might suppose that Jardine withheld the mail from Dent in order to reduce its own losses, thereby perhaps increasing those of Dent. As a result, after decades of mutually extensive cooperation, Dent and Jardine fell into a bitter feud. After Jardine's duplicity with the mails, Dent decided in 1835 "to end the 'ancient custom' of alternate management" of their insurance company and to set up its own competing company.[25] One might suspect that Dent also ceased to cooperate with Jardine in the delivery of mail.

Despite the possibility of such duplicity as Jardine showed Dent, oligopolists commonly collude for their mutual benefit to avoid price

[22] James C. Scott, *The Moral Economy of the Peasant.*

[23] Michael Greenberg, *British Trade and the Opening of China 1800–1842,* pp. 165–173.

[24] Ibid., n. at p. 167. The indigo market collapsed suddenly after much cheaper Prussian blue was successfully used as a substitute dye. (Ibid, p. 166.)

[25] Ibid., p. 173.

competition.[26] Why do they do it? The most obvious answer is that they commonly do not think they face the threat of elimination by their rivals. When there is at least a slight risk of elimination, there may be overlapping activities—as argued in chapter 11—to induce better cooperation among them. Cooperating in the spreading of risks in their shaky capital markets evidently helped Dent and Jardine cooperate in sharing valuable information through cooperative mail delivery in the decades prior to 1830. For contemporary oligopolists, the most important overlapping activities probably include dealing with government and with unions on industrywide issues. Of course, mutual cooperation in these activities through contract by convention could not prevent the violation of market or other collusion by a risk-averse firm facing unusually desperate times—as did Jardine—or by a firm that could eliminate or cripple a major rival.[27] But it could be conducive to building better expectations about rivals' behavior and could therefore help to reduce the sense of risk involved in market collusion. Hence, it might reduce the likelihood of preemptive defection from a collusive arrangement (see the discussion of GRIT in chapter 13, under "Explicit Contract Versus Contract by Convention").

Perhaps railway efforts to build cartels in the years before the Interstate Commerce Commission was created, and similar efforts in many industries in the early years of the depression, often collapsed in short order partly because there were no other overlapping ties on which to build expectations in a threatening environment. Hence, industrywide bargaining with unions, dealings with regulatory agencies in trying to prevent general rules from being adopted, or lobbying government for or against the adoption of legislation may be beneficial to an industry, because it may help undergird efforts at market collusion by tacit contract by convention. For example, a firm that has been backed and would benefit from continued backing by other firms in its wage negotiations may be slower to defect from market collusion with those firms.

[26] For example, see Arthur Thompson, Jr., *Economics of the Firm: Theory and Practice.*

[27] However, given that there are other games in which an oligopolist may be involved, terminating the market Prisoner's Dilemma by eliminating a rival may not be attractive, even in a small-number oligopoly. For example, in an untrammeled market for the sale of cars, General Motors would probably be pleased to see Chrysler go bankrupt. In the actual American market of 1979–80, GM may have favored federal government efforts to save Chrysler from bankruptcy, because the existence of weakling competitors mitigates demands for political action against GM.

Note the peculiar inversion of size effects in the game of market collusion with the threat of elimination. Two firms that dominate a market may have a hard time convincing each other that they would not defect in order to bankrupt one another. Several firms that dominate a market may generally have an easier time, simply because it would be less likely that a firm with a one-tenth market share could, by secretly defecting from price collusion, increase market share enough to bankrupt one or more of the other firms. But the larger the number of firms in collusion, the less the incentive to enter into a price war with any cheater. The potential loss from having others cheat while one innocently cooperates for a while will generally be higher, the smaller the number of firms, so that there will be stronger incentive to react against cheaters in less-numerous industries.

Market collusion as an iterated Prisoner's Dilemma with the threat of termination by elimination of one or more of the parties is obviously reminiscent of the superpower standoff through nuclear deterrence. If there is any prospect of a preemptive strike, the game is unstable and is the analogue of market conflict when bankruptcy is a distinct possibility for one or more firms. If there is little or no prospect of a preemptive strike, however, the game is more nearly like market collusion among secure firms, because the only form termination can take is the elimination of both (or all) parties. Hence, it can be very stable, and the superpowers can engage in mutually cooperative ventures in other realms without great fear that conflict in those realms could lead to nuclear confrontation.

Indeed, a superpower with a viable deterrent can generally take greater risks in virtually all other respects, because almost no offense is worth mutual annihilation. The principal incentive against offensive risk taking is likely to be that it jeopardizes cooperative ventures in *other* realms. Unless the latter are of great importance, risk-taking ventures—such as the American war against the Viet Cong and North Vietnam, or the Soviet occupation of Afghanistan—involve little cost to superpower relations, just because the relations are limited. Suppose, however, that affluence brought a genuine deterrent force to West Germany or Japan. The United States and the Soviet Union might still be distinguished by their being more nearly self-sufficient in all realms. Hence, overlapping cooperative activities between the two of them or between either of them and any other party would not pose severe constraints on their risk taking in situations other than head-on war with another nation with deterrent power. West Germany and Japan, however, would likely face far greater constraints.

Investment in research on new weapons may be a Prisoner's Dilemma with the threat of elimination, because one of the superpowers might discover a weapon capable of destroying the other's formerly deterrent force. In the Dent–Jardine game the cooperation itself did not necessarily increase the likelihood of the elimination of one of the parties. One of the traders would, in the normal scheduling of trips, have had a clipper arriving in Canton sooner with the news of the collapse of Palmer, and that firm could have done what Jardine did. Only if the cooperation caused Dent to forgo risk-averse behavior—sending a clipper from, say, India to China with the news whenever the market turned bad—did the cooperation per se involve an expected risk. Similarly, in market collusion, only if the collusion substantially reduces wariness need it be a source of risk per se. In the superpowers' Prisoner's Dilemma search for new weapons, contract-by-convention cooperation might be a source of risk if active research is not easily detectable—as installation of weapon systems presumably is. Hence, although the level of armaments could be reduced by contract by convention, further risky and costly research may be harder to control. The risk-averse will, like the peasants of Southeast Asia, prefer a deficient outcome to an outcome that appears to be better in the long run, but that is also potentially disastrous.

13

CONTRACT BY CONVENTION
IN SOCIAL THEORY

Social exchange theory is commonly treated as a generalization of economic exchange, where the latter is ideally conceived as exchange in a market. Attention is therefore focused on exchanging like for like, and much of the argument is given over to showing why what one party yields equals in value what the other yields. The result is often an odd distortion of the relationship under study, because that relationship cannot sensibly be seen as a cruder version of a market exchange. The difference between social exchange in general and the ideal type of market exchange is related to the difference between the analysis of collective action in chapters 2 through 7 and the analysis of contract by convention in chapters 10 through 12. Market exchanges and instances of collective action that fit the earlier analysis involve once-only relationships; social exchange and contract by convention involve ongoing relationships. In Ian Macneil's instructive terms, the former are instances of *discrete exchange,* the latter of *relational exchange.*[1]

Many market transactions are almost perfectly discrete in time and, hence, from any other interaction: I buy x from you this minute at the most favorable price for which I can get you to sell it, and we have no further relationship. Each of us has one strategy available to try to affect

---

Portions of this chapter have appeared in an article by the author, "Exchange Theory on Strategic Bases," *Social Science Information* vol. 21, no. 2 (1982) pp. 251–272; reprinted with permission of Sage Publications, London.

[1] Ian R. Macneil, *The New Social Contract.*

the other's price: I can refuse to buy at any price you offer, and you can refuse to sell at any I offer. If finally I buy, I have x and you have my money and that is the end of our relationship. This is a caricature even of many market transactions. First, I often have other strategies available. I can be obnoxious enough to make not selling x to me at my price seem very costly to you. More reasonably, I can threaten the loss of my future patronage. And second, if I later discover defects in x I can generally return it to you with some expectation of your making it right or returning my money. On the other side, you can have established a reputation for fair dealing that makes it pointless for me to hope for a better price and assures me that you will indeed make x right if I do discover defects in it later. Much of what superficially looks like market exchange therefore lacks discreteness.

Given the relative smoothness and efficiency with which market exchange works, one might think that more general social exchanges could be improved by introducing greater discreteness. There are, of course, inherent obstacles to discreteness in many situations. But the law of contracts has traditionally been seen as a vehicle for making as discrete as possible exchanges that will be spread out over time. As Macneil writes, "The ultimate goal of parties to a discrete transaction is to bring all the future relating to it into the present or, to use a rare word, to presentiate. They can then deal with the future as if it were in the present. . . ."[2] That effective presentiation is not necessarily advantageous, however, will be argued in the following section ("Explicit Contract Versus Contract by Convention").

The lack of discreteness means that there is strategic interaction because there is a prospect of applying sanctions in some part of the ongoing relationship other than in the present exchange itself. This point can be expressed more positively (and more accurately in many contexts): ongoing relationships allow us to establish commitments. The law of contracts enables us to make commitments by subjecting ourselves to potential court action. Contract by convention likewise enables us to make commitments—within limits—as discussed in the second section below ("Commitment: A Reformulation of Sanctions"). The more general fact that the lack of discreteness of relational exchange derives from strategic interaction suggests that social exchange theory should itself be based on strategic considerations, as discussed in the third section ("Exchange Theory on Strategic Bases").

Finally, just as discrete exchange may border on the realm of contract by convention from one side, so behavior governed by norms not based in exchange may border on it from another side. And one may have dif-

[2] Ibid., p. 19.

ficulty determining the relative roles of norms and exchange relations in securing outcomes. Indeed, apparent norms may themselves often be explained as contracts by convention, as discussed in the final section below ("Contracts and Norms").

EXPLICIT CONTRACT VERSUS CONTRACT BY CONVENTION

As already noted, very large groups cannot easily develop conventions that are complex or precise in their goals or behavior. For example, the populace of Iran during 1978 could achieve conventional behavior whose "purpose" or intendment was to depose the shah and bring in the ayatollah. It could not have brought itself to coordinate in achieving more extensively defined outcomes, and many of those who cooperated in the simplistic ayatollah-over-the-shah convention must have done so with great unease. To achieve a more precisely detailed outcome would have required some form of more explicit contracting. One might therefore suppose that explicit contracting or its equivalent would be preferred to contract by convention. But this conclusion does not follow. Explicit contracting is generally costly; contract by convention may be considerably less so.

In the abstract, a group is likely to face a trade-off between costs of agreement and precision of agreement. It will have to choose between the higher cost of explicit contracting and the lesser precision of contract by convention. Often, the former will be the greater barrier, so that the imprecision of contract by convention will be acceptable. The costs of organizing Iranian opposition to the shah so carefully as to produce a constitution to succeed him were surely prohibitive, so that a conventional choice of a more crudely defined alternative was the only feasible recourse.

Stewart Macaulay argues that business firms often prefer informal to formal contracts. The sanctions available under contract by convention are sufficient to protect each firm's interests so that the costs of explicit contracting can be avoided. According to one of Macaulay's businessmen, "you can settle any dispute if you keep the lawyers and the accountants out of it. They just do not understand the give-and-take needed in business." Their expectations of future dealings and their need to have reputations for honorable dealing mean that firms can effect mutual savings by avoiding contracts too explicit beyond routine "boiler plate" provisions. To use Macneil's old-fashioned term again, market exchanges that must of necessity be spread over time can as nearly as possible be presentiated under the law of contracts to make them appear to be merely discrete market exchanges. Alternatively, they can be left spread over time and can be governed by contract by convention rather than by contract at law, just as nonmarket exchanges commonly are governed. Indeed, to insist on a complete contract may guarantee performance to the letter, which is likely to be minimum performance.[3]

Among the greatest costs of explicit contract is that it requires clear articulation of what is at issue. As argued above, often what the members of a group can do almost instinctively is likely to be both a more efficient and a more coherent guide to action than what they might be able to agree on after extended discussion. Even if there had been no barriers to open political conspiracy in Iran, opponents of the shah could not likely have reached extensive agreement on an alternative government. Having an ill-defined but real alternative in Ayatollah Khomeini made coordinated opposition to the shah possible. One might suspect that many so-called charismatic leaders are merely necessary conventions: such a leader makes it possible to focus a movement, to seem to reify a tenuous program.

The great appeal of Charles Osgood's GRIT (for Graduated and Reciprocated Initiatives in Tension-reduction) proposal, which involves informally reciprocated steps in mutual arms reduction by the United States and the Soviet Union,[4] is that it avoids the laborious and cumbersome process of treaty negotiations, a process that engenders antagonism and conflict even while it is directed at mutual accommodation. The histories of SALT I and II suggest that treaties can be similar to explicit contracts in encouraging minimum performance. They can also produce so much careful calculating of slight individual advantages and disadvantages that mutual advantages recede from view.

In his GRIT proposal, Osgood sets numerous guidelines for an effective conflict- and arms-reduction strategy. Almost all of these can be seen as helping to establish commitment and to communicate and secure that each side has a clear understanding of the strategic structure of the

[3] Stewart Macaulay, "Non-Contractual Relations in Business," esp. pp. 61, 64. See also Macneil, *New Social Contract*, p. 68; Arthur Allen Leff, "Injury, Ignorance and Spite—The Dynamics of Coercive Collection"; and G. B. Richardson, "The Organization of Industry." For a summary of the issues, see Oliver E. Williamson, *Markets and Hierarchies*, pp. 106–109.

[4] Charles E. Osgood, *An Alternative to War or Surrender,* and Osgood, "GRIT for MBFR: A Proposal for Unfreezing Force-Level Postures in Europe." For a survey of research pertinent to GRIT, and more generally to contract by convention, see Svenn Lindskold, "Trust Development, the GRIT Proposal, and the Effects of Conciliatory Acts on Conflict and Cooperation."

interaction and its implications. For example, Osgood recommends that initiatives be diversified in nature.[5] Diversity may increase the quality of communication, making it seem more likely that there is a commitment to reduce arms. A clearly patterned series of initiatives might seem explainable in other terms as a self-interested program. For example, a serial reduction of forces in Europe might be cynically interpreted as an economic measure or as part of some negotiating ploy with the Europeans. A series of diverse measures may be harder to interpret cynically; hence, it makes commitment to reduction of tension more credible. Most of his other recommendations have similar implications.

Since contract by convention depends on reciprocation for the other's action, inability to observe certain of the other side's activities makes it harder to achieve contract by convention over those activities. Furthermore, if there is an unobservable realm of armaments, any reduction in other armaments might be largely compensated by increases in the unobservable field, so that the prospects for contract by convention are undercut all across the board. Hence, in the era of mutual interest in reducing the costs and the risks of nuclear deterrence, the suggestion that the United States should sooner reward than punish Soviet spies is not altogether facetious.

Would GRIT be preferable to such negotiations as SALT II? Although experience may be too limited to judge with confidence, one particular experience is more than suggestive. On June 10, 1963, President Kennedy put forward "A Strategy of Peace" in a widely reported speech announcing that the United States was unilaterally ending nuclear tests in the atmosphere and would resume them only if another nation did. At that time, negotiations on a test ban treaty had long been stalled. Premier Khrushchev immediately reciprocated and went further, announcing that the Soviet Union would unilaterally cease production of strategic bombers. Numerous other steps were taken unilaterally, and in August a nuclear test ban treaty was signed.[6]

Working against the Kennedy–Khrushchev GRIT episode was the fact that it required deep understanding, so deep as to compel relevant action—on both sides. It was also a short episode—Kennedy was assassinated not six months after his speech, and Khrushchev was toppled soon thereafter. Strategic thinking has not been a notable strength of any of their successors to date. It may also well be that Kennedy and Khrushchev did not feel sufficiently compelled by their

---

[5] Osgood, "GRIT for MBFR," p. 5. Osgood's rationale for this is that we "not weaken ourselves progressively in any one area" (Ibid.).

[6] Amitai Etzioni, "The Kennedy Experiment"; Osgood, "GRIT for MBFR," pp. 11–13.

own grasp of their equivalent of GRIT to carry through with it very far. But they made a beginning, and they achieved surprising momentum in very short order—the SALT negotiations have been glacial by comparison. Perhaps even being compelled to do that much depended on their personally having taken us so near the edge over the Cuban missile crisis that the prospect of nuclear war and its implications carried force for them far beyond what it has carried for subsequent leaders. Obviously, to attempt GRIT or other contract by convention at all requires of the relevant parties that they perceive that there are mutual gains to be made. It is not obvious that certain senators, military leaders, and presidential advisers in the United States and certain of their counterparts in the Soviet Union perceive any such thing. Chairman Brezhnev may have attempted a new round of mutual reductions with his 1979 offer to withdraw some forces from Eastern Europe if new Pershing missiles were not installed in Western Europe. President Carter's dismissal of the proposal must have killed any chance of contract-by-convention arms reduction on that occasion.

The contrast between explicit contract and contract by convention suggests another explanation of the often-noted tendency of popular interest groups to decline soon after their founding. What can be achieved through contract by convention is, again, likely to be general and vague. A spontaneous contract-by-convention creation of a movement with generally defined goals seems to be commonplace. Once the movement generates organizations to prosecute its goals, however, these often must be more precisely defined, even to the point of being given explicit legislative content. At that point, the parties to the original convention may find that they have substantial disagreement. The obverse of the fact that precision—as in a legislative program—cannot be achieved through contract by convention may often be that contract by convention cannot survive precision. The civil rights movement and more recently the women's movement seem to have suffered from their successes, not because there is little left for them to do—as was perhaps true of the Grange movement against the railways once shorthaul rates were regulated—but because success has meant defining their goals more extensively.

COMMITMENT: A REFORMULATION OF SANCTIONS

The success of a small-number contract by convention requires little more than mutual understanding that the small group is in an ongoing Prisoner's Dilemma, because there can be no hope of long-term free riding. The success of a large-number contract by convention requires support from overlapping activities that give rise to opportunities for sanctioning free riders. This condition has what may seem like a perverse implication: if I wish to get others to cooperate with me, I would want to give them power to sanction me. Schelling writes with strategic irony that

> among the legal privileges of corporations, two that are mentioned in textbooks are the right to sue and the "right" to be sued. Who wants to be sued! But the right to be sued is the power to make a promise: to borrow money, to enter a contract, to do business with someone who might be damaged. If suit does arise, the "right" seems a liability in retrospect; beforehand it was a prerequisite to doing business.

In other words, "the right to be sued is the power to accept a commitment."[7] Analogously stated, the problem of sanctioning is a problem of commitment: a very large group can achieve contract by convention if its members can all establish credible commitments to cooperate.

We can recast the entire analysis of contract by convention in terms different from, but strategically equivalent to, those of the discussions in chapters 9 through 12 and in the preceding section of this chapter: we can analyze not how I can sanction others, but how I can commit myself, how I can subject myself to the threat of sanctions. Not surprisingly, when so recast, the argument is similar to the argument for how one may make a threat credible in order to deter certain acts by another. To make a threat credible, one has to make one's commitment to carry it out credible, even though carrying it out once it has failed to deter may not be in one's interest—it may seem "a liability in retrospect," as Schelling says. To make a contract by convention seem likely, all or many of the potential parties to it must make their commitment to cooperate under it seem credible.

Analytically, one can think of numerous ways to establish commitment—for example, by making side-bets, entering into contracts, burning one's bridges, and so forth. In ordinary social life, these are often not suitable devices, and the only available device may depend on whether one has had and credibly expects to continue to have an ongoing relationship with the person or persons with whom one wishes to establish a commitment. Hence, there may be only a small subset of a relevant population with whom one *could* establish commitment. Thus, again, if a large group is to establish or maintain a contract by convention, it is

[7] Thomas C. Schelling, *The Strategy of Conflict*, p. 43.

likely to require overlapping activities that allow credible commitment within small subgroups.

Commitment requires coupling one action with others. We can expect a contract by convention in a small enough group (two members or a few more) simply from the logic of their ongoing Prisoner's Dilemma. That is, we can uncouple their ongoing Prisoner's Dilemma from all *other* considerations and still expect cooperation. We cannot uncouple a large group's Prisoner's Dilemma from other considerations and still expect cooperation on narrow self-interest grounds. In neither case can we uncouple choice at this particular moment from all other considerations and still expect cooperation. Contract by convention implies that a group's actions are somehow coupled: they are coupled over time in repeated plays of the same game, and they may also be coupled across various games.

Finally, even the problem of anomie, on which chapter 12 opened, can be restated as a problem in establishing commitments. In wider social contexts, my reputation depends less on me than on the reputations of others. If almost no one is trusted, then I will not be trusted even if I am—alas, known only to me—utterly trustworthy. In certain communities, no marriage is secure, because no one individual can establish a credible commitment for holding to a more exacting norm than the larger community honors. In some contexts, a very low incidence might destroy everyone's trust for all—this is, again, perhaps the least misanthropic interpretation of Hobbes's view of the state of nature.[8] This much we have in common with used cars: the incidence of enough lemons among us will wreck the reputations of us all.

EXCHANGE THEORY ON STRATEGIC BASES

Social exchange theory is often criticized as a conceptually destitute cousin of economic exchange theory. In a generally lucid and insightful critique of students of the former, Anthony Heath remarks that

> the economic theory is *forward-looking*. Bygones are bygones for the economist. Goods or services are handed over with an eye to the future, not to the past. If I reciprocate it is because I want your help again in future, not because I feel grateful for past favours. In contrast, the sociological theory is *backward-looking*. Bygones are of crucial importance. Services are given and judgements made in recognition of past favours, not in expectation of future ones.[9]

[8] As noted in chap. 11 at n. 27. See Thomas Hobbes, *De Cive*, p. 100.
[9] Anthony Heath, *Rational Choice and Social Exchange*, pp. 59–60.

These remarks tell against many passages and faulty analyses in the work of some notable scholars who have considered themselves social exchange theorists. But they do not tell against a properly framed social exchange theory.

The point of contingent choosing in the contexts analyzed in chapters 9 through the present one is to influence *future* behavior. The role of past behavior is perhaps most important for its contribution to one's reputation, which is valued because future relations depend on it. That economic and social exchange are not particularly different in this respect is seen from the fact that oligopoly pricing above the competitive market price is commonly achieved through convention rather than collusion. The profit-making oligopolist is hardly backward-looking. A more accurate statement perhaps is that the *emphasis* of social and economic exchange explanations is different. In economic exchange on a market, the account books are generally cleared immediately or soon, whereas in social exchange and much of economic exchange, the books are kept open with red and black entries not made in strict order or within strictly determined time limits.

To the extent that both economic and social exchange require information about other parties, both are backward-looking. To the extent that both require incentives to act, both are forward-looking. The most commonplace market exchanges are backward-looking in this respect: I buy a given product with confidence that I will not be cheated in the transaction, because the maker and the seller have reputations based on past behavior, and because their futures depend on maintaining their reputations. We all know that we are likely to be cheated when, as tourists, we buy supposedly valuable handicrafts. We may too readily associate being cheated with dealing with, say, Italians, because we have bought painted plaster—thinking it was alabaster—in San Marino. But we do not get cheated in Florence, while even Florentines get cheated in San Marino. That is because the market in San Marino almost exclusively involves exchanges with transient, one-time-only customers. It is almost impossible for merchants in San Marino to develop reputations for honesty and quality, and it would be pointless for them to behave as though their reputations mattered. (The only reputations at stake in San Marino may be among artisans in fraud. The best frauds will get the best wholesale prices from merchants.) Merchants in an anomic market can no more be expected to strive to be honest than others can be expected to cooperate in collective purposes in anomic settings.

To frame the analysis of contract by convention in terms of rationally committing oneself, as was done in the previous section, is to make the actions strictly forward-looking. It may well be, however, that for many people it works the other way, that is, backward-looking, in that they make no substantial calculation of expected returns, but merely cease to deal with those who do not reciprocate, so that the development of cooperative relationships over the longer term is an evolutionary phenomenon. But in some respects it does not matter how people work out their interactions. They may choose not to deal again with those who have cheated them, or they may choose not to cheat those with whom they expect or hope to deal again. The results will be the same in either case: we will enjoy ongoing cooperative relationships. And in either case, it will be possible to build up to successful, large-number collective actions, although it will be increasingly difficult as the numbers increase.[10]

In general, to the extent that it makes sense to cooperate in single-play Prisoner's Dilemma *if* a binding agreement can be signed, it often makes sense to cooperate in the iterated version of the same game. Social exchange theory is commonly about those cases in which binding agreements would be impossible or costly. It differs from economic exchange theory principally in that it emphasizes the ongoing nature of relationships and, sometimes, the richness of relationships. These are generally necessary features of economic exchange as well, but the latter generally takes place in contexts in which these features are so well understood as to be taken for granted in our explanations of behavior—they need not be emphasized. Social exchange theory explanations commonly involve much more detective work in determining how relationships are ramified in relevant ways to make cooperation or exchange rationally secure. Hence, the explanations are often defective, or plausibly so—as in many of the studies criticized by Heath—for reasons of fact rather than of logic, although the enormity of the factual burden of such explanations may depress the logical faculties of even good scholars. But when one keeps clear what is at stake, one can see that social exchange and economic exchange theories are both deductions from the assumption of self-interest, or narrow rationality.

As Williamson notes, the kind of reciprocity that arises in sociological exchange relationships "is much more common among the members of an internal organization" than in a market. "Market exchange tends predominantly to encourage calculative relations of a transaction-specific sort between the parties. Such transactions are carefully metered; unsettled obligations do not carry over from one contract, or related set of transactions, to the next." The large-number conditions that permit market exchange make transaction-specific relations attractive because they permit selection from large numbers of potential partners to any

---

[10] See further, n. 13 below and related discussion in text.

exchange. But they may also make the rise of Prisoner's Dilemma conventions difficult.[11] To the extent that contract by convention cannot be established, the static analyses of chapters 2 through 7 may be conclusive even for an ongoing Prisoner's Dilemma.

The ongoing interactions of internal organizations permit the easy rise of less specific, more subjectively metered exchange relations. Groups with ongoing interactions among their members similarly permit the rise of sociological exchange relations—that is, exchange without money and with reciprocation deferred to an unspecified future opportunity. To understand such a group in order to explain its extant pattern of stable expectations generally requires knowledge of the group's history.

CONTRACTS AND NORMS

When ongoing cooperation has been established through contract by convention, it may often be difficult either for the cooperators themselves or for observers to separate moral from narrowly rational contractual motivations. One might tend to speak of one's formal contractual obligations as moral, even though the obligations are powerfully backed by sanctions that would make it more costly to violate than to honor them. So, too, one might speak of one's contract-by-convention obligations as moral. One might speak of both as matters of fairness.

One should often distinguish two norms under the rubric of fairness. For example, one may act from a norm of fairness—a norm that is neither based in exchange nor dependent on sanctions—in voting or sending a check to some political group. One may also act from a norm of fairness in dealings with one's associates—but this norm may be a convention solidly based in ongoing exchange relationships. Although a norm of the latter type, which is conventional in the technical sense used here, may govern the provision of small-scale collective goods, it is less likely that it can govern the provision of large-scale collective goods. The former type of norm may govern behavior on any scale, whether it benefits a whole society, a group, an individual, or even no one at all (just as keeping a promise to a dead friend may benefit no one).

The ethical norm of fairness may be reinforced by or may be the spillover effect of the conventional norm of fairness. I may eventually act from considerations of fair play in wider contexts because I have developed the habit of fair play in small-scale exchange interactions.[12]

---

[11] Oliver E. Williamson, *Markets and Hierarchies*, p. 38.

[12] This is roughly Titmuss's argument for the larger values of having blood collected from voluntary donors—the practice may help to breed altruistic be-

One could argue that such spillover is rational in this sense: that the mental cost to me of deciding in each case the costs and benefits of fair play this time outweighs the sometime cost of being fair contrary to my narrow interests. Just as an act-utilitarian, for reasons of bounded rationality, may choose to follow standard rules and hence appear to be a rule-utilitarian, so I may choose to generalize my conventional norms to cover cases in which the convention could not possibly arise. However, this sort of argument—although it might explain my being honest to a store clerk whom I will never see again—is unlikely to explain many important instances of political collective action. Similarly, overlapping relationships and activities may seem to explain the strength of widespread conventions that are norms for behavior in what are generally small-scale interactions—such norms as honesty, keeping promises, fair play, and so forth; it is not so likely that they can explain cooperation in large-scale collective actions to obtain political goods.

The habit of voting, for example, is not readily generalized from everyday conventional norms; nor is the decision to write a check to any of various political groups. Although a substantial part of all voting in national elections may be the easy result of rational choice, much of it surely is not explicable as acting from narrow self-interest. The narrowly rational part consists of those acts of voting stimulated by net gains from private benefits over costs, not by concern for the collective good. For example, in parts of Philadelphia, there are voting machines on almost every block, so that one can hardly claim that going to vote is particularly burdensome. But not going to vote can be burdensome, because party workers will knock at one's door repeatedly and increasingly often —right through dinner if necessary—until one does vote. Conspicuously, however, many people do not live in Philadelphia, and many non-Philadelphians seem to vote strictly voluntarily without heavy social pressure and without suffering costs when they do not vote. One may argue that, in voluntarily voting, they act from a social norm. But that norm is not easily seen as a convention based on exchange relationships; it is not a narrowly self-interested norm, as honesty and fair play often may be. Much of the activity of contributing strictly voluntarily (that is, not as a by-product of the organized distribution of private benefits) to large-scale political interest groups is evidently similar to voluntary voting: it is governed by norms that are not based in self-interested exchange relationships.

---

havior in wider contexts. Williamson defends this position against Arrow and other critics, saying that an "atmosphere" of goodwill and altruism may stimulate cooperative behavior. (Richard M. Titmuss, *The Gift Relationship;* Williamson, *Markets and Hierarchies,* pp. 37–38; Kenneth J. Arrow, "Gifts and Exchanges.")

From the discussion of amalgamation and generalization in chapter 12, one might suppose that how widespread a contract by convention may be depends inversely on the size of the group in which the contractual norm is likely to be exercised. Truth telling is largely at issue in dyadic or very small group interchanges. Hence, the sanctions are dyadic. And the contractual norm of truth telling is widespread. To build up a contractual norm of cooperation in a large-scale collective action is far more difficult. Although one should not too casually claim that it would be impossible in the absence of overlapping small-scale interactions, it seems likely that the latter will be very important. Edna Ullmann-Margalit argues that, in situations having the strategic structure of the Prisoner's Dilemma, norms will emerge to encourage cooperative behavior. She calls such norms *PD-norms*.[13] Unfortunately, ethical generalization may be confused in ordinary understanding. For example, the golden rule may seem to have meaning only in small-number contexts and may not seem to apply in very large collective action contexts. (There is often little sense in which I can do unto a million people what I would have them do unto me.) But the principal role of a PD-norm is precisely in large-number cases, because in small-number cases, contingent choosing will commonly suffice to bring about cooperative behavior (except for one-shot interactions).

The issues of this book are largely in the realm of social exchange theory, which encompasses not the entire realm of self-interested behavior, but only that part involving self-interested exchange behavior. In the by-product theory and in contract by convention, exchange theory goes very far toward explaining collective action, although one would have to be not merely bold, but foolish, to claim that all collective action is motivated by exchange or even by secondary motivations that are themselves rooted in exchange. One can say that our norms are social

---

[13] Edna Ullmann-Margalit, *The Emergence of Norms*, p. 60. For further discussion see Russell Hardin, "The Emergence of Norms," pp. 576–578. However, it does not also follow that norms may not easily govern the behavior of a very large population. They can, especially if they are invoked in small-number interactions. Hence, much of Heath's discussion of the rationality of conforming to, enforcing, and instituting norms is off the mark. (Heath, *Rational Choice*, pp. 154–160.) Similarly, Buchanan's discussion of the effect on norms of population size is valid if at all only for such norms as govern collective action problems. A contractual norm against lying, for example, which is largely enforced in dyadic relationships, can be strongly held in a vast population. Buchanan's numerical assessments of the returns from adhering to or violating a general norm leave out the costs and benefits of sanctions and rewards, to the individual, that derive from small-number interactions under non-collective-action norms. (James M. Buchanan, "Ethical Rules, Expected Values, and Large Numbers.")

creations without implying that they are all built out of self-interested exchange behavior.

Much of the individual contribution to collective action that we see may conceivably be normatively motivated. The person who privately writes a check for a campaign to save whales, children, redwoods, or some foundering candidacy may sensibly expect to receive virtually nothing in return (not even a commensurate level of good feeling, the last resort of failed exchange theorists). One might suppose that exchange relations must have influenced the values and ethical commitments which that person holds, but one should be reluctant to assert that these values could be reduced to a combination of exchange relations that would make any norms apparently guiding the person's behavior narrowly self-interested, just as one would be reluctant to assert that all puritanical urges are merely another form of pleasure seeking.

14

CONTRACT BY CONVENTION
IN POLITICS

"Since one of the best ways to test an idea is to ride it into the ground," Schattschneider wryly observes, "political theory has unquestionably been improved by the heroic attempt to create a political universe revolving about the group."[1] Since the group theory of politics was, in Schattschneider's view, already ridden to death by 1960, perhaps I should be at pains to justify my still trying to saddle it two decades later. The short justification is that I am not concerned with a theory of politics in general, but only with a theory of group action. Given such a theory, one should naturally be concerned with its significance in helping to explain political outcomes, even if one did not think it the only relevant consideration. An irony of the simplistic pluralism—which Schattschneider criticizes—that sees political outcomes as the vector sums of forces from groups is that, if outcomes were merely vector sums, there would be little politics. There would only be the paraphernalia of enforcement. Political science would reduce to such principles as the Coase theorem, which says that in the absence of transactions costs, overall economic efficiency is not a function of *which* governmental institutions or laws we have, because if one of my activities benefits me less than it harms you, you can contract with me to stop it.[2] But political institutions have a partly autonomous existence, and they play enormous roles in determining political outcomes.

[1] E. E. Schattschneider, *The Semi-Sovereign People*, p. 21.
[2] For further discussion of the Coase theorem in this context, see chap. 4 above, under "Dimensions of Collective Action Problems."

220

It is within the context of extant political institutions, then, that we wish to understand the role of groups, and therefore the role of contract by convention. The ways in which the analysis of contract by convention should affect our understanding of political outcomes are discussed below. First, the role of convention in the creation and the life of formal interest group organizations is discussed, and then the weight of convention in a representative system is assessed. Finally, by way of epilogue, differences in the implications, for politics, of contract by convention and the static logic of collective action are briefly discussed.

CONVENTION IN FORMAL INTEREST GROUP ORGANIZATIONS

I have argued that convention is much less likely to have coherent effect on detailed policy than on a general policy stance. It is partly by convention that the civil rights and the subsequent antiwar movements in the United States succeeded as much as they did. And it is partly by convention that Ayatollah Khomeini was substituted for the Pahlavi Shah. The civil rights and women's movements may have begun to dissipate after initial successes because easy conventional agreement on more precise goals was not possible. Social states of affairs are often much more to be explained by what *can* be tacitly coordinated than by what anyone's preferences or reasoned outcomes might be. To achieve more detailed outcomes commonly requires a formal organization with resources at its control.

Does convention then play no role in organized efforts? It has at least two important roles. First, once collective action is being under-taken on any other basis (for example, out of a desire for participation or out of moral motivations, as discussed in chapter 7), convention may then govern much of the form of the action and much of the individual behavior. As a perhaps obvious example, convention may govern procedural rules for reaching organizational decisions. More importantly, it may restrict what the organization can do, especially if contributions are in part morally motivated, because if the organization is perceived to do the wrong thing, it may lose support.

Second, a perhaps far more important role of convention is to underpin the life of a group enough to enable the group to organize and stay organized for political or other action. A quick survey of the environmental movement would lead one to think the San Francisco Bay Area has a much larger proportion of environmentalists than any other region of the country. Why should it? Part of the answer may be a simple function of present circumstances. There is a lot of natural beauty worthy of protection around the Bay. And Bay Area residents are affluent, so that one should expect the arguments about asymmetry of demand (in chapter 5) and moral motivations (in chapter 7) to apply to them more than to most. But a very large part of the answer must be a function of historical circumstances that have contributed to contract-by-convention support of political organizations. Potential environmentalists in the Bay Area are more likely than those elsewhere to find themselves in networks of manifold social relations with organized environmentalists. Many of those who were previously uncommitted will discover their intense preferences for environmental protection in part by acting out, rather than merely by checking, their introspective preference orderings. Therefore, other things being equal, a Bay Area resident is more likely to become an active environmentalist than is, say, a Cook County, Illinois, resident. Moreover, once a Bay Area resident joins the Sierra Club, for example, he or she is more likely to encounter conventional incentives for continued membership, perhaps even for extra contributions or for other forms of action. Many of the club's members-by-mail, those who do nothing other than send in their dues, encounter no such incentives. San Francisco Bay Area members may be more nearly like the members of the American Medical Association (AMA) in that conventional incentives may even be the most important incentives for their membership. (Recall that, as noted in chapter 12, perhaps the most important incentive to contemporary membership in the AMA is conventional: it is the desire to receive referrals from member doctors. The sanction of not giving referrals is not controlled by the AMA, but by its members acting voluntarily.) In its early days as primarily a certifying organization, the AMA was not unlike a local medical clinic dependent on its good reputation. One could turn to it for proof of competence. If such an organization became successful, it would be sure to grow, perhaps even to cover a state. Hence, the AMA grew to its later power through federation, through amalgamation of power by convention.

Note that, to the extent convention can underpin organized group action, Olson's criticism of Marx's theory of class action is not necessarily germane, since the motivations in Marx's theory are not static, but strategic. Olson concludes from his logic of collective action that "class-oriented action will not occur if the individuals that make up a class act rationally," as Marx commonly assumes individuals do act.[3] From Marx's account of why peasants, with their common and perhaps even

___

[3] Mancur Olson, Jr., *The Logic of Collective Action*, p. 105; for related discussion see ibid., pp. 102–110.

commonly recognized interest, fail to become an active class (discussed in chapter 12 under "Failure to Arise"), he appears to presume that more than merely the fact of a common interest and the recognition of it are necessary for class action. The "more" evidently includes the contingent choosing and sanctioning that are possible among those who enter "into manifold relations with one another."[4] If Marx's expectations of class action by workers have not been fulfilled, it need not follow that Marx was illogical in his analysis, that he failed to grasp the logic of collective action, but merely that he overrated the extensiveness of the manifold relations among workers or the ease of their reaching conventionally ordered cooperation toward common ends. Indeed, on a strictly rational analysis, the expectation of the development of class solidarity among workers may have been more fitting in Marx's own time than it is today. The typical industrial establishment has considerably more employees today than in Marx's time, so that the problem of federating a class organization out of local cells is exacerbated by the greater difficulty today of organizing the much larger local cells. Unions may have arisen when they did historically largely because shops were small enough. Thereafter, federation and the vote made large unions possible. They too, like the AMA, have grown by conventional amalgamation.

Finally, recall the discussion of extrarational motivations in the static analysis of chapter 7. In the strategic or dynamic analysis of contract by convention, extrarational motivations may likewise play an important role. Indeed, given the dynamic nature of such contracts, extrarational motivations may be important either before or after a contract by convention is established. First, they may motivate a leader such as Joe Hill, around whom a contract by convention may be coordinated. And second, they may motivate contributions to an extant organization whose existence is substantially rational or contractual. For example, the Sierra Club makes contribution to it a potentially prominent solution to the problem of collective action to support conservation and environmental protection. It does not follow that contributions to the Sierra Club are rationally motivated, because the prominence of the club makes supporting it an easy way to put one's ethically motivated contributions to apparently effective use. One who independently of contract-by-convention interactions with other environmentalists sends in a contribution may be acting, say, from a norm of fairness. Yet the Sierra Club itself may have become a prominent environmentally active organization in large part through contract by convention.

4 Karl Marx, *The Eighteenth Brumaire of Louis Bonaparte,* pp. 123–124.

CONTRACT BY CONVENTION IN A
REPRESENTATIVE SYSTEM

Traditional group theorists have often seemed too ready to assume that all interests will be expressed, and that in the pluralist political system, all interests will be represented. Schattschneider and others have argued forcefully that this is not so: there are biases affecting which interests get expressed in the first place, and which interests are eventually represented in government policies. Olson's logic of collective action explains some of the biases Schattschneider observes, and the asymmetries discussed in chapter 5 and the motivations discussed in chapter 7 are further sources of biases in expression. That these lead to biases in representation is to be explained by several factors, including the kind of venality that seems to have been behind the Perot provision discussed in chapter 5 under "Heterogeneity." But another, often overlooked problem is the difficulty representatives and other government agents may have in learning their constituents' interests if these are not expressed.

Lindblom's comments on the difficulties central planners encounter because they must rely on "computation" rather than on "the acting out of choices" apply, more generally, to representatives:

> Among the difficulties that bar central planners from collecting necessary computations . . . is that consumer and planner preferences are not empirical phenomena to be observed and measured, like rainfall or frequency of alcoholism. They are "not facts to be gathered but choices to be made." Not even the chooser himself knows his preferences until he is confronted with an actual choice, and his understanding of his own preferences is to be doubted unless he is in a real choice situation in which he chooses not hypothetically but actually. Hence the acting out of choices in market systems may be indispensable, and computation of preferences no substitute.[5]

It is commonly taken for granted that organized groups get what they want by influencing elected and other government officials in a very strong sense, with forms of influence ranging from capitalizing on venality to "promising" votes to those who respond to the groups. Once an issue has a central place on the political agenda, these may well be the principal modes of group influence. But just as it is interesting to ask not merely how an organization is maintained, but also how a group comes to be organized, so too it is interesting to ask how an

[5] Charles E. Lindblom, *Politics and Markets*, p. 103.

issue gets on the agenda and how it moves to a central place once there. Often this means to ask how a convention on what is a problem is reached. The mutual signaling and resignaling involved in acting out may often be almost necessary for reaching coordination and a subsequent convention.

If politicians intuit how difficult it is to organize popular collective actions, they may be inclined to weight organized popular interests very heavily—on the reasonable presumption that when tens of thousands organize, perhaps millions share their interest. Even a completely malleable political entrepreneur seeking to represent any popular interest worth a few votes will often have difficulty judging popular preferences in the absence of group activity. Lindblom argues that "societies combine two methods of achieving desired social organization—problem-solving analysis and problem-solving social interaction. People both think their way and act their way to solutions."[6] They also both think their way and act their way to discovering their interests. Therefore, anyone who tries to represent people's interests will pay heed to organized popular groups, not merely because they have resources, but also because they are a credible display of acting out preferences. They are a proof of interests, even though not all interests have an equal chance at such proof.

Aside from informing our understanding of how government agents give credible weight to interests that often might otherwise seem uncertain, the process of the acting out of preferences will also inform a richer understanding of *groups' behavior*. To speak of acting out rather than merely thinking out preferences is preeminently to transcend the static analysis of earlier chapters and raise the issue of dynamic elements in collective action and contract by convention.

Finally, acting out may, like moral action, *itself* be a superior good. Hence, it may be indulged more readily by the upper middle class than by the poor and working classes. Thus the signaling involved in acting out preferences to reach a conventional definition of policy interests will tend to give representatives far more information on the interests of the well-off than on those of the less well-off. As is true in general of moral motivations and of nonfungible goods (as discussed in chapters 7 and 5, respectively), acting out interests to reach policy conventions may produce a substantial upward bias in the effects of public interest group activity. It may also underlie the actual existence of interest group organizations, as discussed above.

To judge the importance of conventional definition of the issues, one would have to judge how much difference the relevant issues make to

6 Ibid.

representatives when they vote on policies. Obviously, that requires a much broader view in which other influences are similarly weighed. No doubt some legislators are for sale, or as a contemporary joke has it, for rent. And in many nations, legislators who might want to represent one side of an issue must first come to represent a geographically defined constituency. Rental fees may be prohibitive for most popular interest groups, and we need not address this problem further here. The more interesting and pervasively important problem is that conventionally defined interests may have to compete at the constituency level with more reliable and more easily tapped sources of support for legislators. This is too big an issue for extended discussion here, but a brief digression will suggest why optimistic versions of the group theory of politics may founder on the facts of actual organizational influence in the American context, even apart from the usual recognition of the preponderance of business influence.

American national legislators—especially in the House of Representatives, but also in the Senate—increasingly wage continuous campaigns for reelection. They spend a large part of their time politicking in their home districts, even when Congress is in session. (Those who take long weekends home away from the House are called the "Tuesday to Thursday Club.") It is widely agreed that such continuous campaigning is necessary, especially in marginal districts, that is, in districts where neither of the two major parties has overwhelming strength.[7] What happens when legislators are back home politicking? Richard Fenno, in *Home Style,* describes the activities of eighteen then current and future members of Congress during the seventies.[8] To oversimplify, the legislators can do two things to meet and woo the electorate: they can set themselves up in various locations for open meetings or open office hours, and they can make appearances before various organized groups. The first device depends on the self-motivations of the electorate and on heavy publicity, and therefore it is almost surely subject to biases in favor of organized groups. But the second device is more pervasively dependent on such groups. Why? Because a campaigner who wishes to appear before organized groups must either organize the groups or fall back on extant groups—those which, consonant with Olson's by-product theory, may generally be organized for purposes other than to influence political outcomes.

The largest groups organized in such fashion at the local level include church groups, unions, business groups, veterans' groups, and perhaps a

---

[7] For accounts, see David R. Mayhew, *Congress: The Electoral Connection;* and Morris P. Fiorina, *Congress: Keystone of the Washington Establishment.*

[8] Richard F. Fenno, Jr., *Home Style: House Members in Their Districts.*

few smaller social groups such as parent–teacher associations. Members of Congress who are continuous campaigners are likely to depend on such groups simply because they are already there.[9] Or rather, one might prefer to argue, candidates with a natural or contrived base in constituencies of such groups will have advantages over candidates who must themselves organize their constituencies. Any legislator whose "home style" is to appear often before local groups will find that available, already organized groups ease the burden of organization. Fenno notes that "the more one observes members of Congress at work in their districts, the more impressed one is by the simple fact that people are hard to find." On the other hand, "although 'people' are hard to find, certain people are not. Those who cluster in structured, organized communities, public or private, do make themselves available for presentations by their representatives."[10]

What happens to representation and representativeness in this system? Fenno writes that in the perceptions of members of Congress, "There is no way that the act of representing can be separated from the act of getting elected."[11] Clearly, however, the effect of the continuous campaign may distort the representativeness of any given representative. More systematically, one might suppose that groups whose basis of organization is local, but whose scope is much wider, perhaps even national, are likely to be very important in influencing the overall cast of Congress. These groups enter with the occasional, conventionally constructed group that is relatively issue-specific and has signaled its backing among voters. A subjective accounting suggests that in the contemporary United States, the former tend to be socially conservative and small business and community-oriented, whereas those of the latter that do not also have a substantial basis in ongoing local organizations tend to be liberal and upper middle class. The growth of the continuous-campaign syndrome generally benefits the former not only against the latter, but also against the larger population.

[9] In *Home Style,* Fenno does not present a systematic account of whom his campaigners see. Presumably he has data in his notes that would be of great interest if they were organized.

[10] Ibid., pp. 234–235. As one of Fenno's campaigners explained: "You can't create crowds. So you go where people meet. That means you spend more time talking to groups like the Chamber [of Commerce] than you do to people who live along the road here. . . . The great mass of people you can't reach. They are not organized. They don't have institutions you can plug into. The leadership, the elite, runs along the top of all the institutions, and you can reach them, but not the people generally" (Ibid., p. 235).

[11] Ibid., p. 233.

CONTRACT BY CONVENTION AND
THE LOGIC OF COLLECTIVE ACTION

Much social analysis is based on a peculiar bit of logical slippage: collectivities such as groups and nations are wrongly treated as though they had certain of the attributes of individuals. In particular, it is commonly clear what constitutes narrowly rational behavior for an individual in a given context, and therefore it is clear what would be a rational choice or outcome for the individual. It is not clear that there is any similar sense in saying of a group or a national "choice" that it is rational. A group choice or outcome can, of course, often be rationally understood, but this is to say that it can be understood as the joint outcome of individual choices that can each be rationally understood.[12]

Among the great values of Prisoner's Dilemma and of Olson's analysis of the logic of collective action is that they show that the analogy from individual to group behavior is wrong. Yet so strong has the grip of that analogy been that individual behavior in the static, single-play version of the Prisoner's Dilemma is commonly viewed as paradoxical. In the context of large-scale collective action, the strategic implications of Prisoner's Dilemma are more readily reconciled with common sense and evidently seem less paradoxical, perhaps for the simple reason that most of us are aware that we typically do not contribute to many collective causes that interest us. But there may be a further reason for our sense that the Prisoner's Dilemma is paradoxical while the frequent failure of collective actions is not: when we think of actual instances of 2-person Prisoner's Dilemma, we may naturally think of Prisoner's Dilemmas that occur in ongoing relationships. In such Prisoner's Dilemmas, our own behavior belies the supposed logic of noncooperation. Hence, our instincts may be to think of one-shot relationships with strangers when we contemplate the problem of large-scale collective action, and of ongoing relationships when we envision 2-person Prisoner's Dilemma problems. As a result, we happily find that our examined intuitions easily correspond to Olson's claim that small groups should and large groups should not be expected to cooperate in collective action situations. However, as we saw in examples in chapter 2, the logic of collective action is not a function of group size, because that logic applies as clearly to relevant two-member groups as it does to very large groups. The greater distinction between small and large groups is not one of Olson's logic, but merely of the likelihood of their being involved in a thick enough network of mutual interactions. Almost any commonsense

---

[12] See further, the epilogue in Brian Barry and Russell Hardin, eds., *Rational Man and Irrational Society?*

assumption of the limits as to how many people one can involve in ongoing exchange relations with oneself would suggest that very large groups might have greater difficulty than smaller groups in acting collectively when there are costs to individual participants. Generalization of such a commonsense conclusion, however, is not easy, because overlapping small-group and large-group relationships may enable even very large groups to achieve cooperation, and because very small groups defined by some common interest may not be bound by any ongoing relationships.

Arguments for Homo economicus explanations of behavior often implicitly assume that individual choices over one set of alternatives are uncoupled from choices over other sets of alternatives. For example, suppose there are two merchants selling eggs equidistant from my house. If I am fully aware of the facts, as a Homo economicus I should buy from the one whose price is lower. Americans seldom have opportunity to test their own behavior in such circumstances, because such circumstances seldom obtain in their lives. In a village, however, where ongoing relationships are thick, choices are often not so straightforward, and one may choose one merchant over another for reasons other than an advantage of price or quality of merchandise. This is not an objection to understanding the choice in rational terms, but only to seeing it as a static problem involving this choice alone, rather than as a problem strategically related to other issues and expectations. The static analysis may be useful because it can at least clarify part of the costs and benefits at stake in a particular choice. But it need not be conclusive for determining what choice will be made.

Olson's logic of collective action is based on a strictly static analysis of the costs and benefits of any given collective action uncoupled from other exchange relationships. As an empirical theory, it is therefore valid only for polar cases characterized by complete discreteness, or for cases that are nearly so. As the goals of collective action become extremely specific and as the groups interested in them become very large, the collective action problem tends to approach the polar case. When issues are narrowly defined, narrowly rationally motivated collective action in politics may therefore be more prevalent at the extremely local level, at which contract by convention works best, than at the national level. But occasional issues are broadly enough defined to support enduring movements, and within these movements contract by convention may motivate a high level of activity, especially, again, if the activity can partly be localized, as in the American civil rights, antiwar, women's, and environmental movements. Alas, to understand such activity in a particular case might require such intensive observation as would try the patience of an anthropologist and such attention to nuance as would frustrate a philologist.[13] At this point, I take comfort in being neither and therefore in leaving the field to others.

[13] In his essay, "Thick Description: Toward an Interpretive Theory of Culture," Geertz notes of thick description, at least as he practices it, that "it is miscroscopic" (Clifford Geertz, *The Interpretation of Cultures*, p. 21). To understand common instances of political activity in rational terms would require "microscopic" descriptions of relevant individuals' behaviors and intentions.

BIBLIOGRAPHY

Akerlof, George A. "The Market for 'Lemons': Quality Uncertainty and the Market Mechanism," *Quarterly Journal of Economics* vol. 84, no. 3 (August 1970) pp. 488–500.

Arrow, Kenneth J. "Gifts and Exchanges," *Philosophy and Public Affairs* vol. 1, no. 4 (Summer 1972) pp. 343–362.

Banfield, Edward C. *The Unheavenly City Revisited* (Boston, Little, Brown, 1974).

Barone, Michael, Grant Ujifusa, and Douglas Matthews. *The Almanac of American Politics 1978* (New York, Dutton, n.d.).

Barry, Brian. *Political Argument* (London, Routledge and Kegan Paul; New York, Humanities, 1965).

———. *Sociologists, Economists and Democracy* (London, Collier-Macmillan, 1970; reprint ed., Chicago, University of Chicago Press, 1978).

———. "Is It Better To Be Powerful or Lucky?" *Political Studies* vol. 28, nos. 2 and 3 (June and September 1980) pp. 183–194, 338–352.

———, and Russell Hardin, eds. *Rational Man and Irrational Society?* (Beverly Hills, Calif., Sage, 1982).

Bartky, Ian R., and Elizabeth Harrison. "Standard and Daylight Saving Time," *Scientific American* vol. 240, no. 5 (May 1979) pp. 46–53.

Baumol, William J. *Welfare Economics and the Theory of the State* (Cambridge, Mass., Harvard University Press, 1952).

———. "Environmental Protection and Income Distribution," in Harrold M. Hochman and George E. Peterson, eds., *Redistribution Through Public Choice* (New York, Columbia University Press, 1974) pp. 93–114.

Becker, Gary S. *The Economic Approach to Human Behavior* (Chicago, University of Chicago Press, 1976).

Bendix, Reinhard. *Max Weber: An Intellectual Portrait* (Garden City, N.Y., Doubleday, 1960).

———. *Nation-Building and Citizenship* (Garden City, N.Y., Doubleday, 1969).

Benn, Stanley I. "The Problematic Rationality of Political Participation," in Peter Laslett and James Fishkin, eds., *Philosophy, Politics and Society*, 5th ser. (New Haven, Yale University Press, 1979) pp. 291–312.

Bentham, Jeremy. *An Introduction to the Principles of Morals and Legislation* (1823; reprint ed., New York, Hafner, 1948).

Berlant, Jeffrey L. *Profession and Monopoly* (Berkeley, University of California Press, 1975).

Blum, Walter J., and Harry Kalven, Jr. *The Uneasy Case for Progressive Taxation* (Chicago, University of Chicago Press, 1953).

Bowman, John R. "New Deal, Old Game: Competition and Collective Action Among American Capitalists 1925–1934." Unpublished paper. University of Chicago, February 1979.

Bradley, F. H. *Ethical Studies* (2nd ed., London, Oxford University Press, 1927).

Brecht, Bertolt. *Stücke* [Plays] vol. 3 (Berlin, Suhrkamp Verlag, 1955).

Buchanan, James M. "An Economic Theory of Clubs," *Economica* vol. 32 (February 1965) pp. 1–14.

———. "Ethical Rules, Expected Values, and Large Numbers," *Ethics* vol. 76, no. 1 (October 1965) pp. 1–13.

———. *The Demand and Supply of Public Goods* (Chicago, Rand McNally, 1968).

Chamberlin, John. "Provision of Collective Goods as a Function of Group Size," *American Political Science Review* vol. 68, no. 2 (June 1974) pp. 707–716.

———. "A Collective Goods Model of Pluralist Political Systems," *Public Choice* vol. 33, no. 4 (December 1978) pp. 97–113.

Clark, Kenneth B. "The Civil Rights Movement: Momentum and Organization," *Daedalus* vol. 95, no. 1 (Winter 1966) pp. 239–267.

Coase, R. H. "The Problem of Social Cost," *Journal of Law and Economics* vol. 3 (October 1960) pp. 1–44.

Cohen, Kalman, and Richard Cyert. *Theory of the Firm: Resource Allocation in a Market Economy* (Englewood Cliffs, N.J., Prentice-Hall, 1965).

Comte, Auguste. *Auguste Comte and Positivism*. Edited by Gertrud Lenzer (New York, Harper & Row, 1975).

Congressional Quarterly. *Guide to Congress* (2nd ed., Washington, D.C., Congressional Quarterly, 1976).

Coombs, Don. "The Club Looks at Itself," *Sierra Club Bulletin* (July/August 1972) pp. 35–39.

Council on Environmental Quality. *Environmental Quality 1972: The Third Annual Report of the Council on Environmental Quality* (Washington, D.C., U.S. Government Printing Office, 1972).

————. *Environmental Quality 1978: The Ninth Annual Report of the Council on Environmental Quality* (Washington, D.C., U.S. Government Printing Office, 1978).

CQ Almanac (Washington, D.C., Congressional Quarterly, various years).

Deutsch, Morton. *The Resolution of Conflict* (New Haven, Yale University Press, 1973).

Dorfman, Robert. "Incidence of the Benefits and Costs of Environmental Programs," *American Economic Review* vol. 67, no. 1 (February 1977) pp. 333–340.

Downs, Anthony. *An Economic Theory of Democracy* (New York, Harper and Brothers, 1957).

Edelman, Murray. *The Symbolic Uses of Politics* (Urbana, University of Illinois Press, 1964).

Etzioni, Amitai. "The Kennedy Experiment," *Western Political Quarterly* vol. 20, no 2 (June 1967) pp. 361–380.

Fenno, Richard F., Jr. *Congressmen in Committees* (Boston, Little, Brown, 1973).

————. *Home Style: House Members in Their Districts* (Boston, Little, Brown, 1978).

Findlay, J. N. "The Structure of the Kingdom of Ends," The Henrietta Hertz Lecture for 1957, in Findlay, *Values and Intentions* (London, George Allen and Unwin, 1961) pp. 419–435.

Fiorina, Morris P. *Congress: Keystone of the Washington Establishment* (New Haven, Yale University Press, 1977).

Flood, Merrill M. "Some Experimental Games," *Management Science* vol. 5, no. 1 (October 1958) pp. 5–26.

Freeman, Jo. *The Politics of Women's Liberation* (New York, David McKay, 1975).

Freeman, Stephen, Marcus R. Walker, Richard Borden, and Bibb Latané. "Diffusion of Responsibility and Restaurant Tipping: Cheaper by the Bunch," *Personality and Social Psychology Bulletin* vol. 1, no. 4 (Fall 1975) pp. 584–587.

Frohlich, Norman, and Joe A. Oppenheimer. "I Get By with a Little Help from My Friends," *World Politics* vol. 23, no. 1 (October 1970) pp. 104–120.

————. *Modern Political Economy* (Englewood Cliffs, N.J., Prentice-Hall, 1978).

————, and Oran R. Young. *Political Leadership and Collective Goods* (Princeton, Princeton University Press, 1971).

Fuller, Lon L. *Legal Fictions* (Stanford: Stanford University Press, 1967).

————. *The Morality of Law* (rev. ed., New Haven, Yale University Press, 1969).

————. "Law and Human Interaction," in Harry M. Johnson, ed., *Social System and Legal Process* (San Francisco, Jossey-Bass, 1978) pp. 59–89.

Gaddis, William. *JR* (New York, Knopf, 1975).

Gamson, William A. "Experimental Studies in Coalition Formation," in L. Berkowitz, ed., *Advances in Experimental Social Psychology* vol. 1 (New York, Academic, 1964) pp. 82–110.

Geertz, Clifford. *The Interpretation of Cultures* (New York, Basic Books, 1973).

Georgescu-Roegen, Nicholas. *Analytical Economics* (Cambridge, Mass., Harvard University Press, 1967).

Gompers, Samuel. "Discussion at Rochester, N.Y., on the Open Shop—'The Union Shop is Right'—It Naturally Follows Organization," *American Federationist* vol. 12, no. 4 (April 1905) pp. 221–223.

Gouldner, Helen P. "Dimensions of Organizational Commitment," *Administrative Science Quarterly* vol. 4, no. 4 (March 1960) pp. 468–490.

Greenberg, Michael. *British Trade and the Opening of China 1800–1842* (Cambridge, At the University Press, 1951).

Guttman, Joel M. "Understanding Collective Action: Matching Behavior," *American Economic Review* vol. 68, no. 2 (May 1978) pp. 251–255.

Haefele, Edwin T. "A Utility Theory of Representative Government," *American Economic Review* vol. 61, no. 3 (June 1971) pp. 350–367.

Hansen, W. Lee, and Burton A. Weisbrod. "The Distribution of Costs and Benefits of Public Higher Education: The Case of California," *Journal of Human Resources* vol. 4, no. 2 (Spring 1969) pp. 176–191.

Hardin, Russell. "Collective Action as an Agreeable *n*-Prisoners' Dilemma," *Behavioral Science* vol. 16, no. 5 (September 1971) pp. 472–481.

———. "The Emergence of Norms," *Ethics* vol. 90, no. 4 (July 1980) pp. 575–587.

———. "Rationality, Irrationality, and Functionalist Explanation," *Social Science Information* vol. 19, no. 4/5 (1980) pp. 755–772.

———. "Groups in the Regulation of Collective Bads," in Gordon Tullock, ed., *Public Choice in New Orleans* (Blacksburg, Va., Public Choice Society, 1980) pp. 91–102.

Harsanyi, John C. "Rationality Postulates for Bargaining Solutions in Cooperative and in Noncooperative Games," *Management Science* vol. 9, no. 1 (October 1962) pp. 141–153.

Hart, H. L. A. "Are There Any Natural Rights?" *Philosophical Review* vol. 64, no. 2 (April 1955) pp. 175–191.

———. *The Concept of Law* (Oxford, Oxford University Press, 1961).

Hayek, Friedrich A. *Law, Legislation, and Liberty* vol. 1 *Rules and Order* (Chicago, University of Chicago Press, 1973).

Heal, Geoffrey. "Do Bad Products Drive Out Good?" *Quarterly Journal of Economics* vol. 90, no. 3 (August 1976) pp. 499–502.

Heath, Anthony. *Rational Choice and Social Exchange* (Cambridge, Cambridge University Press, 1976).

Heller, Joseph. *Catch-22* (New York, Simon and Schuster, 1961).

Hirschman, Albert O. *Exit, Voice, and Loyalty* (Cambridge, Mass., Harvard University Press, 1970).

Hobbes, Thomas. *De Cive* in Hobbes, *Man and Citizen*. Edited by Bernard Gert (Garden City, N.Y., Doubleday, 1972).

Homans, George C. *Social Behavior: Its Elementary Forms* (New York: Harcourt, Brace and World, 1961).

Hume, David. *A Treatise of Human Nature*. Edited by L. A. Selby-Bigge and P. H. Nidditch (2nd ed., Oxford, Oxford University Press, 1978).

————. *An Enquiry Concerning the Principles of Morals* in Hume, *Enquiries*. Edited by L. A. Selby-Bigge and P. H. Nidditch (3rd ed., Oxford, Oxford University Press, 1975).

Ionesco, Eugene. *The Hermit*. Translated by Richard Seaver (New York: Viking, 1974).

Kafka, Franz. *Tagebücher* [Diaries] (Frankfurt am Main, S. Fischer, 1967).

Kahneman, Daniel, and Amos Tversky. "Prospect Theory: An Analysis of Decision Under Risk," *Econometrica* vol. 47, no. 2 (March 1979) pp. 263–291.

Kaplan, David, and Richard Montague. "A Paradox Regained," *Notre Dame Journal of Formal Logic* vol. 1, no. 2 (July 1960) pp. 79–90.

Laslett, Peter, "The Face to Face Society," in Peter Laslett, ed., *Philosophy, Politics and Society*, 1st ser. (Oxford, Blackwell, 1956) pp. 157–184.

Leff, Arthur Allen. "Injury, Ignorance and Spite—The Dynamics of Coercive Collection," *Yale Law Journal* vol. 80, no. 1 (November 1970) pp. 1–46.

Lewis, David K. *Convention* (Cambridge, Mass., Harvard University Press, 1969).

Lindblom, Charles E. *Politics and Markets* (New York, Basic Books, 1977).

Lindskold, Svenn. "Trust Development, the GRIT Proposal, and the Effects of Conciliatory Acts on Conflict and Cooperation," *Psychological Bulletin* vol. 85, no. 4 (July 1978) pp. 772–793.

Lipset, S. M., Martin Trow, and James S. Coleman. *Union Democracy* (New York, Free Press, 1956).

Locke, John. *The Second Treatise of Government*. Quotations are from Locke, *Two Treatises of Government*. Edited by Peter Laslett (Cambridge, Cambridge University Press, 1963).

Luce, R. Duncan, and Howard Raiffa. *Games and Decisions* (New York, Wiley, 1957).

Macaulay, Stewart. "Non-Contractual Relations in Business," *American Sociological Review* vol. 28, no. 1 (February 1963) pp. 55–70.

MacAvoy, Paul W. *The Economic Effects of Regulation* (Cambridge, Mass., MIT Press, 1965).

Mackie, J. L. "Fallacies," in Paul Edwards, ed., *The Encyclopedia of Philosophy* vol. 3 (New York, Macmillan, 1967) pp. 169–179.

Macneil, Ian R. *The New Social Contract* (New Haven, Yale University Press, 1980).

Mandeville, Bernard. *The Fable of the Bees; or Private Vices, Publick Benefits*. Edited by F. B. Kaye (6th ed., Oxford, At the Clarendon Press, 1924).

Manzer, Ronald. "Selective Inducements and the Development of Pressure Groups: The Case of Canadian Teachers' Associations," *Canadian Journal of Political Science* vol. 2, no. 1 (March 1969) pp. 103–117.

March, James G. "Bounded Rationality, Ambiguity, and the Engineering of Choice," *Bell Journal of Economics* vol. 9, no. 2 (Autumn 1978) pp. 587–607.

————, and Herbert Simon. *Organizations* (New York, Wiley, 1958).

Margolis, Howard. "A New Model of Rational Choice," *Ethics* vol. 91, no. 2 (January 1981) pp. 265–279.

Marshall, Alfred. *Principles of Economics* (8th ed., London, Macmillan, 1920).

Marwell, Gerald, and Ruth E. Ames. "Experiments on the Provision of Public Goods. I. Resources, Interest, Group Size, and the Free-Rider Problem," *American Journal of Sociology* vol. 84, no. 6 (May 1979) pp. 1335–1360.

———. "Experiments on the Provision of Public Goods. II. Provision Points, Stakes, Experience, and the Free-Rider Problem," *American Journal of Sociology* vol. 85, no. 4 (January 1980) pp. 926–937.

Marx, Karl. *The Eighteenth Brumaire of Louis Bonaparte* (New York, International Publishers, 1963).

Mayhew, David R. *Congress: The Electoral Connection* (New Haven, Yale University Press, 1974).

McGuire, Martin C. "Group Size, Group Homogeneity, and the Aggregate Provision of a Pure Public Good Under Cournot Behavior," *Public Choice* vol. 18, no. 2 (Summer 1974) pp. 107–126.

Menger, Karl. "The Role of Uncertainty in Economics," in Martin Shubik, ed., *Essays in Mathematical Economics in Honor of Oskar Morgenstern* (Princeton, Princeton University Press, 1967).

Milgram, Stanley. *Obedience to Authority* (New York, Harper & Row, 1975).

Mill, J. S. *Principles of Political Economy*. Edited by W. J. Ashley (1909; reprint ed., New York, A. M. Kelley, 1965).

Mishan, E. T. "The Relationship Between Joint Products, Collective Goods, and External Effects," *Journal of Political Economy* vol. 77, no. 3 (May/June 1969) pp. 329–348.

Mitchell, Robert Cameron. "National Environmental Lobbies and the Apparent Illogic of Collective Action," in Clifford S. Russell, ed., *Collective Decision Making: Applications from Public Choice Theory* (Baltimore, Johns Hopkins University Press for Resources for the Future, 1979) pp. 87–121.

Moe, Terry M. *The Organization of Interests* (Chicago, University of Chicago Press, 1980).

Morgenstern, Oskar. "The Collaboration Between Oskar Morgenstern and John von Neumann on the Theory of Games," *Journal of Economic Literature* vol. 14, no. 3 (September 1976) pp. 805–816.

Mumey, G. A. "The 'Coase Theorem': A Reexamination," *Quarterly Journal of Economics* vol. 85, no. 4 (November 1971) pp. 718–723.

Newman, James R., ed. *The World of Mathematics* vol. 1 (New York, Simon and Schuster, 1956).

Nozick, Robert. *Anarchy, State, and Utopia* (New York, Basic Books, 1974).

Olson, Mancur, Jr. *The Logic of Collective Action* (Cambridge, Mass., Harvard University Press, 1965; reprinted with a new app., 1971).

Osgood, Charles E. *An Alternative to War or Surrender* (Urbana, University of Illinois Press, 1962).

———. "GRIT for MBFR: A Proposal for Unfreezing Force-Level Postures in Europe." Unpublished manuscript. University of Illinois at Urbana, n.d.

Pareto, Vilfredo. *The Mind and Society*. Edited by Arthur Livingston (New York, Harcourt, Brace, 1935).

Pauly, Mark V. "Clubs, Commonality, and the Core: An Integration of Game Theory and the Theory of Public Goods," *Economica* vol. 34, no. 135 (August 1967) pp. 314–324.

Picard, Max. *Die Welt des Schweigens* [The world of silence] (Erlenbach-Zurich, Eugen Rentsch, 1948).

Plato. *The Republic*. Translated by G. M. A. Grube (Indianapolis, Ind., Hackett, 1974).

Proust, Marcel. *Remembrance of Things Past* vol. 1. Translated by C. K. Scott Moncrieff (New York, Random House, 1934).

Quine, Willard V. *The Ways of Paradox and Other Essays* (New York, Random House, 1966).

Rapoport, Anatol. *Two-Person Game Theory* (Ann Arbor, University of Michigan Press, 1966).

———. "Editorial Comments," *Journal of Conflict Resolution* vol. 12, no. 2 (June 1968) pp. 222–223.

———. "Prisoner's Dilemma—Recollections and Observations," in Rapoport, ed., *Game Theory As a Theory of Conflict Resolution* (Dordrecht, Holland, D. Reidel, 1974) pp. 17–34.

———, and Albert M. Chammah. *Prisoner's Dilemma* (Ann Arbor, University of Michigan Press, 1965).

Rapoport, Anatol, and Melvin Guyer. "A Taxonomy of 2 × 2 Games," *General Systems* vol. 11 (1966) pp. 203–214.

Raven, J. E. *Plato's Thought in the Making* (Cambridge, At the University Press, 1965).

Rawls, John. *A Theory of Justice* (Cambridge, Mass., Harvard University Press, 1971).

Rhys, Jean. *Quartet* (First published in 1928 as *Postures;* New York, Random House, 1974).

Richardson, G. B. "The Organization of Industry," *Economic Journal* vol. 82, no. 327 (September 1972) pp. 883–896.

Rousseau, Jean-Jacques. *The First and Second Discourses*. Edited by Roger D. Masters; translated by Roger D. and Judith R. Masters (New York, St. Martin's Press, 1964).

Runciman, W. G., and Amartya K. Sen. "Games, Justice and the General Will," *Mind* vol. 74, no. 296 (October 1965) pp. 554–562.

Ryle, Gilbert. "Conscience and Moral Convictions," *Analysis* vol. 7, no. 1 (January 1940) pp. 31–39. Reprinted in Ryle. *Collected Papers* vol. 2 *Collected Essays 1929–1968* (New York, Barnes and Noble) pp. 185–193.

Samuelson, Paul A. "The Pure Theory of Public Expenditure," *Review of Economics and Statistics* vol. 36, no. 1 (November 1954) pp. 387–389.

———. "Diagrammatic Exposition of a Theory of Public Expenditure," *Review of Economics and Statistics* vol. 37, no. 1 (November 1955) pp. 350–356.

———. "Economists and the History of Ideas," *American Economic Review* vol. 52, no. 1 (March 1962) pp. 1–18.

Schattschneider, E. E. *The Semi-Sovereign People* (New York, Holt, Rinehart and Winston, 1960).

Schelling, Thomas C. *The Strategy of Conflict* (Cambridge, Mass., Harvard University Press, 1960).

————. "Hockey Helmets, Concealed Weapons, and Daylight Savings," *Journal of Conflict Resolution* vol. 17, no. 3 (September 1973) pp. 381–428.

————. *Micromotives and Macrobehavior* (New York, W. W. Norton, 1978).

Schmertz, Herbert. Letter to the editor. *New York Times,* Jan. 15, 1978, sec. 3, p. 14.

Scholem, Gershom. *Sabbatai Sevi: The Mystical Messiah* (Princeton, Princeton University Press, 1973).

Schur, Max. *Freud: Living and Dying* (New York, International Universities Press, 1972).

Scott, James C. *The Moral Economy of the Peasant* (New Haven, Yale University Press, 1976).

Selznick, Philip. *Leadership in Administration* (New York, Harper & Row, 1957).

Shibutani, Tamotsu. "On Sentiments and Social Control," in Herman Turk and Richard L. Simpson, eds., *Institutions and Social Exchange: The Sociologies of Talcott Parsons and George C. Homans* (Indianapolis, Bobbs-Merrill, 1971) pp. 147–162.

Sierra. Various issues, 1978–80.

Sierra Club Bulletin. Various issues, 1976–78.

Smith, Adam. *The Wealth of Nations.* Edited by Edwin Cannan (New York, Random House, 1937).

————. *The Theory of Moral Sentiments.* Edited by D. D. Raphael and A. L. Macfie (Oxford, Oxford University Press, 1976).

Snidal, Duncan. "Public Goods, Property Rights, and Political Organizations," *International Studies Quarterly* vol. 23, no. 4 (December 1979) pp. 532–566.

Starbuck, William H. "Organizational Growth and Development," in James G. March, ed., *Handbook of Organizations* (Chicago, Rand McNally, 1965) pp. 451–533.

Stigler, George J. *Essays in the History of Economics* (Chicago, University of Chicago Press, 1965).

————. "Director's Law of Public Income Redistribution," *Journal of Law and Economics* vol. 13, no. 1 (April 1970) pp. 1–10.

————. "Free Riders and Collective Action: An Appendix to Theories of Economic Regulation," *Bell Journal of Economics and Management Science* vol. 5, no. 2 (Autumn 1974) pp. 359–365.

Taylor, Michael. *Anarchy and Cooperation* (London, Wiley, 1976).

Thompson, Arthur, Jr. *Economics of the Firm: Theory and Practice* (Englewood Cliffs, N.J., Prentice-Hall, 1973).

Titmuss, Richard M. *The Gift Relationship* (New York, Pantheon Books, 1971).

Trollope, Anthony. *Phineas Finn* (London, Oxford University Press, 1962).

Tucker, William. "Environmentalism and the Leisure Class: Protecting Birds, Fishes, and Above All, Social Privilege," *Harper's* (December 1977) pp. 49–56, 73–80.

Ullmann-Margalit, Edna. *The Emergence of Norms* (Oxford, Oxford University Press, 1977).

Village Voice, Sept. 15, 1975, p. 40.

von Neumann, John, and Oskar Morgenstern. *The Theory of Games and Economic Behavior* (3rd ed., Princeton, Princeton University Press, 1953).

Wagner, Richard E. "Pressure Groups and Political Entrepreneurs," *Papers on Non-Market Decision-Making* vol. 1 (1966) pp. 161–170.

Wall Street Journal, Oct. 28, 1975, p. 3; Nov. 7, 1975, p. 1; June 11, 1976, p. 2; July 20, 1976, p. 4.

Waltz, Kenneth N. *Man, the State, and War* (New York, Columbia University Press, 1965).

Weisbrod, Burton A. "Toward a Theory of the Voluntary Non-Profit Sector in a Three-Sector Economy," in Edmund S. Phelps, ed., *Altruism, Morality and Economic Theory* (New York, Russell Sage, 1975) pp. 171–195.

Whitney, Simon. *Trade Associations and Industrial Control* (New York, Central Book Company, 1934).

Williamson, Oliver E. *Markets and Hierarchies* (New York, Free Press, 1975).

Windham, Douglas M. *Education, Equality and Income Distribution* (Lexington, Mass., Heath, 1970).

Wittgenstein, Ludwig. *On Certainty*. Edited by G. E. M. Anscombe and G. H. von Wright (Oxford, Basil Blackwell, 1969).

INDEX

Acting out preferences, as superior good, 225
Altruism, difference from trust, 186
Amalgamation, and contract by convention, 195–197
Ambiguity, in notion of R, 162
American Medical Association, 192, 222
Ames, Ruth E., 114
Analogy, individual to group behavior, 228
Anomie, 190, 213
Antinomy. *See* Paradox
Armaments
reduction, 209
research investment, 205
Asymmetries
and collective action, 81
political effect of, 68, 83
and private goods, 80

Banfield, Edward, 109
Barry, Brian, 13, 125*n*
Baumol, William, 7, 21
solution of, 52, 63, 84
Welfare Economics and the Theory of the State, 21*n*
Bendix, Reinhard, on sanctions, 177

Benefits. *See* Costs and benefits
Bentsen, Lloyd, 80
Bernoulli, Daniel, on St. Petersburg Paradox, 139, 144
Blackout, as step bad, 65
Blake, William, 22
Bradley, F. H., 108
Buchanan, James, 44
Business Roundtable, 77
By-product theory, 31–35, 39, 101.
See also Olson, Mancur, Jr.

Cage, John, 61
Calcutta credit crisis, of 1829–1834, 202
Catch-22 (Heller), 8
Chamberlin, John, 44
contradiction of Olson, 127
on group size, 126
Chammah, Albert, 13, 148
Charismatic authority, 177
Chicago-East Coast Railways, 201
Civil rights organizations, 11, 110
Class-oriented action, 222
Clean air. *See also* Pollution
benefits asymmetry, 71
as superior good, 69

241